FOLENS GCSE
P.E.
For WJEC

Julie Walmsley

Acknowledgements

The publishers would like to thank the following for permission to reproduce photographs:

Actionplus on pp. 7b, 44, 57b, 68, 71, 127, 178a, 218, 219; Action Images on pp. 52, 70; Alamy on pp. 5, 59b, 60c, 163, 194; Corbis on pp. 10, 16, 49, 75, 82, 135, 147, 180, 194, 209a; DeVereGroup on/Greens Health & Fitness on p. 24; Digital Vision on pp. 7a, 8b, 11b, 90, 112, 133; Empics on pp. 8a, 50a, 50b, 64, 66, 86, 91, 103, 104, 136, 161, 186, 188, 196, 211, 218; Getty Images on pp. 45, 50, 51, 54, 58, 77b, 97, 100, 101a, 101b, 101c, 106, 119, 145a, 145b, 145c, 145d, 147e, 178b, 178c, 191a, 191b, 203a, 203b, 203c, 203d, 206a, 206b, 209b, 212, 213a, 213b; Istock on pp. 13, 15, 25a, 40, 130, 138, 154, 169, 171, 189; Rex features on pp. 145c, 155b, 177a; Science Photo Library on p. 116; Nacivet on p. 210; SW Pix on pp. 42, 105; Paul Doyle/Photofusion on p. 47; 57a; PhotoLibrary on pp. 47, 62; Photodisc r.f. on pp. 7c, 9, 26a, s6b, 32, 38, 41, 46, 139, 140, 143, 148, 151, 155, 175, 185, 191c, 191d

United Kingdom: Folens Publishers, Apex Business Centre, Boscombe Road, Dunstable, LU5 4RL.

Email: folens@folens.com

Ireland: Folens Publishers, Greenhills Road, Tallaght, Dublin 24.

Email: info@folens.ie

Poland: JUKA, ul. Renesansowa 38, Warsaw 01-905.

Editor: Mandy Tragner

Illustrations by Roger Goode, Colin Brown and Maggie Rammage – Beehive Illustration and Mark Stacey Jamil Dar, Planman Technologies

Cover design: Duncan McTeer

Cover image: C J Farquharson WomensCycling.net

Nicole Cooke – World Number 1 (2006–2007)

'Over the past decade Nicole Cooke's unprecedented achievements have set new standards in international cycling. Nicole's wins include the Tour de France and Giro D'Italia stage races which are the ultimate test of endurance, and precision performance enroute to winning medals at all major championships. In 2006 Nicole was Britain's first rider to be ranked World Number 1.'

Index compiled by Claire Shewbridge

Layout by Planman Technologies

First published 2007 by Folens Limited.

British Library Cataloguing in Publication Data. A catalogue record for this publication is available from the British Library.

ISBN 978-1-85008-250-7

Contents

Introduction

The contents of this book cover the theory and content for WJEC GCSE in Physical Education and help with the written examination, which is divided into two papers.

This material has been endorsed by WJEC and offers high quality support for the delivery of WJEC qualifications. While this material has been through a WJEC quality assurance process, all responsibility for the content remains with the publisher.

Written Paper 1 is in two sections and is allocated $1^1/_2$ hours to complete.

Section A:

A maximum of 12% of marks are available in this section. The candidate will be set a series of compulsory questions based on video extracts of people taking part in the physical activity. This aims to test the knowledge and understanding of:

Section 5.1 – Physical Fitness.

Section B:

A maximum of 8% of marks are available in this section. The questions here are all compulsory and aim to test the candidate's knowledge and understanding of:

Section 5.2 – Factors Affecting Participation, Provision and Performance.

Written Paper 2 is allocated $1^1/_2$ hours to complete.

Section C:

A maximum of 20% of marks are available in this section. All the questions are compulsory and aim to test the candidate's knowledge and understanding of:

Section 5.3 – Assessment and Evaluation of Physical Fitness

Section 5.4 – Effects of Training/Nutrition/Hydration on the Body's System

Section 5.5 – Skill and Psychological Factors Influencing Performance.

The book layout

The book is set out so that it matches the WJEC specification. The headings of each of the sections and the order in which topics are covered relate directly to the specification. This means that if you carefully work your way through this book you will cover everything that the exam board requires of you. To help you further, the material is presented in small, easy-to-digest chunks that are broken down using frequent sub-headings.

There are many photographs, illustrations and diagrams used to give you a visual way of remembering the work. There are also numerous learning features built into this book.

What you will learn in this section

At the beginning of each section, you will find a list of all the topics you will learn about in that section. Each topic is numbered, which is especially useful when you are revising, as it will be quicker to find relevant information and to check you know all the points you are supposed to.

Tasks

Each section of work involves completing a series of numbered tasks. Completing tasks involves referring to the work just read or discussed in class. Tasks need to be recorded in your own book or file.

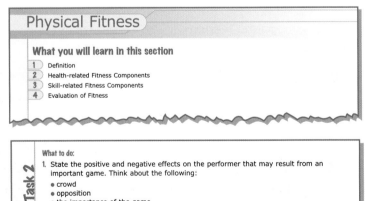

Physical Fitness

What you will learn in this section
1. Definition
2. Health-related Fitness Components
3. Skill-related Fitness Components
4. Evaluation of Fitness

Task 2

What to do:
1. State the positive and negative effects on the performer that may result from an important game. Think about the following:
   - crowd
   - opposition
   - the importance of the game
   - personal desire to do well.

By keeping your book up-to-date and tasks complete, the work recorded will build up into your personal revision document. It is important that when you are working, information you write down can be read easily when you refer back to it. Take enough time to make your words legible.

Active Challenge

These are thought-provoking tasks, which often involve working with a partner. Completing these tasks will open your mind to the section being worked on and give you the chance to add verbally to the topic.

Using a spidergram

Spidergrams are quick and easy to complete. They are an excellent way of recording and remembering the main points of a section.

Key Terms

Wherever there are words in **bold** in the book they will be found in the key terms section. This indicates important words for you to remember together with their definitions.

Summary

At the end of each section there is a summary that rounds up the essential information that you need to remember from the topics covered. It acts as a short collection of the ideas that are the most important to the section. When revising, the summaries can be used as a starting point to remind you of the main ideas. You can then add to them with more detailed information from memory or by re-reading the text.

Glossary

Many words that you come across in the text are explained in the glossary. When you come across a word for which you are unsure of its meaning – look it up in the glossary.

You and the exam

You could view the exam as a competition – a competition to get a better grade than pupils nationwide who have chosen to take this exam. So give yourself the best chance. If you are absent it is up to you to copy up any work missed. Gaps in work are gaps in knowledge. Pupils who have completed all of the work give themselves the best chance of success.

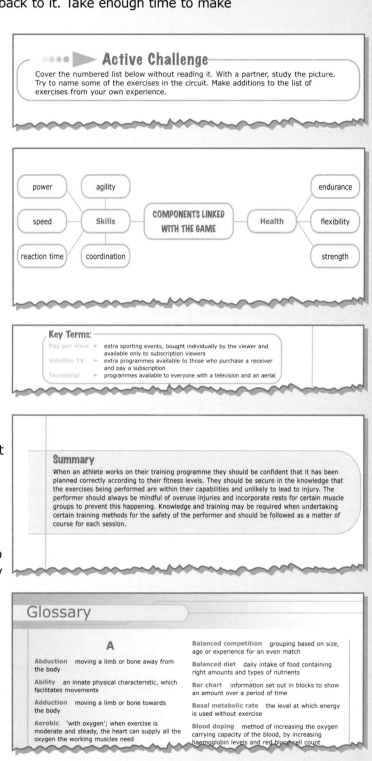

Active Challenge

Cover the numbered list below without reading it. With a partner, study the picture. Try to name some of the exercises in the circuit. Make additions to the list of exercises from your own experience.

Key Terms:

Pay per view ► extra sporting events, bought individually by the viewer and available only to subscription viewers

Satellite TV ► extra programmes available to those who purchase a receiver and pay a subscription

Terrestrial ► programmes available to everyone with a television and an aerial

Summary

When an athlete works on their training programme they should be confident that it has been planned correctly according to their fitness levels. They should be secure in the knowledge that the exercises being performed are within their capabilities and unlikely to lead to injury. The performer should always be mindful of overuse injuries and incorporate rests for certain muscle groups to prevent this happening. Knowledge and training may be required when undertaking certain training methods for the safety of the performer and should be followed as a matter of course for each session.

Glossary

A

Abduction moving a limb or bone away from the body

Ability an innate physical characteristic, which facilitates movements

Adduction moving a limb or bone towards the body

Aerobic 'with oxygen'; when exercise is moderate and steady, the heart can supply all the oxygen the working muscles need

Balanced competition grouping based on size, age or experience for an even match

Balanced diet daily intake of food containing right amounts and types of nutrients

Bar chart information set out in blocks to show an amount over a period of time

Basal metabolic rate the level at which energy is used without exercise

Blood doping method of increasing the oxygen carrying capacity of the blood, by increasing haemoglobin levels and red blood cell count

Physical Fitness

What you will learn in this section

1. Definition
2. Health-related Fitness Components
3. Skill-related Fitness Components
4. Evaluation of Fitness

1 Definition

Fitness is different from health. It can be defined as:

'the ability to meet the demands of the environment'.

Having the minimum level of fitness will allow a person to go about their everyday life and meet its demands without tiring. Fitness, therefore, is concerned with the physical condition of a person. Walking to the bus stop and completing tasks at work are both actions that should be completed without exhaustion. Each person has a different set of physical demands in their day, so each person's minimum level of fitness differs.

2 Health-Related Fitness Components

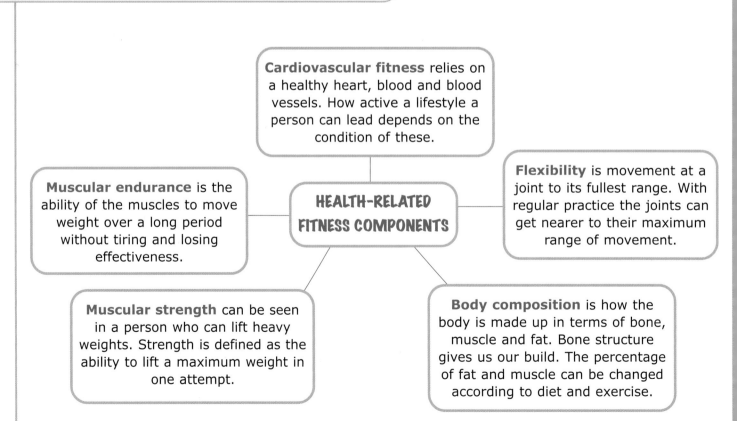

Cardiovascular fitness relies on a healthy heart, blood and blood vessels. How active a lifestyle a person can lead depends on the condition of these.

Flexibility is movement at a joint to its fullest range. With regular practice the joints can get nearer to their maximum range of movement.

Muscular endurance is the ability of the muscles to move weight over a long period without tiring and losing effectiveness.

HEALTH-RELATED FITNESS COMPONENTS

Muscular strength can be seen in a person who can lift heavy weights. Strength is defined as the ability to lift a maximum weight in one attempt.

Body composition is how the body is made up in terms of bone, muscle and fat. Bone structure gives us our build. The percentage of fat and muscle can be changed according to diet and exercise.

Health-related fitness components and the performer

The condition of the five components of health has a great effect on the amount and quality of exercise, training and performance a person can achieve.

Cardiovascular fitness

Ice skaters need good cardiovascular fitness.

The good condition of the cardiovascular system allows for efficient transportation of blood to the necessary parts of the body in order that the body can meet the extra demands of exercise.

In training, if the cardiovascular system is not fit then the ability to keep working is reduced and so the required skill level is less likely to be reached. In competition, fatigue and breathlessness would prevent a person from playing to the required standard or even continuing the activity in some instances.

Muscular strength

Lennox Lewis uses his muscular strength to overpower Mike Tyson.

Muscular strength, in itself, can be used to overpower an opponent. A player who can combine strength with speed can create power, which is especially useful when playing a forehand drive down the line in tennis, in order to pass an opponent at the net, for instance.

Having poor strength may prevent a player shooting with the required amount of power to beat a goalkeeper. In contact sports, like judo, a weak player gives little resistance to an opponent with muscular strength.

Muscular endurance

Good muscular endurance prevents the body tiring quickly.

Muscular endurance is essential for long-distance events such as 10 000m racing. The body is able to keep working for a long time without tiring and so the performer has more chance of winning.

Flexibility

Controlled use of the full range of movement available at joint can allow for the execution of the correct technique, improving performance and lessening the risk of injury. Where resistance to a force is necessary, the muscles must be strong enough to prevent over-extension beyond the fullest range. For example, players in a rugby scrum must have muscles strong enough to prevent over-extension of their shoulders.

Romanian Dana Carteleanu demonstrates her flexibility.

Body composition

Success in sport can depend on choosing the most appropriate sport for your build. The amounts of fat, muscle and bone in the body will change the shape of a person, making them more or less suitable for a particular activity. A particular-sized skeletal frame may lend itself to a certain sport or position in the team. The longer the bones making the frame, the taller a person is; this would be advantageous to a basketball player or goal shooter in netball. Shorter skeletal bones make for a smaller frame, suiting the needs of a jockey for example.

Most jockeys have a small skeletal frame and a minimal fat component.

> ◀●●●● ▶ **Active Challenge**
>
> With a partner, for each of the health-related fitness components, list five activities/sports that mostly depend on that component for success.

3 Skill-related Fitness Components

The idea of various levels of fitness applies to different sports too. To take part in any sport requires a combination of fitness and performance. Exercise is a series of physical activities that improve health and fitness. A person may be fit to play badminton, but not fit in the necessary way for tennis. Each activity has its own set of requirements that the player must meet in order to succeed. The exercises, therefore, for each activity's training session will be different in order to fit with the requirements of the sport. The performance will improve by choosing and working on the most appropriate exercises.

Most sports have a combination of all the components of fitness. Each sport has its own special mix of **skill-related fitness** components to master in order for a player to be successful. These are the specific requirements unique to successful performance or participation of that sport. Some sports need more power and strength, like throwing events in athletics, whereas others, like badminton, need agility and co-ordination.

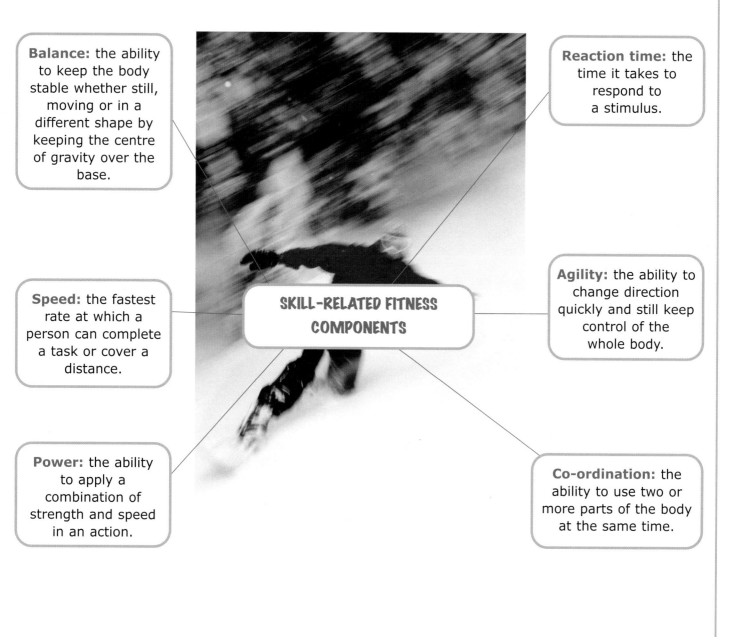

Balance: the ability to keep the body stable whether still, moving or in a different shape by keeping the centre of gravity over the base.

Reaction time: the time it takes to respond to a stimulus.

Speed: the fastest rate at which a person can complete a task or cover a distance.

SKILL-RELATED FITNESS COMPONENTS

Agility: the ability to change direction quickly and still keep control of the whole body.

Power: the ability to apply a combination of strength and speed in an action.

Co-ordination: the ability to use two or more parts of the body at the same time.

Why test?

Testing will give an assessment of the current state of health and fitness of the performer. This knowledge, from the first results of testing, provides the baseline information required for the levels of intensity for the initial training sessions.

A thorough test will focus on measuring each component of health and skill/fitness appropriate to the sport. These results will provide knowledge of the strengths and weaknesses of the individual. This knowledge will mould the training to the individual's needs.

As the training progresses the athlete's body will adapt. Further testing is necessary to see how much the body has developed. The intensity of the training sessions must increase to take these changes into consideration so that further progress can be made.

The statistics of the test can be an indicator of the next performance results.

Tests often have performance tables with scores showing what a performer of a certain age and gender should be achieving. These recognised norms are a clear guide to the performer and comparisons with these statistics show where and how well they are doing with those in the same category.

Re-testing can indicate what progress has been made. Seeing how the training is working can give confidence to the performer and motivate them, making them even more determined to reach higher goals.

A sportsperson can use testing in the following ways:

- Show how intense the initial training session should be
- Regular testing shows the adaptation of the body and indicates how the intensity of the training sessions should be increased
- After injury a performer can be re-tested so that training sessions are set at the appropriate levels to prevent further injury and take into consideration loss of fitness.

Testing is rigorous and aims to show the maximum performance an athlete can reach. Therefore the athlete should be in a condition to perform at the most demanding level. For their safety, before any test can take place, a full warm-up is necessary.

What to do:

1. Create a spidergram of all the uses of testing. There should be at least six reasons for testing included.

Task 1

What can be measured?

All the components of health-related and skill-related fitness have a bearing on the performance of an athlete. Therefore each can be useful to the sportsperson depending on the activity they are undertaking.

How the components can be measured

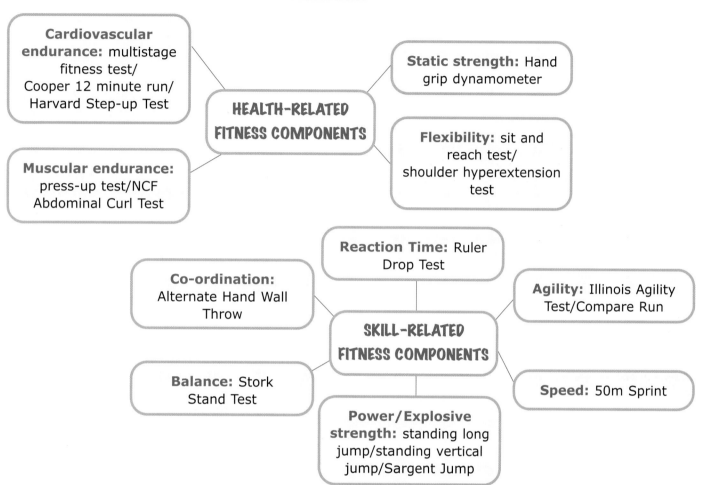

When testing it is vital that the test follows, exactly, the method prescribed in the protocol. These instructions can include:

- measuring devices to use
- equipment for the performer to use
- distances/size of a course
- the most suitable area or surface on which to test
- how many people are needed
- time limits for performance.

Each of the protocols are set out in section 5.3 Assessment and Evaluation of Physical Fitness

Note

Every time the test is performed it should be the same as previously carried out. This will give validity and reliability to the results. Surface and weather conditions have a bearing on performance and therefore need to be neutral each time too.

Why test?

- to provide information on the performer's current state of health and fitness
- to provide a base starting point for training
- to show strengths in the performer
- to show weaknesses in the performer
- to show how the body has adapted and improved to training
- to show how performance compares with recognised norms
- to show success of training and results in motivation
- to give confidence.

TESTING

How to evaluate

- choose the component to measure
- choose a recognised way of measuring it
- record the results
- work out what the results imply
- decide on the changes to the training programme based on the results
- apply the changes to the training.

How to test

- test one component
- the test should be easy to repeat
- performer should completely understand the test
- ensure safety
- follow the prescribed protocol
- use the same equipment
- test in neutral weather conditions
- the test should be carried out the same way every time.

Key Terms:

Skill related fitness ► Physical abilities of the body adapted to specific sports

Summary

Testing is important to the athlete, as it will show a level of ability at a particular moment in time. Equipped with the knowledge of the results of the test, changes to the training programme can be made so further progress can occur. When analysing the results and comparing them with recognised norms, the athlete can see how their performance measures up to others of a similar age and gender.

It is crucial to test components that are appropriate to the activity. There will probably be several areas to test and these should all be addressed for a thorough evaluation. It is essential to use a recognised test, which will focus on one health or skill component.

The tests will have to be carried out several times as the performer's body adapts to the training and so in turn requires the sessions to increase in intensity in order that further progress can be made. It is vital that on each occasion the tests are carried out, they follow the same protocol. This will give a true result of the performance providing validity and reliability to the procedure and results.

Recording results and comparing them with previous ones will show how the athlete's body has adapted and will indicate the changes needed in the programme in the future. Analysing the results will also show to what degree the performer has progressed which can be a guide to possible future levels of improvement.

Principles of Training

What you will learn about in this section

1. How the Principles Help the Performer
2. Specificity
3. Progression
4. Overload (frequency, intensity, time)
5. Reversibility
6. Tedium

1 How the Principles Help the Performer

When a coach or athlete designs a fitness training programme there are guidelines to keep to in order to ensure the training suits the performer and they achieve the desired results. These are called 'principles of training' and are the rules to follow when exercising, to improve the body gradually, safely and appropriately through exercise.

The type and intensity of a training programme depends on the condition, fitness and needs of the performer. It is important that the existing capabilities of the performer are known so that the training can be set appropriately.

There are five principles that will influence the performer and their training programmes: Specificity, Progression, Overload, Reversibility and Tedium. These principles are easy to remember as the initials make the word SPORT.

2 Specificity

This principle requires an understanding of the needs of the game, for example, a goalkeeper will include lots of reaction work in their training. When applying this principle the activity is usually practised at the pace required in the sport. If a person trains too slowly then their skills will only be reproduced at the slower pace and the action will be unable to match the requirements of the game. At a school practice for your team, if you repeat the skills slowly then when you get to the game the other team may be quicker than you are. So, speed up your practices!

The actions in training should copy the actions used in the game. If a person needs good leg strength, simply making them strong may not be enough. A cyclist will train their legs, whilst cycling, in a different way from a long-distance runner; both need muscular endurance but the method of training is different. In order to become a better swimmer a person needs to spend most of their time in the water! Therefore the 'type' of exercise is essential – it must match the actions of the activity being training for.

3 Progression

Exercising at the same degree of difficulty all the time will only maintain current fitness levels. As training starts to change your body tolerances, the same session will not have the same effect. Your body needs to be put under slightly more pressure to continue to improve. This is the idea behind the principle of progression. The need to increase the amount of difficulty of exercise gradually is reflected by the ease with which you complete tasks for cardiovascular fitness, the same amount of exercise will not bring your pulse rate into the **target zone**. After about five to six weeks there may be a need to change the programme. The resting heart rate decreases the fitter a person becomes; this indicates fitness improvement.

What to do:

1. Write, in your own words, why the principles of specificity and progression are important to the performer and their training.

4 Overload

Muscle strength can be improved by making the muscles work harder than normal. Putting greater demands on the body by exercising can improve fitness. The point where exercise is demanding enough to have an effect on the body is called the 'threshold of training'.

Whether a person is training for muscular endurance or muscular strength, their aim is to train between 60–80% of their maximum. Working between these levels will put enough stress on the athlete to bring about improvement. For older people the threshold of training decreases. Working at 50% of their maximum heart rate will often have a positive effect on their cardiovascular fitness.

There is a combination of three targets (frequency, intensity, time and type) that a performer can overload their body with in order to meet the **minimum level of fitness**. Training is adapted by changing any one or more of the **FITT** combinations.

There are three ways in which the intensity of the exercise can be increased:

Frequency

Frequency is the number of times exercise is undertaken per week. The more times a person exercises the more often their body is put under stress. Three or more times a week is the recommended number of times extra exercise should be repeated, to reach the minimum level of fitness. Top-class sportspeople would have to train a lot more frequently than this if they are to achieve results good enough for their aspirations.

But remember that the body also needs time to recover from training. Training very hard, every day, may be harmful even for a top-class athlete.

Friday 8–9am

Monday 6–7pm

Wednesday 7–8pm

Intensity

This is the level of difficulty of the exercise. For instance, when considering cardiovascular fitness your pulse rate can show you how intensely you are working.

Working in a target zone of 60–80% of the maximum heart rate is the level where fitness will usually increase. When training for strength the intensity is calculated in the same way. A person trains within the target zone by finding the maximum weight they can lift and working to 60–80% of that weight. As the amount of weight lifted increases, with training this adds to the intensity.

After the warm-up, exercising regularly for 20 minutes to 60–80% of maximum heart rate will increase the body's fitness.

Time

This is the length of time the exercise session lasts. Keeping your pulse at 60–80% of its maximum for 20 minutes is the target. Warming-up is not included in the 20 minutes. The time begins when the pulse is at 60% of its maximum.

What to do:

1. Explain how 'Overload' is important to the athlete.
2. Write three sentences on ways to overload the exercise intensity.

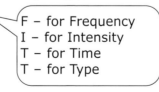

F – for Frequency
I – for Intensity
T – for Time
T – for Type

5 Reversibility

Just as the body will increase in strength, tone and skill with exercise, it will lose them without it. The body needs to be stressed to maintain and increase strength. After an injury or illness, an athlete may have lost their strength and skill. Although a person can quickly improve on their endurance capability, it can be lost three times faster than it can be gained. Remember, if you don't use it you lose it!

In order to keep the athlete motivated it is essential that the contents of the training sessions vary. This will prevent tedium setting in.

Some coaches of team activities include mini games based on different sports in the training programme. This varies the activity, changes the mood of that part of the session – often they are approached in a much more light-hearted way – and can promote team spirit within the squad.

Round-up of ideas

All the principles are important when devising a training programme. The individual needs of the performer are taken into account and an exercise programme is set out solely for their capabilities.

When training for a specific event, specificity is a key principle. A swimmer will mainly swim; a runner will mainly run.

To gain from any training, overload must be applied. Muscles and body systems need to be subjected to stress. This is training above the threshold of training. The threshold is 60% of the maximum heart rate.

Once the performer is used to the exercise programme, then the principle of progression is applied. When applying progression the changes are planned systematically. This will make each change at the correct level and not injure the performer.

The **FITT** factors are vital to the success of the exercise programme. The regularity of exercising leads to improvements in fitness. Generally, the more frequent the exercise, the better the results that will follow. A person working towards more than the minimum level of fitness would train five times a week for 30 minutes at a time, with their pulse rate above 60% of its maximum. A serious sportsperson would need to ensure that their pulse was above 80% of its maximum when training for endurance. Moderating the number of training sessions strikes the balance between training too much – and causing overuse injury – and too little, when insufficient stress is put on the body to show progression. Once training has stopped then reversibility may occur. This is when the muscles **atrophy** – or weaken – due to lack of work.

●●●● ▶ Active Challenge

In pairs, prepare two questions with answers, ready to ask another pair on the principles of training.

Summary

People deciding to train need to think carefully about the type and intensity of the exercise they are to do. The training programme should be designed specifically for the individual and the activity. Age, ability, gender and experience will all play a part in making the programme unique. A clear awareness of the reason for training will influence the type of activities included. For the minimum level of fitness to take place, a person needs to participate in three exercise sessions per week each lasting for 20 minutes and increasing the heart rate to 60% of its maximum. For higher levels of fitness the frequency, intensity and duration should increase.

Different sports require distinct types of fitness. Long-distance events and players in the outfield for most games need aerobic fitness. Developing aerobic fitness allows a person to work for the whole game without losing form. Anaerobic fitness is needed in athletic field events and for single actions within games play, such as a single penalty kick or forehand drive in racket sports. Most games events need an element of muscular endurance. This allows the muscles of the body to keep working for a long period without tiring. The various sports require different types of muscular strength. Explosive strength (power) is used in events such as shot put and javelin; static strength is employed when holding the body still and dynamic strength is utilised in moving actions over a period of time, such as the leg action in cycling.

Many sports require the body to move the joints into extreme positions. The training programme should concentrate on the specific movements and develop the best range of actions. Having good flexibility often prevents injury but in some sports, too much flexibility can be dangerous.

Key Terms:

FITT	► Frequency, Intensity, Time and Type
Atrophy	► when muscles atrophy, they weaken and lose their strength and size because of lack of exercise
Minimum level of fitness	► the resulting fitness level when someone exercises over a period of weeks, three sessions of 20 minutes, raising the heart rate to 60–80% of its maximum
Target Zone	► level of effort applied keeping within aerobic levels

Methods of Training

What you will learn about in this section:

1. Continuous Training Methods
2. Interval Training Methods
3. Plyometrics
4. Altitude Training
5. Mobility Training

An athlete chooses training methods that can be adapted to their chosen activity.

The method should:

- match the needs of the sport by training the appropriate body systems
- adapt to the skills required by the activity
- provide development to the appropriate level of the performer.

During training the performer may use a mix of methods. This will help to develop all health and skill-related components necessary for the activity. When training over a long period, varying the methods used will reduce the risk of overuse injury and keep the athlete interested and fresh for each session. For example, long distance runners, who train mainly on their own, may enjoy group circuit training sessions where they can work with others.

With all the training methods results of performance should be recorded. When analysed, these will show any changes and development the athlete has made and will indicate changes needed to the training for the future.

Some methods work on a continuous basis – no stops from start to finish. Others have periods of activity and then recovery phases. Some are based on improving mobility.

1 Continuous Training Methods

Types of training include:

Fartlek and Continuous Training.

Fartlek

As the periods of work and rest imitate the game, the principle of specificity is applied. To keep the performer improving when using interval training, the principle of progression is used. There are several ways to do this:

- The amount of recovery time may shorten and competitive pace work may be increased
- The intensity or difficulty of the work may increase; this could be increasing the distance covered or amount of time run
- The number of repetitions or sets completed may increase.

What to do:

1. Choose and name a sport.
2. Design a 30-minute interval training session for that sport.

> If designing a session for long interval training, include 5 repetitions and 4 sets. If using short interval training, use more repetitions and sets.

Task 1

About the training method: Fartlek Training

Fartlek is a Swedish word meaning 'speed play'. It involves exercise, often running, varying in time, distance and effort.

What the training develops

Due to the changes of intensity of the exercises, it trains both aerobic and anaerobic fitness. The athlete becomes increasingly capable of meeting the changes of pace in a competition or game.

How the method works

It covers: speed, distances covered and the amount of time spent exercising change. In general, the session has work of varying intensity taking place over a minimum of a 20-minute period.

Fartlek can be an introduction to interval training and sometimes both can be combined to form a programme of exercise, owing to their similar content. This would suit a games player. The content of the session is flexible. The repetitions in the sessions, therefore, are made different to add interest to the training. Rest periods or less strenuous exercise give time to recover so training can continue.

The exercises involved

Sprints, jogs and runs make up the session. These may have times set for them or may be for a certain distance. The session can be continuous with periods of intense work followed by easier work, which gives the body a chance to recover. Sometimes the session can include periods of complete rest.

In Sweden, where this method originated, athletes use the surrounding hills and forests to train in. Many areas large enough to run in can be used to vary the training session such as in a park, at the beach and in the countryside. Fartlek training can be adapted to running, cycling and swimming.

Possible fartlek session

0–15 minutes	warm-up
15–35 minutes	sprint 10 seconds on flat
	jog on flat
	sprint 10 seconds uphill
	jog/walk downhill on flat
	run 150m on flat for 1 minute
	jog
	sprint 80m on flat
	jog
	sprint 20m uphill
	jog downhill on flat
	sprint 10 seconds on flat
	jog/run downhill on flat
	sprint 10 seconds uphill
	jog/run downhill on flat
35-45 minutes	cool down

As an athlete's fitness improves the session will be planned to include increased intensity.

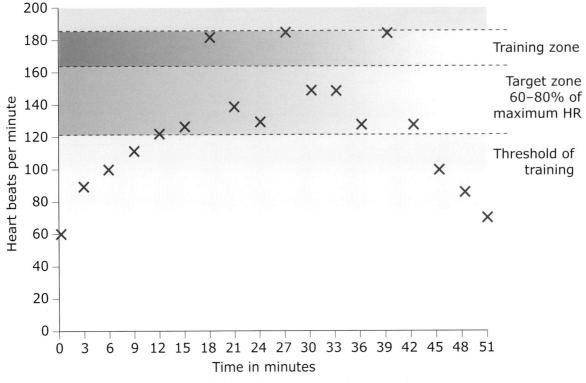

The heart rate rises and falls regularly in a fartlek session.

What to do:

1. From your understanding of fartlek training, copy and complete the paragraph below.

   The word fartlek means _____ _____ in _____ where this training method originated. Athletes can use _____, _____, and _____ to run in. By using the natural changes in the countryside and beach the demands on the athletes _____. Uphill work increases the _____ of the exercise and the heart rate will rise. Sprinting to set markers trains _____. Periods of slower running help the athlete to _____ so that training can continue and the athlete uses _____ respiration.

Who benefits from the training?

Due to the continuous nature of the method together with the changes of speed and intensity, the method resembles changes in a game situation. There will be times to jog/walk for position; run into a covering space and sprint to beat an opponent. Therefore games players benefit from this method.

Continuous training

This method exercises the body at a moderate rate, keeping the pulse at a constant level between 60–80% of maximum.

What the training develops

This training works the body aerobically and keeps the pulse at a high rate. Its effect is to improve the cardiovascular and respiratory systems. It can be adapted for both the health and fitness performer and the top athlete.

Task 2

The exercises involved

The types of activity that suit this training include cycling, swimming, exercise classes (aerobics), running and jogging. Many sports centres and gyms have specialised machines that adapt to continuous training. Treadmills, exercise cycles, rowing machines and steppers all lend themselves to this type of training. The activities are a good way of developing general fitness and can be adapted to suit both individuals and groups of people. If running is the exercise chosen, then it is inexpensive to start: changing the place of training is easily arranged, adding interest to the session.

How the training principles apply

After several training sessions, the body will have adapted to the strains of the exercise. Checking the pulse rate during exercise will show if it is in the 60–80% zone, showing that the heart has become stronger as a result of the exercise. The speed of the exercise should be increased, in order to get the pulse rate into the target zone and continue to have an effect on the performer.

For the more advanced performer, greater stresses and demands are made on their body. By keeping in the training zone of 80–90% of their maximum heart rate and working for 15–20 minutes, the training will be effective.

Who benefits from the training

Continuous training suits a person who is training for the first time or returning to exercise after a period of non-activity, such as after injury. A person who specialises in long-distance events can use this type of training out of season to maintain a good level of cardiorespiratory fitness. At the start of the season, continuous training can adapt as a gentle way to re-establish the cardiorespiratory levels. At this level, the work is moderate but can be adapted to be harder at a later time.

An endurance athlete, like a marathon runner, would use this method as part of their training programme.

What to do:

1. Write six facts about continuous training.
2. How can the training method be adapted for beginners and more competitive performers?

> Think about: How hard does the body work? What effect does the exercise have on the heart? What types of activity can adapt to this method? Who would use this method of training?

2 Interval Training Methods

Types of training include:

- Circuit training
- Weight training
- Interval training.

The interval method of training works the body in phases of action and recovery. The athlete performs sudden bursts of activity, followed by intervals of rest.

Circuit training

Circuit training is a series of exercises completed for a certain amount of time after one another.

What the training develops

Circuit training can be useful in different ways. Depending on how the circuit is set up, it can develop power, strength, flexibility and endurance. At a basic level, it can improve the general fitness of the heart and lungs as long as the rests in between the activities are kept short. It can be adapted to incorporate skills for a particular game. Top-class performers, however, do not benefit much from circuit training as it does not allow them to achieve a high enough level of skill.

Circuit training can develop aerobic and anaerobic respiration. When using large muscle groups at each station (moving the whole body), aerobic respiration is in operation and this will develop the cardiovascular system. If exercising small muscle groups (such as the biceps and triceps) in turn at the stations, this is anaerobic, which builds strength.

How the method works

A circuit is made up of several activities. Each activity is given its own space in the gym or sports hall; this space is called a 'station'. Each activity is completed as many times as possible; these are called 'repetitions'. There is a set time for each activity; this is usually between 30 and 60 seconds. In this time as many repetitions of the activity are performed as possible. When all exercises at each station are completed, the circuit is finished. By repeating the circuit or adding exercises, the session increases in intensity. For general fitness the sequence of exercises works different muscle groups at each station. For beginners one circuit is usually enough.

Circuit training can be used in different ways:

Partners partner A performs activity in the time, partner B counts and records

score partners change over and repeat. This is good for beginners as there is plenty of recovery time.

Target At each station a card shows several levels for that activity, each level has the number of repetitions required to achieve that level. Each performer is allocated or chooses the level at which to work. If the target is reached within the stipulated time the performer rests and waits at the station for the remaining time. This variation requires the performer to be aware of their own ability, which will influence the chosen level of performance. The performer can also increase the intensity by working at a higher level when the circuit is repeated.

Pyramid circuit The circuit is set out conventionally and the performer works for:

- first time round 30 seconds
- second time round 20 seconds
- third time round 10 seconds.

This variation suits experienced and fit athletes as the intensity of repetitions is increased.

●●●●● ▶ **Active Challenge**

Cover the numbered list below without reading it. With a partner, study the picture. Try to name some of the exercises in the circuit. Make additions to the list of exercises from your own experience.

1. Step-ups
2. Skipping
3. Sit-ups
4. Benchlifts
5. Bench activities
6. Leg raises
7. Push-ups
8. Squats
9. Star jumps
10. Shuttle runs

Circuit training in school.

How the training principles apply

A circuit can be set for individual needs. Each person doing the circuit can have their own targets. This means that beginners and fitter people can work at the same time because they can work within the same time limits, but they each complete a different number of repetitions.

Completing a circuit can be competitive and motivate people to work harder and achieve more repetitions. Even with inexpensive equipment, a successful general fitness circuit can be set up.

What to do:

1. List the advantages and disadvantages of circuit training.
2. Look at the circuit training picture. Change four exercises from general fitness to skills using a named sport.
3. How can circuit training be adapted to Overload?

> Choose skills from a sport. Can the skills be repeated in the same way? Place them in the circuit.

Weight training

The training involves shifting weight to increase the strength of muscles, using a programme of repetitions and sets.

What the training develops

A person setting up a **weight training** programme needs to think about the following questions: What is the reason for doing the training? Is it for aerobic or anaerobic development? Which parts of the body are to be exercised? The answers to these questions will shape the whole programme.

Lifting heavy weights with few repetitions develops strength and power. This will build up strength, increase muscle size and use anaerobic respiration.

Lifting lighter weights many times develops muscular endurance. This way of adapting weight training can help a person who is rehabilitating after injury. By moving light weights, the muscles gradually get used to working and taking weight again in a safe and controlled way.

Weight training machines are always set up and fully adjustable.

How the method works

Organising a weight training programme:

Assess the performer's strength and fitness. Once the maximum a person can lift is known, the programme can start to develop.

Weights light for aerobic and endurance, heavier for anaerobic strength and size.

Number of exercises the usual range is between 8 and 12.

Repetitions complete 12–17 repetitions at 60–70% of maximum lifting ability for an anaerobic beginner. Use many repetitions for lighter, aerobic work.

Number of sets a beginner might complete 1 set for anaerobic, building up to 2 sets after 2 weeks. More repetitions are completed for aerobic training.

Rest between sets about 2 minutes.

Number of sessions per week 3–4 sessions should show an improvement with up to 48 hours between each session.

Training to get the best results speed of exercise: to lift and lower takes 2 seconds.

Safety factors use of straps, adjustments to the seats, setting the correct weight and correct technique are essential for safe weight training.

Review when the body has adapted to the stresses of the programme, changes are made. The strength of the performer is re-tested. If the programme has been set at the right level, the performer will have increased in strength.

New programme changes are made to the programme. As a result, a combination of weights, repetitions and sets increases slightly.

Examples of weight training cards

% of maximum lift	Repetitions
60%	17
65%	14
70%	12
75%	10
80%	8
85%	6
90%	5
95%	3
100%	1

Good for beginners.

Complete 1 set of above (starting with easiest).

After 3 weeks, increase sets.

Weight training repetitions – the performer works through the order from 60%–100% in a session.

Lift 70% of max.

8 repetitions

3 sets completed

Good for novice.

Level of effort required means weights are lifted properly.

Little risk of injury.

Simple sets – the performer works at the same intensity throughout the session, completing 3 sets of 8 repetitions.

---

start →

160kg x 1 rep
150kg x 2 reps
140kg x 3 reps
130kg x 4 reps
120kg x 5 reps
100kg x 10 reps

Good for experienced lifters.

Pyramid sets – the performer starts at the easiest weight working their way to heavy weights but with fewer repetitions.

The exercises involved (two ways of training)

Machine weights

Using machines, rather than free weights, can be a safer way of weight training. They are technically designed to move in the correct way and are adjustable for different sizes of user. They are safe as they are steady and do not vary position apart from the designed range. This also has the effect of not training the stabilising muscles that may be needed for a sport. They usually have supports and belts to make sure the body is prepared in the correct position to shift the weight. They are always set up so they are ready to use. Users starting a weight training programme find them easy to work. One drawback is that extra weights cannot be added to the machines. This limits their use for the advanced performer.

A variety of exercises in the gym.

Free weights

Free weights can be used in a weight training programme. The use of such weights is specialised and needs lots of training so the performer works safely. Many top sportspeople use free weights. A person training with heavy weights must always use a spotter; this is a person who helps steady the performer and is ready to catch the bar or assist if the performer is struggling.

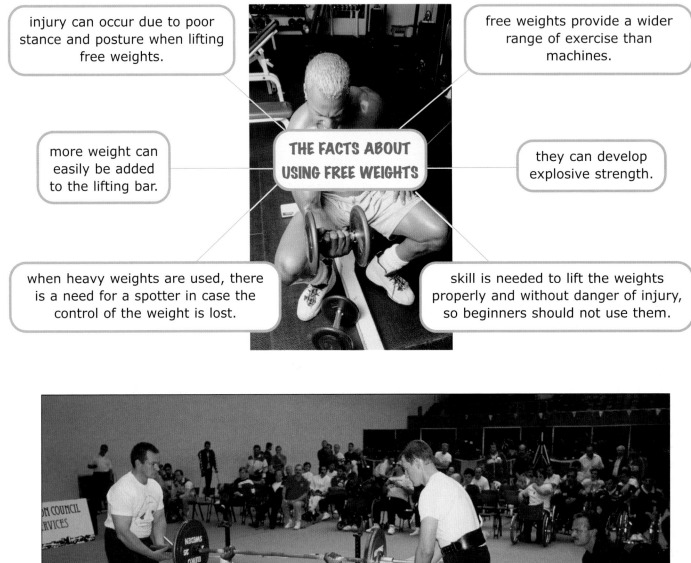

injury can occur due to poor stance and posture when lifting free weights.

free weights provide a wider range of exercise than machines.

more weight can easily be added to the lifting bar.

THE FACTS ABOUT USING FREE WEIGHTS

they can develop explosive strength.

when heavy weights are used, there is a need for a spotter in case the control of the weight is lost.

skill is needed to lift the weights properly and without danger of injury, so beginners should not use them.

Spotters help make free weight training safe, as shown here at the British Disabled Powerlift Competition.

How the training principles apply

With both types of **weight training** method, regular training improves the muscles' ability to move the weight. As the body adapts, the progression, overload and FITT principles are applied and the weights, repetitions and sets are gradually increased. This allows improvement of the muscles to continue. Lifting 60–80% of the maximum weight a person is able to lift will keep the performer within the target zone. Each session should last for no longer than 45 minutes.

A weight training card helps the performer to train safely and see progress

NAME	PERSONAL TRAINER		DATE PROGRAMME STARTED	
VISITS	1 2 3 4 5 6 7 8 9 10 11 12 13 14			
WARM-UP OPTIONS	JOG 5 MINS	CYCLE 5 MINS	EASY ROW 5 MINS	STEPPER 5 MINS
THEN	STRETCHES:	ARMS/SHOULDERS	LEGS/HIPS	ABDOMINALS
EXERCISE	STARTING POINT	PROGRESSION 1	PROGRESSION 2	PROGRESSION 3
TRICEP PULLDOWNS				
SQUATS				
HIP FLEXORS				
LATERAL PULLDOWN				
HAMSTRING CURLS				
HIP EXTENSORS				
BENCH PRESSES				
SEATED LEG EXTENSIONS				
COOL DOWN OPTIONS	WALK/JOG 5 MINS	EASY CYCLE 5 MINS		EASY ROW 5 MINS
FINISH	WITH STRETCHES			

What to do:

Answer these questions:

1. What makes each weight training session different?
2. How do free weight training sessions compare to machine weight training sessions?

> The training principles change the sessions: say how they do this. When comparing each type, think of the special features each method has.

Interval training

This method of training involves times of work followed by times of rest.

What the training develops

This method can be adapted to develop different types of fitness. Short bursts of pace, using anaerobic respiration, needed in games play, use short interval training. Prolonged moderate to hard pace, using aerobic respiration, needed in middle-distance running events, uses long interval training.

Interval training is suited to individuals working on their own, small groups of people and to larger numbers like teams of players. Many sportspeople can benefit from interval training. The sessions can be adapted to practise the skills used in a particular game. Whether a runner, swimmer, footballer or netball player, interval training can be adapted to your sport.

The work is intensive and should be performed with accuracy and at competition pace. The times of rest allow performers to regain energy so they do not become too tired and can no longer carry on training. The times of work are repeated to form repetitions. Four or five repetitions make up a set. There may be four or five sets in a session.

An example of an interval training activity

Time limit for activity →	Complete 4 sets of the following	Time limit for return ←
6–10 seconds	dribble and shoot →	
	jog, return and rest ←	60–180 seconds
6–10 seconds	dribble and shoot →	
	jog, return and rest ←	60–180 seconds
6–10 seconds	dribble and shoot →	
	jog, return and rest ←	60–180 seconds
6–10 seconds	dribble and shoot →	
	jog, return and rest ←	60–180 seconds

How the method works

Interval training can be adapted for different types of athlete and event. The working periods copy those in the event. The rest periods allow time for recovery in the same way that there would be quieter times during a game.

Long interval training

Work time is 15 seconds to 3 minutes. Games players and middle-distance athletes benefit from this type of training. The training copies the events in the need for bursts of maximal effort within the 15-second and 3-minute time spans. Even the best athletes cannot work at full pace for longer than 60-second periods so, when using this method, performers work at 80–85% of their maximum.

The resting times match the working times so the longer they work the longer they rest. The resting times are important to enable a performer to recover and continue the session. When working in larger groups it is more difficult for everyone to keep together due to the longer time limit and the variation in ability.

A 4-minute-mile runner could use interval training in the following way: repeat 10 × 60 second $\frac{1}{4}$ mile distances with 2 minutes rest between each run.

Short interval training

This training works on short bursts of maximal effort. The working times may be as short as 15 seconds. The performer aims to work all out for the whole of this time. Sprinters and racket sport players use this method to match the short bursts of maximal effort used in their events. A sprinter goes all out to reach the line as fast as possible and a squash player hits the ball with a burst of maximal effort. Due to the effects of the intensive effort on the body, rests of two minutes are necessary. In this time, the body has a chance to recover enough to carry on training.

The exercises involved

You will have used interval training in school already. Shuttle runs, dribbling relays, lay up shot drills and swimming 25m are all examples of exercises used for interval training. In a games or athletics lesson, you will have used shuttle runs. As you complete your shuttle run, that is one repetition. You rest while your teammates complete theirs. You may also complete four repetitions before you are stopped; those make up a set. The teacher may give you another chance to complete the shuttle run after resting and so you will then have completed two sets.

How the training principles apply

As the periods of work and rest imitate the game, the principle of specificity is applied. To keep the performer improving when using interval training, the principle of progression is used. There are several ways to do this:

- the amount of recovery time may shorten and competitive pace work be increased
- the intensity or difficulty of the work may increase; this could be increasing the distance covered or amount of time run
- the number of repetitions or sets completed may increase.

What to do:

1. Choose and name a sport.
2. Design a 30-minute interval training session for that sport.

> If designing a session for long interval training, include 5 repetitions and 4 sets. If using short interval training, use more repetitions and sets.

3 Plyometrics

Plyometrics are exercises designed to develop power such as:

- explosive strength

What the training develops

- Training for explosive strength (a combination of speed and power)
- Designed for performances requiring explosive maximal contractions

How the method works

Plyometrics uses an eccentric muscular action followed by a concentric muscular action to create a maximum force.

When a muscle stretches a lot of the energy used in the action is lost in heat, however, some of this energy can be stored in the elastic component of the muscle. This energy is solely available for use in the next contraction only or it is lost. To get the best use of this energy, the next contraction should be performed as quickly as possible. The eccentric and concentric action of these exercises is called the 'stretch shortening cycle'. By using this cycle the force generated by the muscle can be dramatically increased.

The emphasis of this method is on the quality of work. Therefore a Plyometric session should be divided into sets with plenty of recovery time in between.

After a good warm-up a session could involve exercises developing the following types of strength in the subsequent order:

● exercises to develop elastic strength – (low drop jumps and low hurdle jumps)
● exercises to develop concentric strength – (standing long jump and high hurdle jumps)
● eccentric strength – (high drop jumps).

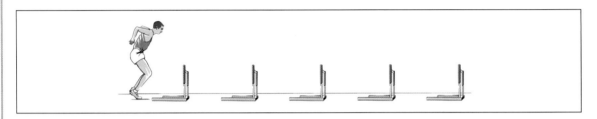

The exercises involved

For explosive leg strength development jumping, bounding and hopping exercises are appropriate. Volleyball players, football goalkeepers and rugby players jumping in the lineout will need vertical jump skills. They could use 'Drop jumping' or 'Box jumping'.

Javelin throwers will need to use upper body plyometric exercises. They could use 'Press up and clap' or 'Medicine Ball Work'

Lower body example - drop jumping

The action is as follows – dropping from a box to the ground and then immediately jumping up.

The phases of the action are:

● Drop – pre-stretches the leg muscles
● Vigorous/explosive drive upwards – secondary concentric contraction.

The effect the exercise has is to condition the lower leg muscles.

Upper body example – press-up and clap

The action is as follows – press-up with a clap in between keeping contact with the ground to a minimum

The phases of the action are:

- Pre-stretch – when arms arrive back on the ground and chest sinks
- Explosive phase – upward action in order to make the clap action

The effect the exercise has is to conditions the arms and chest.

⚠ A note of caution

The impact of landing in some exercises is great, so the floor surface should be able to cushion these. Cement surfaces should be avoided, as there is no cushioning at all. Due to the higher forces put on the muscles and joints of the body the athlete should have a sound base of strength and endurance; these are developed by weight training for the expert performer. For beginners, undertaking lower level plyometrics, certain exercises can be part of a circuit training session, so gradually conditioning the body. Caution should be made when working with preadolescent athletes as the forces on the under-developed bone structure could have detrimental effects.

How the training principles apply

It is important that the correct type of exercise is chosen, suiting the activity, so applying specificity. If the event depends on forward motion then bounding and hurdling plyometric exercises would benefit the performer.

Young athletes using plyometrics would begin by subjecting their body to lighter loads. In the drop example the load is governed by the height of the box. Beginners would start with two-footed landing on the spot with no box. As progression is made a box would be introduced. The height of the box would start low and gradually increase as development is made.

4 Altitude Training

This method needs the athletes to travel to areas where the altitude is higher than they are used to and to train there.

What the training develops

At high altitude there is less oxygen in the air, so for the body to carry enough oxygen for its needs it produces more red blood cells. This increased capacity of blood to carry oxygen is then available in the body to use aerobically, by the athlete when he or she returns to a lower altitude. This improves the athlete's level of endurance and therefore improves performance for long-distance events, until the red blood cell level returns to normal.

How the method works

For the first few days at altitude athletes experience some side effects when training. They find it difficult to complete sessions and tire quickly. This is because with the change in air pressure not as much oxygen mixes with the haemoglobin; therefore, there is not as much oxygen carried to the working muscles of the body. Due to the reduced amounts of oxygen available, the athlete's aerobic ability is affected. For a short time, athletes find they cannot complete the same amount of training as they did at sea level. But as the number of red blood cells increase, their performance improves. Endurance athletes who have recently been at high altitude are able to carry more oxygen in their blood when they return to lower altitude levels, and this helps their performance.

The exercises involved

When athletes train in areas of high altitude, they complete their specific training scheduled for their event.

How the training principles apply

As with all training programmes, when the body adapts to the sessions then the FITT principles apply. This may be that more sessions are performed in a week, sessions may last longer or the type of work completed may make the heart rate beat faster.

Some athletes partake in altitude training several times a year.

What to do:

1. Write three statements a person may make about the following training methods:

   a. altitude training   b. interval training

> You could use speech marks as though a person is actually saying the statements.

5   Mobility Training

About the training method: mobility training

The athlete performs a series of dynamic mobility exercise drills. These drills are designed to warm-up, stretch out and keep the body moving, providing a slick transition from rest to high-energy activity.

The training aims to prevent injury and improve performance.

What the training develops

'Dynamic mobility exercises' work on quick and efficient movement.

How the method works

Performed as part of the warm-up period, it prepares the body for vigorous movement.

Mobility drills stimulate the nervous system, muscles, tendons and joints by the movement of the exercises. The drills aim to match the forceful and strenuous actions of the activity to follow in the main session.

The exercises involved

- Joint rotations
- Continuous warm-up activity – Aerobic activity for 5–7 minutes
- Dynamic mobility exercises – series of swings, rotations, bends, twists and bounces working the joints of the body.

Example mobility training session

Duration – 10–15 minutes

Exercise order	time	specific	movement description	repetitions
1 Rotations Fingers, Wrists, Elbows, Shoulders, Neck, Trunk and Shoulder Blades, Hips, Knees, Ankles, Feet and Toes	2 minutes	name of area exercised	flex, extend and/or rotate	6–10 repetitions of each
2 Warm-up Activity	5 minutes	walking, jogging, cycling, skipping, side-stepping		6 each way
3 Upper Body Mobility	2 minutes		a) Arm Swings – Overhead/Down and Back, Side/Front Crossover	6 each way
			b) Neck Movements – Forward and Back, Look Left then Right, Tilt to Left then Right	6 repetitions of each

Exercise order	time	specific	movement description	repetitions
			c) Trunk and Shoulder Movements – Flexion/Extension, Lateral Flexion, Rotation	6 repetitions of each
4 Lower Body Mobility	3 minutes		a) Hip Circles and Twists – Circles and Twists	12 repetitions
			b) Leg Swings – Flexion/Extension, Cross-body Flexion/Abduction	10 repetitions each leg
			c) Ankle Bounces – Double-Leg Bounce, Single-Leg Bounce	12 repetitions

How the training principles apply

When first working on Mobility Training perform all the exercises slowly and within a comfortable range for the joint. After about four weeks use progression to gradually increase the speed and range of the exercises – this will make the movements more dynamic.

SAQ

About the training method: SAQ

SAQ stands for Speed, Agility and Quickness.

A session of SAQ work involves progressive exercises and instructions to improve ability in the three areas. The method aims to make the athlete more skilful, faster and work with greater precision. Studies showed that the three elements of speed, agility and quickness are often inherent in competitive games activities and so the method was developed.

What the training develops

- Improve quality of movement so actions are more efficient and less prone to injury
- Speed and quickness of movement increased
- Quality is combined with quickness of movement
- Quickness and control of response is improved
- Movement skills are developed in a practical way.

How the method works

The session can be divided into 6 phases:

- Dynamic flexible warm-up
- Mechanics
- Innervation
- Accumulation of potential
- Explosion
- Expression potential.

The exercises involved

1 **Dynamic flexible warm-up**

Exercises here include walks, runs, skips and flexing, and shoulder and hip mobility movements.

2 **Mechanics** – developing coordination and agility

This phase uses a combination of plyometrics, little shuttle runs, zigzag runs and drills designed for agility development.

3 **Innervation** – this phase activates the neural pathways

Exercises like the 'Fast foot ladder', dance-like actions and reaction drills are combined in this phase.

4 **Accumulation of potential** – can focus on conditioning the body

Included here are appropriate combinations of drills, direction change exercises and obstacle course runs.

5 **Explosion** – developing explosive strength (power)

This phase includes a series of:
- agility exercises
- medicine ball throws
- high quality plyometrics
- short maximal sprints
- resistance training.

6 Expression Potential uses appropriate skills at the quickest, competition rate
This is short phase but imperative to the performers. It demands maximal effort
and so needs lots of rest. It has the potential to end the session leaving performers
exhilarated as they have been involved in exercises which have asked them to
move fast, in a controlled manner.

It also applies chosen skills of the session to high quality, sport specific movements –
rugby would use short, high intensity tag games for instance.

How the training principles apply

Specificity is the key. Working on actions of the activity and applying them to the
exercises and drills is essential. All drills must be performed as max effort to simulate
the competition speed.

What to do:

1. Choose a drill that will fit the 'Accumulation of Potential' phase.

2. Describe how it works.

3. Draw a diagram to help show the actions involved.

Key Terms:

Altitude training	► training in places where the height above sea level is much greater than the athlete is used to
Circuit training	► a series of exercises completed in order and for a certain time
Continuous training	► aerobic exercising, at a moderate to high level, with no rests
Fartlek training	► 'speed play', changing speed, distances and times of exercise in the same session
Interval training	► mixing periods of hard exercise with rest periods
Weight training	► progressively lifting heavier weights to improve strength or lifting weights more often to improve stamina

Summary

The method of training can be a personal choice or it can be sport specific. Some
methods suit certain kinds of event or game. People exercising for leisure can make
any choice they want. People needing specialised training must choose the method
that will improve their body systems and skills to the best of their ability. In this
case, knowledge of the requirements of the sport is essential. By combining the
knowledge of the sport and the abilities of the individual, an appropriate programme
can be designed.

Individuals need their own programme of exercise as everyone is different and has
their own reasons for training. The key is to work the heart above the threshold of
training. Working in the target zone will help general fitness; working in the training
zone is for more serious athletes.

The principles of training create guidelines for improving the body. Plan progression
carefully by reviewing the improvements made by the athlete. Systematically plan
new programmes, increasing the intensity of the exercise when old levels have been
adapted to. Remember, training at the correct levels will improve the body but it will
reach a stable state from time to time and progress will stop temporarily.

Task 8

Applying Methods of Training

What you will learn about in this section

1 Apply Methods to Different Sports/Activities

2 Knowledge of Correct Stages and Procedures of a Training Session: Warm-up, Main Activity and Cool Down

3 Have Knowledge of How to Peak for a Sport/Physical Activity

4 Have Knowledge of the Correct Skills/Techniques and Safety Procedures

1   Apply Methods to Different Sports/Activities

Each sport is different and puts different demands on the performer. Each will have a different blend of both health and skill-related fitness components. What makes each activity unique comes about from the rules, equipment, playing area, duration and number of players involved in the activity.

Identifying the selection of components and then devising a training programme around them makes training sessions meaningful and appropriate.

Types of activities in training sessions

The types of activities in a training session will be a mix of both health and skill-related fitness components. Each exercise or activity will be adapted to the game in an attempt to train the body in the way it will be required to move in the game situation. For instance, the game requires both aerobic and anaerobic respiration so adapting Fartlek training to some sessions would help the player.

> **Example**
> Basketball

Health-related fitness components

Endurance needs aerobic respiration so sustained activity keeping heart rate between 60–80% of max should be incorporated into the programme.

Strength – weights for general strength improvement – plyometrics for lower and upper body strength.

Flexibility – dynamic exercises to increase the range of movement at a joint.

Skill-related fitness components

General speed off the mark is essential in basketball. This requires anaerobic respiration. So short, sharp bursts of maximal effort are used; these sprints can be combined with turns and changes of direction simulating the actions reproduced in the game.

Sessions often include a series of drills sharpening actions and skills simulating the game situation. Drills require the performer to work all-out and then rest, waiting for their next turn. Working and resting in this way is the interval training method. The components used in the game are identified and put into the programme:

Coordination ● Reaction time ● Power ● Agility ● Speed

What to do:

1. Choose a sport.
2. Follow the headings and identify the health and skill-related components of the activity.
3. Describe four training methods/drills which would suit your chosen game.
4. Prepare to discuss your work with others.

Task 1

2 Knowledge of Correct Stages and Procedures of a Training Session: Warm-up, Main Activity, Cool Down

Three parts to an exercise session

An exercise session consists of a warm-up, a main activity and a cool down.

Warm-up

There are three phases to a warm-up; aerobic phase; stretch and flexibility phase; skills and intensive exercise phase.

The time immediately before the main activity is crucial. This is the period when the body can prepare for the rigorous physical activity. There is no set time for a warm-up. It should be adapted to the demands of the sport and the age of the performer.

By warming up, the body systems, muscles and joints gradually become used to working harder. This gradual increase of stress on the body reduces the risk of injury. The pulse and body temperature are raised to nearer the working rate.

Concentrating on the warm-up activities will concentrate the mind. By focusing in this way an advantage may be gained over the opposition by having a better start to a match.

In the warm-up phase of team sports there needs to be an opportunity to practise the basic skills of the game and to start to think collectively as a team. The warm-up creates a link between rest and the main activity. The timing between the two is important. If there is too long a gap the effects of the warm-up will be lost. If actions stressing the muscles and joints, like sprinting, are used in the event then these should be included at the end of the warm-up session.

Applying Methods of Training

Types of movement to include in a warm-up

Light aerobic work

This type of activity, such as marching on the spot, starts a session in order to get the heart and lungs working harder.

Stretches

Stretches and flexibility exercises are next. Stretches ease the muscles and joints used in the activity into action.

There are different types of stretches and those performed in the warm-up should, for safety, be performed in the following order: static – assisted – dynamic.

Athletes using static stretches ease the muscles gradually into the stretched position and hold it there for 10 seconds.

Assisted stretching is when the action is helped by pushing against another person or a wall. A specialised way of stretching is often used in gymnastics. Here, the coach helps the performer by pushing the limb and so stretching the joint further. These are called 'proprioceptive neuromuscular facilitation (PNF) techniques'. These should only be undertaken by an expert and with great care.

Dynamic stretches are the most complex to perform. Care needs to be taken as injury can occur if these are misused. The athlete moves into the stretch position and 'bounces' the muscle. This starts at half pace for two to three repetitions. These gradually increase to full speed. These movements are used when the event or activity needs rapid, explosive movements.

Flexibility exercises

These exercises increase the mobility of the joints of the body – rotating shoulders and hips, for example. Each joint should be given some time, although certain sports may need some joints warmed more than others.

Skills and intensive exercises

Basic skills related to the sport can help co-ordination in a game. The exercises gradually increase in intensity. If the sport includes times when bursts of pace are necessary then, at the end of the session, some short sprints can be included. By warming up, a person will increase their awareness and reaction time ready for the game. Preparing the body will increase the level of work the person is capable of producing in the event. Note that professional football teams have set warm-ups which they perform on the pitch before a match.

Main activity

The warm-up leads to the main activity. This can be a training session, skills session or a competition, match or performance. Once the body systems are trained they become fit enough to complete the skills practised. When the body is pushed to the limit in competition, the skills can be put to the test without breaking down because of inadequate fitness levels.

Cool down

There are two phases to the cool down: gentle aerobic and stretching.

After the main activity, the body is given the chance of gradually returning to its resting state; the cool down helps to do this. The heart and muscles of the body take advantage of this. By completing a cool down the heartbeat reaches its resting rate sooner; this is called the 'recovery time'. The heart, therefore, does not have to work too hard for longer than it needs to. The speed of the recovery rate is influenced by several factors:

- The older a person is, the slower the recovery rate will be.
- If the exercise is new, then the new stresses will be harder to recover from.
- How 'in shape' the performer is: the fitter a person is, the quicker the recovery.
- Women tend to recover more slowly than men.

Like the warm-up, there is no set time for a cool down; keeping the blood circulating prevents it from having the chance to 'pool' or collect in areas of the circulatory system; this prevents light-headedness.

Gentle stretching stops the build-up of lactic acid in the muscles and so prevents immediate cramp and aching and soreness the following day. Stretches in a cool down should be held for about 30 seconds and should concentrate on the muscles used in the event. Freestyle swimmers will concentrate on cooling down their arms; runners will stretch their legs. A controlled, restful cool down can have a calming effect on a person after the excitement of a competitive match.

Task 2

What to do:

1. Give three reasons why a warm-up helps a performer.
2. List three types of exercise that would be included in a warm-up.
3. Draw a spidergram of the main points and reasons for a cool down.

Summary

There are many advantages to taking part in physical activity. A person in the habit of regular exercise could benefit from their healthy lifestyle. Physically, the body and its systems can increase in fitness, and be able to meet the demands of their environment and the added demands of the activity. A stronger body may increase life expectancy.

Personal development can come about through the challenges of exercise. A person may develop determination, courage and a positive attitude as a result of taking exercise; in turn this may spill over into general life and positively affect a person's confidence. Co-operation, teamwork and friendships may develop from being a member of a group, club or team.

Periodisation

The training programme for the year needs detailed planning. The plan will change according to the sport, the individual and the facilities available. The coach should make the team or individual familiar with the plan and, although it may have to change due to injury or postponed fixtures, the general outline should create goals to achieve and keep the performers motivated. The training differs greatly between the pre-season, peak season and out of season (closed season).

The performer will need to consider the following:

- What is the overall aim of the training?
- When does the training year start?
- What results am I working on – personal best or qualifying performance?
- When is the competition I am training for?

Planning for an individual event

If an athlete is training for a competition taking place in August, then the training starts in the previous October and is divided into six phases each with their own goal.

The timetable sets out with specific plans to develop each of the following areas: condition of the body, strength, technique, mobility, endurance and speed. Each of the activities are building blocks worked on to ensure there is no injury. The goals or objectives of each phase are as follows :

Phase 1 – starts October for 16 weeks. General development of strength, mobility, endurance and basic technique.

Phase 2 – starts February for 8 weeks. Development of specific fitness and advanced technical skills to do with the event.

Phase 3 – starts April for 8 weeks. Competition experience: achievement of indoor objectives helping to bring an edge to performance.

Phase 4 – starts June for 8 weeks. Adjusting technique for the event and preparation for the main competition.

Phase 5 – starts July for 8 weeks. Competition experience and achievement of outdoor objectives.

Phase 6 – starts September for 4 weeks. Active recovery from the season's efforts changing the amount and type of training. Planning preparation for the next season.

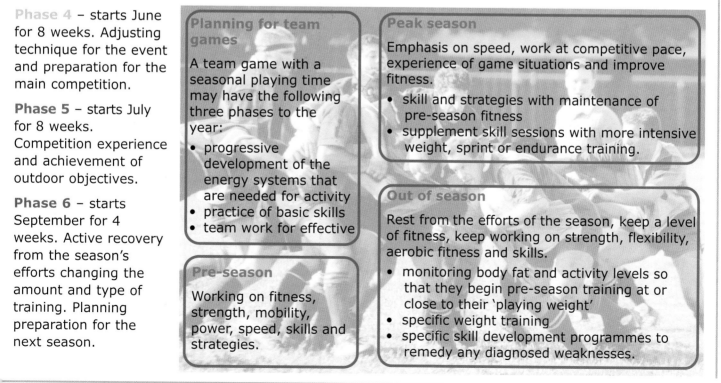

Planning for team games

A team game with a seasonal playing time may have the following three phases to the year:

- progressive development of the energy systems that are needed for activity
- practice of basic skills
- team work for effective

Pre-season

Working on fitness, strength, mobility, power, speed, skills and strategies.

Peak season

Emphasis on speed, work at competitive pace, experience of game situations and improve fitness.

- skill and strategies with maintenance of pre-season fitness
- supplement skill sessions with more intensive weight, sprint or endurance training.

Out of season

Rest from the efforts of the season, keep a level of fitness, keep working on strength, flexibility, aerobic fitness and skills.

- monitoring body fat and activity levels so that they begin pre-season training at or close to their 'playing weight'
- specific weight training
- specific skill development programmes to remedy any diagnosed weaknesses.

Out of season

Mid May–July

Time without competitive matches

Light general fitness work completed

Different sports played to keep the mind fresh

General levels of fitness maintained by a moderate aerobic training programme

Pre-season

July–August

Time before the matches start

Training intensity increases

Netball skills and techniques improved and refined

Initial work on 'set plays'

Increased anaerobic training – with progress comes confidence in self and team

Mental preparation

Some rest periods before the season starts

Diet changes according to the intensity of the training

Peak season

September–April

Regular competitive matches

Time spent training and resting between matches

Peak of performance reached

Fitness levels maintained

Continued work on mental preparation – focusing prior to the game

Continued keeping to strict diet

Early season

Mid August–September

Aerobic and anaerobic training continues

Skill and technique training continues and intensifies

Set plays modified for each game

Continued work on mental preparation for matches

Strict and specific diet kept to for the level of training and competition

4 Have Knowledge of the Correct Skills/Techniques and Safety Procedures

When a performer decides to use any training method careful planning is needed. Before they begin it is crucial they have knowledge of their own fitness levels and limitations. This knowledge will be a safety guideline for the well-being of the performer.

Each method will demand different levels of intensity, frequency, time and type of the exercise used. Applying the training principles of specificity, progression and overload according to the performer's fitness levels will keep the training safe.

When working with equipment it is important to be trained in its use and adhere to the correct procedures each time. When designing and using circuit training there are several essential safety considerations to apply. Often a group of performers will work out at the same time. Spacing the stations correctly in the gym will reduce the possibility of injury. Mobile equipment used in the exercises, like netballs, need secure placement at the station before the athlete moves on. This will prevent it rolling away and being a hazard to others. Mat placement can also make certain exercises included in the circuit safer, for example, sit-ups. Lifting weights can also cause a problem. Always keep the body in line and take the weight with the leg muscles when appropriate.

Summary

When an athlete works on their training programme they should be confident that it has been planned correctly according to their fitness levels. They should be secure in the knowledge that the exercises being performed are within their capabilities and unlikely to lead to injury. The performer should always be mindful of overuse injuries and incorporate rests for certain muscle groups to prevent this happening. Knowledge and training may be required when undertaking certain training methods for the safety of the performer and should be followed as a matter of course for each session.

Factors Affecting Participation, Provision and Performance

What you will learn about in this section

1. Popularity and Participation Levels
2. Gender, Race and Social Issues

1 Popularity and Participation Levels

Many factors influence the reasons for participation. Sports rise and fall in popularity from time to time, the reasons for which are wide and varied. Where in the country a person lives and what tradition that area has can have a bearing on the sport a person takes part in.

Cultural influences

An area may have a sport as part of its cultural heritage – for years, the Welsh valleys produced many world class rugby union players and had a successful national side. The success of a rugby, gymnastics or hockey club, for example, may be an attraction for new players or competitors and coaches, and so help maintain the traditional high standards of the club.

Family traditions may encourage children in a particular sport, even to the detriment of other sports. By focusing on one activity, there is a chance that talents for other sports are missed or overlooked.

Tradition, interest and facilities lead to a gold medal for the women's British curling team.

When success in new sports does emerge, the local authority may allocate more money for it in their budget or private sponsors may finance efforts to raise the profile, standards and participation levels.

In the Salt Lake City Winter Olympics, the British curling teams were solely made up of people from Scotland. This was due to the long tradition of curling in Scotland, where there are many curling rinks and the interest is high.

Activities in and out of fashion

The popularity of an activity can change quickly as **trends** in sport fall in and out of fashion. In the short term, during Wimbledon week more people can be seen using local tennis facilities inspired by what they are seeing on the TV. A more long-term effect can come about by a national side doing well in a major tournament, which causes an increase in popularity in that sport, which may encourage local authorities to fund new facilities.

If a **minority sport** begins to receive greater coverage on the television this will lead to an increase in its popularity. In recent years snooker has gained in popularity, perhaps due to the coverage of the top personalities within the sport inspiring and attracting youngsters to the game. A sport could also decline in popularity with less people taking part; squash in recent years has taken such a downturn. Courts in local sports centres, rather than remaining unused, are being adapted for trendier activities such as aerobics and yoga.

Age

The age of a person may influence their chances of taking part in certain activities. There may be age limits for participation or joining of some clubs, such as for golf, netball or rugby. Depending on the size of the club, each age group usually has its own section with separate competition and coaching. Guidelines may be set by the sports governing body to help organisation.

As the trend for a healthier lifestyle continues, older people see the need to keep exercising. Although they may be carrying an injury or a condition, if they are properly educated about the problem and are sensible about how much they take on, they will continue to benefit from exercising.

An older age group enjoying sport.

Older people have the chance to learn new skills as many public and private centres now cater for older age groups. More people are planning for their retirement but money may still be a problem for the older generation. In some cases, concessions are made for older participants and off-peak times are set aside for them.

●●●●● ▶ Active Challenge

Discuss with a partner events in the media which may affect the popularity of sporting activities.

Facilities available

The provision of indoor and outdoor facilities depends on many factors. All areas of the country would like excellent local facilities but providing these would not be financially or practically workable. There are many issues taken into consideration when deciding on new facilities:

Location – certain sites naturally lend themselves to various activities. Outdoor pursuit centres are situated where there are hills, rivers, lakes and forests suited to the particular activities involved. The beautiful countryside of North Wales is popular for mountaineers. It provides challenges for all abilities and has excellent facilities to support this area of the tourist industry. Plas y Brennin, in Snowdonia, is the National Mountain Centre for Wales.

The National Mountain Centre for Wales, Plas y Brennin, in Snowdonia.

Funding – money to increase or improve the facilities can come from different sources: the government may set aside money in their annual budget; the lottery may meet part of the cost; an individual may personally finance a team.

Expected use and demand – whether it is private or publicly funded, the aim is to have as many people use the facility for as much of the time as possible. When deciding on a site for a new facility enough people should be available in the area to make full use of it.

Access

Where facilities for certain activities are good, there may be more chance that more people will participate. The greater the involvement, the better the possibility of a higher standard which then attracts more players and coaches. In small communities, there may be an interest but not enough people to make it viable. Unless transport is available to towns with established clubs, the opportunity to play is lost.

The Welsh assembly has produced a 20-year plan, 'Climbing Higher' promoting a healthier lifestyle for all residents, making physical activity a part of everyday living. The plan covers school children, adults and the elderly, of all abilities, raising the barriers which existed to prevent people taking part.

Some of the operational priorities include:
- Funding for primary schools to the Dragon Sport scheme
- The support of the free swimming initiative
- Mass participation in sporting events in Wales
- Making maximum use of the natural beauty of North Wales in outdoor activities
- The introduction of new coaching plans:

In July 2005 the Coaching Plans for Wales were launched. The two main aims are:
- to increase the number of coaches, leaders and instructors both voluntary and professional
- to improve the quality of coaching in Wales by increasing opportunities for education, training and qualifications.

The new plans aim to raise the profile of coaching and adopt the UK Coaching Certificate (UKCC) which will standardise the coaching qualifications over all sports. The certificate will be recognised throughout the UK, it can be transferred across to other sports more easily. Training will be quality assured and the structure and management of administration will be quality assured. 31 sports are targeted with the first twenty were ready to deliver the certificate in 2006.

Other courses will include:
Sports coach UK (scUK) – providing general coaching workshops at all levels
Continuous professional development – for coaches at all levels
Coach scholarships – supports coaches working with top class, elite athletes
Mountain Leadership – taking advantage of the unique natural environment of Wales with the following
- Sports leader UK – is a basic expedition leadership award for teachers, youth workers and members of the community
- Mountain Leader training Wales – the course involves all skills that would be required to lead a group in the mountains

Economic constraints and participation

In order to participate in most sports there needs to be a certain financial commitment. Some sports are relatively cheap to sustain. The major essential for running is a good quality pair of running shoes and you're off. Other activities are more technical and complicated to complete so taking part in these sees the expense increase. There are sports that are just too expensive to finance individually and membership of a club is the only way to take part.

> "I want to play tennis but there are no facilities close by."
>
> "I can win against girls four years older than me, but I am too young to join my local club."
>
> "Everyone says I am a talented rugby player, but my family are enthusiastic that I follow family traditions and play football."

What to do:
1. Read the three comments in the box made by keen and talented sportspeople.
2. Study their problems.
3. Think of possible ways they could overcome them and play the sport of their choice.

Task 1

What to do:

Think about different types of physical activity.

Make three lists of activities and their costs to take part in

1. Those requiring less than £150
2. Those requiring between £151 and £300
3. Those requiring more than £300

For a lot of people an amount of disposable income is necessary to finance a physically active pursuit. If a person wants to keep taking part over a long period of time then there needs to be a plan in place to cover the cost. Money to pay possible joining fees and annual subscriptions are required in order to join a club. Equipment will need replacing; new innovations may be made in the sport and equipment needs updating to keep competitive.

What to do:

1. Choose five different activities.
2. For each, list the expenses that each may incur in order that a person may regularly participate.

The initial expense of buying high quality equipment may be great, but once purchased, only transport costs remain in order to participate.

2   Gender, Race and Social Issues

The Welsh Assembly set out clear plans for a healthier Wales in the 'Climbing Higher' document. In the plan they made the Welsh Sport Council a key contributor by giving them the task of taking away barriers to sporting opportunities. They targeted women and girls, those with disabilities, black, minority ethnic communities and deprived areas. Equality of opportunity was key to any funding being granted.

Gender

Both males and females are encouraged to participate in most sports. Ideally everyone who has an interest should be able to participate and compete in their chosen activity. However, there are constraints: some clubs may only offer single sex teams due to a lack of facilities and qualified coaches.

Although most sports are available to both sexes, generally each sex competes separately. This is for safety, due to the physical differences of size and strength and fair play. Some sports have their own governing bodies for each sex; tennis and golf, for example. Two of the few major sporting events to have male and female competitors in the same event are show jumping and mixed-doubles matches in tennis.

Males and sports

Boys often start playing sport because they regard the activity as great fun. In the controlled environment of a game situation an activity may provide an outlet for aggression and act as a release valve for youth, energy and enthusiasm. Sport can also provide opportunities to express natural tendencies for competition. Some sports are popular with men due to the nature of the game. Rugby attracts some males because it is a physically demanding contact sport.

Activities readily available in the area may have reputations for success, good facilities, excellent coaching, social events and the like. These will be well known in the community and so new, young members (attracted by these reputations), will help keep the traditions and the strong continuation of the activity going in the locality.

Training for an activity often develops skill, physique and competitiveness in sport and is often chosen by men for its physicality.

Often men state that a reason for joining a club is to be part of a team. They enjoy the feeling of togetherness and camaraderie brought about by being in a group of similarly minded people all working to the same end. Many activities have a social side. Often teams will have a club house where everyone can mix after a game. Some clubs still have the tradition of providing a meal after the match for the players. When the speeches are over all can have a drink together, this gives the possibility of making new acquaintances and friends. Many clubs often arrange special social events enabling all members and friends to be involved and feel part of the club.

Males often choose a sport for its physicality.

What to do:

1. From the information in Males and sports create a spidergram of the key points which explain why males participate in sport.
2. Discuss the information with others.

Girls and sports

Women have a different mix of reasons, although just as valid as men, for participating in physical activity.

Some women like the competitiveness of a team game. To be part of a group with similar interests and the same aim gives a sense of belonging. The popularity of ladies hockey and netball teams exist as a result.

Often the sports most attractive to women are those with less body contact with other players. These can include netball, gym, dance, racket sports.

Many women enjoy less competitive physical activities like aerobics or weights. These activities involve great amounts of effort but do not require aggression geared towards others. What is required, especially in weight training, is self-determination to overcome the resistance of the weights. The emphasis with these activities is on the personal look the effects have on the shape of the body. The effects on the body – keeping a balanced weight/height ratio – may make the women more attractive to men.

Table of participation of girls 2–11 years out of school time at least once

	2–11 yrs	2–11 Yrs	2–11 Yrs
	1994	**1999**	**2002**
Games	85%	86	88
Team Games	71	78	76
Invasion games	58	32	67
Football (inc.5-a-side)	35	46	46
Netball	29	32	28
Basketball	19	26	28
Striking games	53	58	54
Cricket	22	27	24
Rounders	45	48	46
Volleyball	14	15	16
Racket sports	64	59	64
Tennis	51	46	53
Badminton	31	29	31
Table Tennis	25	20	27
Golf (all types)	19	20	22
Swimming activities	84	81	83
Dance and ice skating	53	48	52
Dance classes	27	25	32
Ice skating	36	32	34
Gym and Trampolining	13	13	16

Source – From MORI published in 'Young People and Sport' report by Sport England 2003

Although aerobics and weights are more individual in nature, there is still scope for meeting other people with similar interests – a group aerobics session is just one example.

Women, wanting to participate in physical activity, often choose activities that will maintain their feminine image.

For young girls, often the pressure from peers not to take part in exercise can prevent them from taking part at all; here the need to remain popular in a group outweighs the desire for exercise.

Many women will take part in physical activities which have a bearing on their health and weight.

•••• ▶ Active Challenge

Ask all the girls in the class about the sport/exercise activities they participate in.

Collate all the data.

Prepare a bar chart to reflect the data.

Women in sport

Women's opportunities in sport are steadily increasing and becoming more financially rewarding. There is greater representation for women in the national authorities. The Sports Council supports women's participation in sport and has in place ways to raise levels of achievement. More governing bodies are recognising women's place in their sport.

In 1972 the Women's Football Association (WFA) was formed, supporting female talent for the game. The Women's Sport Foundation (WSF) founded in 1984, also pioneers the female cause, working hard to increase media coverage, raising the awareness of top class women's sporting success. Events such as the Women's Rugby World Cup showed the highest level of women's sport, helping it to become more popular. There are increasingly more opportunities for women to have careers linked with sport in the media. This may be a first career or an occupation taken up after competitive life is over. On a local level, many sports centres make time during the day for women's activities. They may provide crèche facilities to help as many women as possible take part.

More women's sports are being televised, raising the profile of those activities. Sports such as the Women's FA Cup final, WTA tennis, Golf, Aerobics and Rhythmic Gymnastics are regularly televised on for Sky viewers.

In recent times companies are more ready to use high profile, successful women to advertise their products.

Kelly Holmes' double Olympic success made her extremely desirable as a person to promote a company's product.

What to do:

1. Using Kelly Holmes as an example, say why a company would want to use her for promotional purposes.

Use the following ideas to help you:

What efforts she had to make to achieve her state of fitness

What she achieved

Where she achieved it

What it meant to the country

Personal qualities

Both the company and women's sport benefit from this association:

- The women used give a wholesome image to the product being advertised.
- The women are seen as role models to look up to and emulate. This in turn can encourage people to lead a healthy lifestyle which includes exercise.
- The activity associated with that woman, is brought to the public eye too. The effect can make that activity more popular.

Success on the track promotes a successful image to a product.

Current trends hope to make the majority of sports accessible to all groups. These trends have allowed women to access a broader range of sports. There are less bans on women taking part in certain activities, for example, athletics has seen women's pole vault added to their competition list in recent years.

Media images of fit and healthy women can influence female participation and popularity levels in exercise. Activities such as aerobics, weight training, which focus on body shape and lifestyle are increasingly popular with women and can be accessible at local public and private gyms.

Sponsors fund sport raising its profile and can, as a result, increase the popularity and participation in that activity.

What to do:

1. Look in the sports pages of a variety of media – newspapers, magazines, Internet and so on.
2. Collect news items to do with women in sport.

Promoting women in sport

There have been many campaigns and programmes promoting women in sport. These have included a wide range of participants from young novice to top level coach.

Disabled and sport

The Sport for All campaign encourages all groups to participate in sport. One such group is the disabled. The campaign makes all people aware that those with a disability have a need to participate in sport. Encouragement is given to this group to join in physical activity. They take part in their own special groups, or mix with the able bodied, showing it is to everyone's benefit, that they participate.

Established facilities are adapted to accommodate the varied needs of the disabled. Ramps, stair lifts, changing areas and toilets are modified to make using these areas easier.

Lottery grants for sports facilities have helped usage for the disabled as often part of the deal for funding is to make sure disabled facilities are in place.

Special groups are formed to help participation — Disability Sport Cymru is focused on sport and recreation opportunities for the disabled in Wales.

Tanni Grey-Thompson sponsored by Norwich Union, is a role model for all women with disabilities.

Media coverage

Increasingly more sports with disabled athletes are being broadcast. For example, the Paralympics had its own slots and the London Marathon coverage increasingly shows the wheelchair athletes in action. This coverage shows how well people with disability can overcome their problems, adapt, enjoy and succeed at sport. People who rise to the top of their sport are positive role models for others to aspire towards.

Some sports have no segregation of able and disabled athletes and so both groups can compete alongside each other. For instance, wheelchair athletes can achieve as high standards as standing athletes in archery.

The young and participation levels

In 2003 Sport England initiated a survey of the young population and how they were involved in sport. It recognised the need to find ways of starting children sooner in physical activity; this would benefit the population's health and social welfare in the long run. In that year they had a survey carried out by MORI (an organisation specialising in surveys, polls and statistics) headed – 'Young people and sport in England — Trends in Participation'. The survey deals with the changes that have come about in participation rates of the young since 1995. The key points to its findings follow.

The survey showed that children's attitudes are changing and they are less inhibited by the social nature of sport. Children increasingly and willingly will take part in physically active situations, feeling more comfortable to be seen joining in. It was also evident that young people more happily associate themselves with group situations and team play, generally being more confident about their involvement.

Attitudes to sport

In 2002 youngsters took part in more sports lessons than in 1995 with more young people realising the importance of physical activity. The youth understand the implications and benefits of regularly taking part in exercise. Many young people agree that keeping fit is important and they readily link this with exercise and sport.

Younger people are becoming more resilient to the adverse weather conditions and the aggressive nature of some activities. Fewer children are now put off by playing sport in the rain or the chance of getting tackled or hit by a ball.

Extra-curricular

There has been a rise in the numbers taking part in extra-curricular activities in school. Children are encouraged to get involved so much so that two in five children participated in these activities in 2002 in comparison with one in three in 1994. This increase has been attributed to the increased involvement of coaches, specialists and sports organisations linked with school. There are now more after school sessions creating greater opportunity and increasing involvement. 51% of boys and 36% of girls now involve themselves in sports clubs.

The majority of the boys still enjoy the more competitive activities whilst many girls still favour dance and swimming. Football is the most popular extra-curricular activity with 51% of children taking part in that activity in 2002. Almost a quarter of boys play football and it is second only in popularity to netball for girls. In general, young people are becoming more competitive.

Fewer children are put off sport by bad weather and the dangers of injury.

Leisure

Such are the changing attitudes of young people that more are likely to take part in sport in their leisure time. Not only is there an increased number of children making sport their leisure pursuit, but they also spend more time per week doing that physical activity too. In 2002, young people on average spent 8.1 hours per week being physically active in comparison with 7.5 hours in 1999. This figure rises in the summer holidays to about 10 hours per week for children aged 7–11 years. As a result of the changing attitudes to sport many school leavers want to continue to take part in exercise, making it part of their young adult life.

PESS (Physical Education and School Sport) project in Wales

The Welsh Assembly's Minister for Education and Lifelong Learning supports the PESS 'Action Plan for Wales'. The project aims to establish development centres across Wales aiming to raise the standard of physical education in schools and continue this in the community through leisure activities.

What to do:

1. Make a list of the above information of the changes in the young and participation levels.

PESS Development Centres and new initiatives have been created and implemented to create a seamless link between physical activity in school and the community. It is hoped that the opportunities created will allow every young person an hour of physically active leisure time. These opportunities may range from activities in the playground at lunch break to the use of facilities at local clubs after the school day.

Sport England has developed the Active Sports Programme which links young people with the sport of their choice. It enables the player to develop their skills in the community to the best level they are capable. It links school sport with local clubs and through development courses provides the best possible coaching.

Task 7

Race

The government realise there is an imbalance of participation in ethnic minority groups. They have assembled action groups to look at the issue of equality in sport. A massive government campaign targeting football, headed 'Kick racism out of football' is a way of making people aware of the problem and to show that it is unacceptable.

Reasons for lack of participation

Many ethnic minority groups like taking part in sport but they live in poorer areas. These areas have very few facilities for sport and so the opportunity to participate is reduced. In fact 70% of the ethnic minority live in 88 of the country's poorest areas. For greater participation, financial issues relating to disposable income and facilities available need resolving for a difference to be made.

Sport specific stereotyping

There are sporting myths that exist implying that certain races are less adaptable to particular activities. African Caribbeans are said to be less successful at swimming and the physical make-up of Asians is said to cause them to injure easily despite the fact that many Asians are successful in sports.

Gender

40% of women from the ethnic groups do not participate in sport. Their reason is that their home and family commitments are put first. For this to change governments have to address the child care provision for these groups to give more time for exercise leisure pursuits.

There are government guidelines available to clubs and institutions giving them ideas of how to reduce racial inequality.

Ways of stopping racism:

Institutions are encouraged to combat racism by doing the following:

- Make all feel welcome who come to the club
- Make everyone feel secure when participating
- Make public their intention of preventing racism
- Make procedure for complaints easy and straightforward
- Show images of people from different races involved in their sport
- Encourage people from ethnic minorities to have roles in administration, decision making and coaching.

Efforts are made so that all feel welcome in the club.

Family influences

Youngsters who grow up in a family, who have had good sporting experiences as part of their life, can be encouraged to follow the same interests. The adult's enthusiasm, interest and enjoyment, experienced through the activity, can often be enough to start the appeal.

If introduced to an activity at an early age and regularly participating in it, sport is shown as a usual part of life. It follows that the youngster could regard sport as part of their lifestyle and keep taking part when they get older and make more decisions for themselves.

Some parents use club membership not only to develop their children's physical skills but their social ones too. By regularly meeting at the club, training and competing, the child mixes with youngsters of their own age, with others who have similar interests and often in the presence of similar minded adults providing role models to copy.

A family keen on a particular activity may be as such because of the family traditions passed on through the generations. In this instance, family pride and experience are added to all the benefits of the pursuit.

Some families have a tradition in certain sports.

> ●●●● ▶ **Active Challenge**
>
> With a partner think of any competitions you know of where there are different generations taking part at the same time.

A role model provided by a family member may be an inspiration to copy. Their lifestyle shows a healthy, social, active and happy life brought about by their involvement in sport. This way of life could be appealing to the young so they aim to pursue happiness in the same way and take up physical activity. A relative could have been extremely successful in a sport and so a younger nephew/niece may want to try to emulate their victories for themselves.

Many families provide the financial backing so their child can pursue their interest. Lack of funds can inhibit some participation, but for those families who can find the money, they make a commitment to support their child for as long as the youngster is interested.

To fund a child's participation parents often need to find money for:

- Kit
- Equipment
- Joining fees
- Subscription fees
- Travel costs.

Getting their children to and from training and competition venues is often taken on by parents. This duty comes with a certain financial cost, but also involves dedication by the parent who often devotes a large amount of time too.

Some dedicated parents will adapt their child's diet to support training and competition. Although there are only a small percentage of families who do this, they recognise the need for the correct type of diet needed for success.

What to do:

1. Search the Internet for any reports on the increase of participation in physical activity in the young.

2. Print out and keep the item as evidence of your search.

Task 8

Barriers to participation in physical activity

There are many factors which can prevent people participating in physical activity. Although a person may want to take part their personal circumstances, commitments, finance and locality may get in the way.

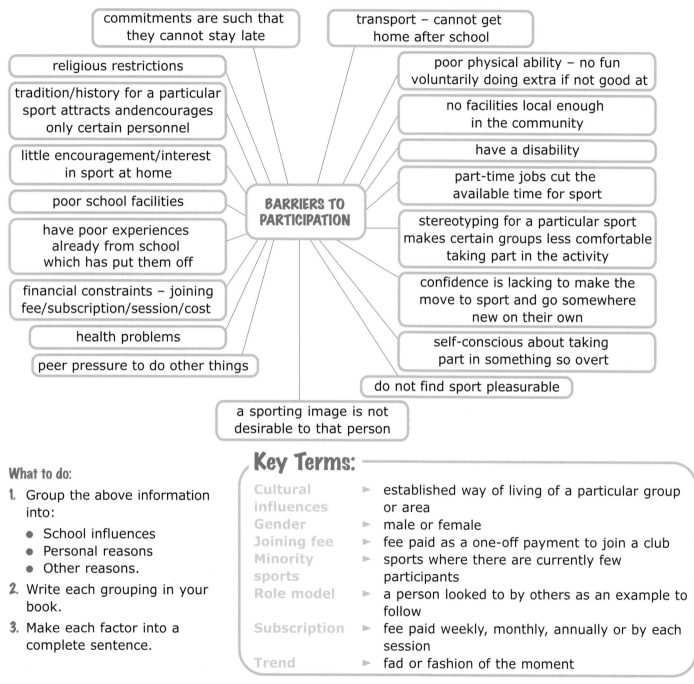

commitments are such that they cannot stay late

transport – cannot get home after school

religious restrictions

poor physical ability – no fun voluntarily doing extra if not good at

tradition/history for a particular sport attracts andencourages only certain personnel

no facilities local enough in the community

little encouragement/interest in sport at home

have a disability

poor school facilities

part-time jobs cut the available time for sport

BARRIERS TO PARTICIPATION

have poor experiences already from school which has put them off

stereotyping for a particular sport makes certain groups less comfortable taking part in the activity

financial constraints – joining fee/subscription/session/cost

confidence is lacking to make the move to sport and go somewhere new on their own

health problems

self-conscious about taking part in something so overt

peer pressure to do other things

do not find sport pleasurable

a sporting image is not desirable to that person

What to do:

1. Group the above information into:
   - School influences
   - Personal reasons
   - Other reasons.
2. Write each grouping in your book.
3. Make each factor into a complete sentence.

Key Terms:

Cultural influences	► established way of living of a particular group or area
Gender	► male or female
Joining fee	► fee paid as a one-off payment to join a club
Minority sports	► sports where there are currently few participants
Role model	► a person looked to by others as an example to follow
Subscription	► fee paid weekly, monthly, annually or by each session
Trend	► fad or fashion of the moment

Summary

Many factors influence participation. These factors can relate to:
- the sport – its appeal, nature and popularity
- the person – what their influences, interests and personality are like
- the circumstances – finance, location and tradition of the area.

For some people a good start in sport with pleasant experiences to look back on can be the key to a life including physical activity; others realise when they are older what the benefits of exercise (and possibly competitive/outdoor adventurous situations) can bring.

The Influence of School Physical Education Programme

What you will learn about in this section

1. Benefits of School P.E. Programme

All the separate governments of the UK have recognised the need for new measures to create further opportunities and encourage greater participation in physical activity for all the population. Special groups have been formed liaising with linked bodies to plan for and implement new schemes and directives.

Under the umbrella of Sport UK, each country's body – Sport Wales, Sport England and Sport Scotland have created their own way forward best suiting the needs of their country.

In 2000, the Welsh Assembly Secretary for Education and Children established a special advisory group, which is governed by the Welsh Assembly to support school sport. The group is called the Physical Education and School Sport (PESS). Liaising with several other health-related bodies it created a plan to make participation in physical activity easier and more readily available for all levels of ability.

ESTYN: Her majesty's Inspectorate for Education and Training – Aims to raise the standards and quality of education and training in Wales through school inspection, support and advice.

Girl's First: The Girl's First Scheme offers new extra curricula opportunities for girls and physical activity. The areas of opportunity include – Sports – Physical activity and – Active recreation. 15,000 girls took part in Girls first activities in 2004/5, with 142 schools being involved. The overall aim is to increase opportunities for over 64,000 girls.

Higher education Institutions: provides education beyond A level standard.

PESS (PHYSICAL EDUCATION AND SCHOOL SPORT)

DELLS: Department for Education, Lifelong Learning and Skills – advises on education and external qualifications in Wales (not NVQ's). In March 2006, merged with Education Department of the Welsh Assembly and re-named.

Further Education colleges: these institutions provide education for people over the age of 16 years.

BAALPE: Wales – Welsh section of the British Association of Advisors and Lecturers in Physical Education (to be renamed Association for Physical Education (afPE). The association provides a support network for advisors and lecturers in physical education.

PESS liaises with the above bodies.

There are many factors affecting a person taking part in sport. What we see on the TV, or read in newspapers or magazines, may sway us in our thinking. The more we are in contact with an influence may result in it having more effect on us. School, consequently, can have an important part to play in the encouragement of exercise.

1 Benefits of School P.E. Programme

Promotion Schools actively encourage participation in sport. Not only is it a legal requirement for all pupils to take part, but pupils can gain many personal benefits from sport at school. A school's physical education programme can encourage participation on several levels. By being given the opportunity to enjoy sport in school a pupil may decide that they want to do more in their own time.

Demonstrates fitness levels Schools provide up to two hours of P.E. lessons a week for all pupils; statistically this is insufficient to improve a person's fitness. However, P.E. lessons can educate young people about safe levels and the amount of exercise that can be undertaken to have a positive effect on fitness.

Encourage a healthy lifestyle Some P.E. lessons involve general instruction on a balance of exercise, diet and the need to avoid harmful substances for a healthy life. A good health education can help young people make sound life choices which continue throughout adulthood. A good P.E. programme can show pupils how to be healthier and fitter, this knowledge can be used in the future to combat obesity and other diseases.

Offer a range of activities By offering a wide range of activities, schools provide a variety of experiences for pupils where progress and achievement can be made. The mix of sports gives more chance of finding an area of interest and success for as many pupils

Sports day brings the whole school together through physical activity.

as possible and, hopefully the confidence to continue taking part in physical activity after they have left school. A mix of competitive and non-competitive activities on the timetable provides a balance that may suit a wider variety of personalities. By being given the chance to take part in activities they like, young people may voluntarily choose to do more.

A school P.E. programme can present pupils with unique opportunities. Pupils may have the chance to experience camps and various other outdoor activities not readily available. Residential visits develop both physical and social skills. Whilst knowledge, understanding and application of the new activities progress away from the home environment, the pupils learn to deal with others in both a learning and social situation.

Extend skills learnt in class Many schools offer pupils the chance to join a school club or team. This provides an opportunity to improve and extend skills learnt in lessons through competition. Sometimes participation is purely for fun. Some clubs may be set up for a completely new activity not on the P.E. timetable to further extend pupils' interest. Using local facilities as part of the P.E. programme shows pupils what is locally available, what is expected there and who they are going to meet.

This experience can equip pupils with enough knowledge, understanding and confidence in an activity that they have the self-assurance to pursue it on their own, in their own time, independent of school.

Leisure pursuits By providing a wide variety of activities on the timetable and extra sessions after school, pupils may be sufficiently interested in exercise to continue participation after they have left school. The experience of visiting a local gym or sports centre whilst at school may provide the knowledge and confidence to go to these centres independently. Well over half the adults that go skiing had their first skiing experience from school.

Experience different ways to enjoy sport Schools recognise the importance of giving pupils a chance not only to play the games but to take part in different ways too. Members of a class may regularly experience how to judge, coach, observe, officiate, captain, lead, organise or choreograph. These different experiences may appeal to children and lead to an interest in sport beyond actually playing the game.

Outdoor and adventurous activities.

Experience healthy competition Some activities provide the opportunity for competition. The rules governing that game allow for healthy competition whilst supplying a framework for safe and fair play. The players know the boundaries and rely on the umpire/referee to implement them consistently.

Develop a variety of skills By providing a balanced curriculum, a full range of skills can be learnt. From experience and knowledge of a variety of activities, a person may choose their favourites – those providing the most satisfaction and enjoyment – and pursue them throughout adulthood.

Develop social skills and friendships Many activities involve people coming together to train, organise or compete. Meeting people of similar interests can develop social skills and make it more likely to create friendships.

In game situations each person has their own role to play. Team members learn that working hard themselves contributes to group success. Each player relies on the others to do their job and when necessary tracks back and covers space on the pitch when errors are made – in football a midfield player may have to run back to cover the defender.

Often after a match, when the facilities are available, all involved meet together socially. This gives a chance not only to talk about the game, but also to chat socially and to establish old and new friendships.

Various school activities involve all personality types and abilities.

The Graham diagram

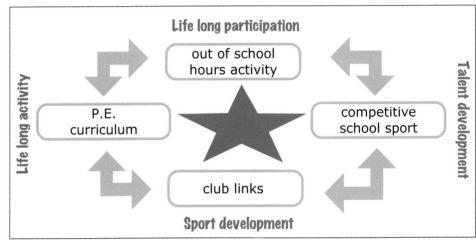

Sport development on all levels.

Education for lifelong learning A long term aim of P.E. is to see people take part in physical activity into adulthood. Schools aim to give a positive experience of exercise and provide pupils with the knowledge, skills and understanding giving them confidence to apply this to their lifestyle after they have left school. The programme should show a person how they can use physical activity for leisure, recreation or career and should aim to be a lifelong learning experience.

Positive experiences P.E., for most people, provides both winning and losing situations. Any success can boost a person's self-esteem. For that moment their standing in the group rises and they can take that feeling away and build on it for the future.

The chance to learn about and cope with losing is also a valuable lesson. In this way sport prepares people for coping with high and low situations, possibly helping them with the ups and downs of life they may experience as they get older.

Develop stars of the future At school level a teacher can recognise a child's ability and potential to do well early on. These skills can be nurtured and developed within lessons and extra-curricular activities.

Through school, staff can point a child in the direction of a club or coach so that their skills can be further advanced. By linking different institutions, at this stage, gives the performer the opportunity to experience a higher level of coaching and competition. This progressive development, in the long term, can prepare performers for major events and competitions.

What to do:

1. Use the headings from the section 'Benefits of School P.E. Programme' to form a spidergram. This will help you remember the main points.
2. Below each heading, write out a sentence, using your own words, expanding the idea.

Teacher

By relating their enthusiasm for the subject, a P.E. teacher shows all of the good reasons for taking part in exercise. Although some pupils are not enthusiastic about physical education, a positive approach by staff can encourage most of the class to join in. By using different ways to deliver the information and encouraging more than just the acquisition of skill, the teacher can plan their lessons to inspire enthusiasm in their class.

In class

The classroom can be a place where information is given, skills, to perform the activity, are practiced and put into operation. Opportunity to learn a wider range of skills is available too. These skills can include:

planning gymnastics and dance routines or strategy in a game
working out finding answers to problems, such as how to beat the opposition
observing learning the correct technique and looking for it in performances
communication discussing useful instructions or **coaching points**
leadership of a small group in class, as a captain or an organiser
choreography in dance, children have the chance to make up their own routines
external examination to increase the understanding of P.E. and aid the career of pupils
achieve awards results in class may contribute to a recognised award scheme
cross-curricular links made with other subjects to enhance the teaching
outside visits links to see sports events, clubs and providers.
ICT gives the opportunity to use the latest technology and link it with sport. Practice in finding information and results of performances on the Internet and recording their own results on computer gives pupils key skills in technology. Searching the Internet gives access to the heroes of the time and creates interest.

▶ Active Challenge

Think of a lesson where you have a role or job to do.
Put a name to the job using the previous section.
Briefly tell a partner what you did and what skills you developed as a result.
Try to think of three examples.

Extra-curricular activities

As an extension to P.E. lessons many schools provide extra sessions after school; these are called 'extra-curricular activities'. These provide even more benefits to the pupils, because they:

- become a member of a team
- have a chance to be a captain or leader of a team
- visit other schools and venues for matches
- may join organised trips to see top-class sport
- become a member of a club or society taking part for the fun of the event and not for the competition
- develop links with clubs and providers; for example, local coaches come into school to help coaching and local clubs offer their facilities to the school
- increase their sports performance by joining after school clubs to increase skill and in some cases reach a standard for awards and proficiency tests.

Awards

Athletics Sainsbury's in association with English schools athletics. association Primary award scheme and secondary award scheme.
Swimming Kellog's – in association with the Amateur Swimming Association.
Gymnastics run by 'British Gymnastics' the governing body.

The organisers of the scheme provide information and activity packs, pointing out the skills of the game/activity to the teacher and performer. These supply a base of skills to learn, practice and hopefully apply to competition. Working for an award gives performers a goal for which to aim and can often keep them focused, interested and motivated to do well.

There is often a structure to the award scheme involving several levels of achievement. Having different levels makes success attainable for all and the grade reached allows the child to experience feedback in that activity. The chance to progress from one stage to another can provide motivation and interest to the performer in a particular season or from year to year.

The presentation of a certificate or badge is tangible feedback of the skills achieved. The award reached shows a competency and can give the incentive to build on that success and earn a higher award in the future.

Key Terms:

Choreography	►	creating a series of steps and teaching others to follow
Coaching points	►	instructions given to improve technique
Extra-curricular activities	►	activities outside the regular school timetable
Healthy lifestyle	►	conducting life adhering to care on mental and physical well-being
National Curriculum	►	government instructions on what is to be taught in schools

Risks of Extremes of Exercise Levels

What you will learn about in this section

1. Risks associated with Sedentary Lifestyle
2. Risks associated with Excessive Forms and Amounts of Exercise

1 Risks Associated with Sedentary Lifestyle

Sedentary lifestyle is one that involves little physical activity.

Office working people who sit a lot in their job are classed as sedentary workers. These people could be at risk of physical health complaints especially if they have a poor imbalanced diet too.

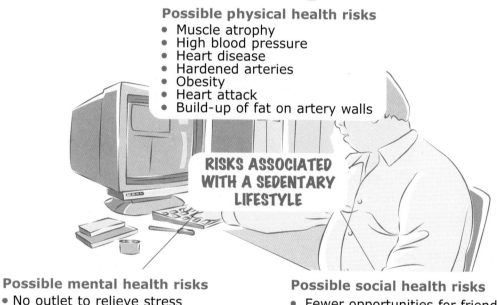

Possible physical health risks
- Muscle atrophy
- High blood pressure
- Heart disease
- Hardened arteries
- Obesity
- Heart attack
- Build-up of fat on artery walls

RISKS ASSOCIATED WITH A SEDENTARY LIFESTYLE

Possible mental health risks
- No outlet to relieve stress
- No outlet for aggression
- Lose self-esteem

Possible social health risks
- Fewer opportunities for friendships
- Less able to integrate with others
- Less able to work as a team

What to do:

1. Put the above information into sentences making a paragraph for each section.

2 Risks Associated with Excessive Forms and Amounts of Exercise

For those who are sedentary (mainly sit down during their working day) and unused to exercise, excessive vigorous exercise can be unwise as it can risk Cardiac Heart Death (CHD). To be safe whilst exercising, they must start at a low intensity level, allowing the body and heart to adjust to the increased intensity.

Exercise for changing lifestyles

Older people restarting exercise after a lengthy break, also need to pitch the exercise at the right level or they may be at risk of CHD as well.

Undertaking new and excessive exercise can also result in musculoskeletal injury. The strain on the muscles and bones is too extreme and they are not strong enough to cope with the forces put on them. Tears, sprains and strains can often occur if the exercise is too excessive.

The older, less fit person also needs to guard against musculoskeletal injury. They can do this by carefully choosing the activities they undertake. Swimming and walking would be better than running as they put less impact on the joints (avoiding musculoskeletal injury). Tennis would be a better game to play than squash as it does not raise the blood pressure as much (avoiding CHD).

Sedentary workers or people returning to exercise after a break need to have a programme appropriate to their fitness.

Often the problem to the heart is the increased demand of oxygen to the working muscles; this can be overcome by following appropriate, correct and thorough warm-up and cool down routines. If the activity programme is carefully planned and followed, exercising can be safe and allow the maximum benefit to the individual. CHD and musculoskeletal injury, therefore, is only a temporary hazard in the initial stage of new, excessive exercise. If the body and heart are allowed to adapt to physical stress then the risk to health is greatly lessened.

Dangers of excessive strenuous activity

Excessive strenuous activity like marathon running can lead to fatigue fractures. A period of rest is necessary to resolve this problem. In women athletes, training for long distance events, can cause amenorrhoea (bone demineralisation). This condition can be put right by the athlete decreasing the amount of exercise undertaken. Training for prolonged periods of time, especially for events that take a long time to complete can cause overuse injuries. A period of rest can rectify the problem but in extreme cases medical advice and treatment are necessary.

When activities like weightlifting and squash are performed intensely, the blood pressure is raised. Such activities cause plaque to break off in the arteries. When plaque builds up and causes blockages in this way it can result in heart attacks and vascular disease. It is important for the performer to exercise at an intensity which is light to fairly hard avoiding feelings of fatigue; they may be sweating and breathing hard but not gasping for breath.

Whilst working at an excessive rate there may be a risk of using the incorrect technique. This may result in muscular injury.

Financial Constraints

What you will learn about in this section

1. Financial Constraints on Clubs
2. Media Coverage

1 Financial Constraints on Clubs

Ways to fund sport

Whether large or small, amateur or professional, money is necessary to keep a club running. Financial input is needed for general day-to-day running and special events.

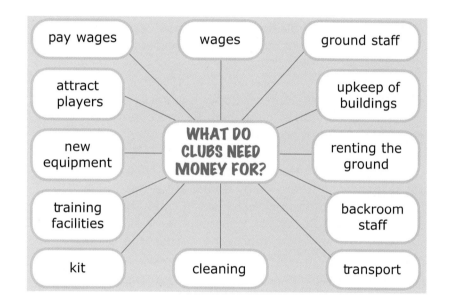

Some ways of financing sports

Charging club membership fees Paying to be a member of a small club allows a person to use what facilities the club has to offer, be eligible for team selection and join in social events. This money goes towards the general running of the club.

Charging entrance money Allows a person to watch the match, use the grounds facilities; some of these may include shops, restaurants, bars and fast food outlets.

Large teams like Manchester United make a lot of money from gate receipts. The capacity crowd at Old Trafford is 76 000, if this is multiplied by the average cost of a ticket, around £30, then the revenue for a home game is about £2 280 000. This money goes towards the high running costs of the club a large portion of which is players' wages.

Grants from agencies Foundations and trusts sports (specific and general) may award money to a club if it meets with the criteria set out.

Governing body Each sport's governing body may give money to individuals or teams for sport development.

Television rights For top flight clubs or sport events attracting a large audience, companies will pay large sums for the rights to broadcast the event on their network.

For larger clubs that generate national interest, television rights can be extremely rewarding and clubs in the best leagues at home and in Europe will make a lot of money in this way. Each team in the Premier League, for instance, received money according to their final position. England's Premier League received more than a billion pounds over three years from the BSkyB contract. Half of this money was divided equally between the clubs, a quarter paid to teams at the end of the season depending on their leagues position and a quarter paid out for live games.

Premier League teams are rewarded at the end of the season according to their position in the league.

Fund raising Club members can organise fund raising events themselves. These can include raffles, open days and social events. Larger clubs have supporters' clubs that regularly help with fund raising.

Lottery Lottery money is distributed through the different sports councils on application to sports clubs. The sport aid foundation gives help to improve the grounds, playing surface, buildings and disabled access and usage.

Merchandising Professional clubs use merchandising sales as part of their income. Football clubs often have a shop selling these items. Many goods are available for purchase such as scarves, mugs, calendars and the like. For some clubs the biggest selling items, by far, can be replica kits. These sales are boosted after a signing of a new star player when supporters want to show their approval and wear the team shirt with the recently acquired superstar's name on the back.

Sales often rely on the popularity of the team, its players and how well they are performing.

Donations Clubs may benefit from donations made by keen and loyal supporters wanting to contribute to the upkeep or development of the club. For many people their local club may have been a main part of their life providing them with fun and a sense of belonging. These life long supporters and club members may make bequests in their will to further support the club after death.

Government grants/local grants Government and local authorities have provision to award money within the community. A club may meet the criteria for new or established schemes to help with finance.

What to do:

1. Using your experience and knowledge of local clubs you know, say how they fund themselves.

Task 1

Sponsorship

Companies can choose to sponsor sport in different ways. Some prefer to put their name to leagues, events or sports facilities. Others choose to sponsor particular individual or team sports. Within a team, players may also have personal deals with their own sponsor and be used to endorse a particular brand or company. **The Institute of Sports Sponsorship (ISS)** predicts that the worldwide market for sports sponsorship will rise to $50 billion (approximately 25 billion) by 2010. This increase will be due to more attractive spectator and corporate facilities but mostly from televised coverage and sponsorship deals.

Advantages of sponsorship

Although football and motor sport dominate the market for sports **sponsorship** in the UK other sports like rugby, cricket, athletics, golf, tennis, equestrian, swimming and snooker enjoy significant support from sponsors.

Advantages for the sponsor

There are several reasons why companies sponsor sport. The most important is for financial gain. Before a sponsor puts their name to a sport, individual or team they work out the financial benefit of making the link to their product. This is usually in the form of increased sales of their product. In competition, which can range from local events to worldwide exposure with television coverage, the sponsor's logo is clearly seen. **Advertising** the brand name in this way saves companies money in comparison with the expense of using adverts in various forms of media.

What to do:

1. Using the information in this section, make a spidergram of key ways to finance sports.

Year	Value (£m)	% change	No. of sponsors	% change
1991	238	–	759	–
1992	238	+ 0.4	659	– 13.2
1993	250	+ 4.6	745	+ 13.1
1994	265	+ 6	818	+ 9.8
1995	285	+ 7	939	+ 14.8
1996	302	+ 6	977	+ 4
1997	322	+ 6.6	995	+ 1.8
1998	357	+ 9.6	969	– 2.6
1999	377	+ 6.8	1172	+ 20.9
2000	400	+ 6.1	1200	+ 2.4

Trends in professional sports sponsorship expenditure.

Here, major and minor sponsors supporting rugby are advertised around the grounds.

By linking the brand name with a certain sport, it can develop a healthy image, making it more popular in the public's eyes. Sports can also benefit from being linked to a company with a good image, as they can be regarded as being successful in the same way.

To promote a caring image the sponsors can help promote minority sports. In schools, a company may provide sports equipment or put their name to an award scheme to help the interest and participation in a particular activity. This can be seen as a gesture of **goodwill** to help get people involved in the sport, whilst at the same time advertising their product.

The money sponsors make available to the sport can improve its standards by helping to provide better coaches, facilities, training and administration. Companies can become more popular and well respected because of their positive and loyal involvement with sport. Many companies finance a showcase event, like a league or a major competition. This can increase the size and standard of the competition, attracting the best performers in the world. The sponsors not only finance the organisation, but the prizes or prize money too.

Norwich Union became a sponsor of UK Athletics between 2001 and 2006.

A company may gain financially through tax relief if they sponsor a sport. The amount they sponsor can be claimed against the tax that they pay and so save them money over the year.

In certain cases a sports equipment manufacturer may be researching and developing a new product. They will back a performer in return for them using the new product and giving feedback on its effectiveness. In this way improvements are made in the sport and the performer is supported in their training and competition.

In some cases, a company may sponsor a person or sport with no thought of financial return. **Goodwill** gestures such as these are a sign of a company's passion for the sport and its commitment to maintaining its standards and further progress. A company who sponsors an event can usually take advantage of corporate hospitality for their employees. They will be allotted good seats and sometimes meals at the events.

What to do:

1. Create a spidergram of the ways sponsors gain from advertising in sport.

Task 3

Advantages for the performer

Taking part and competing at the highest level of sport is expensive. To reach the necessary standard an individual performer needs sponsorship so that they do not have financial worries, leaving the performer to concentrate on training and competing. The obvious way sponsorship helps is by supplying the equipment, clothing and training for the event.

There are other ways sponsors can help the sportsperson. Linked with training, the cost of special diets, to help the athlete's performance, can be expensive. Funds can be made available or local businesses can provide appropriate food direct to the athlete. The expense of travelling to an event may be paid for, whether by road or by air. Car firms or garages may even supply a car for the exclusive use of the athlete. When Michael Owen, the ex Liverpool footballer, became successful and popular, Jaguar provided him with a car for his own use.

The cost of the expenses and the entry fee necessary for a sportsperson to be involved in an event can be substantial, so the sponsors will take care of these financial outgoings. In some cases, an amount of money is given to the athlete, to distribute at their own discretion. Once all of the outgoings are paid, any excess money left acts as an extra income for the sportsperson.

Sponsorship is still vital for many new, young competitors in sport in order that they can reach levels of performance with those best in the world. With well-established performers, a sponsorship deal involves much more money. There can be extra money left over after all the sporting expenses are settled, so this goes to pay for a better lifestyle for the performer.

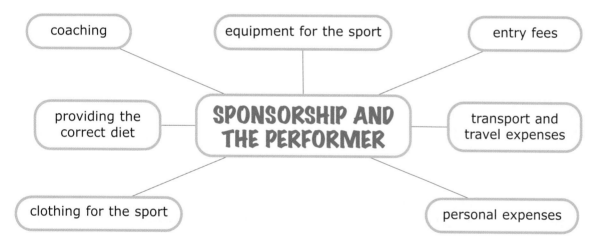

The top-class performers are sponsored for completely different reasons. Their faces are popular and companies want their name linked with them in order to sell more of their product. The individual will still receive clothing for their sport, but will also be provided with leisure clothing like baseball caps, trainers, sweatshirts and so on. These accessories, not directly linked with the sport, are given to the athlete so that they can further advertise the product. Many cricketers and athletes now wear designer sunglasses, tennis players receive watches to wear as they are playing and many sportspeople, in their leisure time, wear baseball caps with the sponsor's logo clearly shown.

What to do:

1. Write five sentences on how a young, promising sportsperson may benefit from sponsorship.

Advantages for the teams

A team may solely receive **sponsorship** from one company or may have several sponsors helping with different aspects of the sport.

A football team may have all their equipment provided by one company. This will include the team strip, training strip, footballs and other necessary equipment.

Bolton Wanderers' football ground is called the Reebok Stadium and the Surrey County cricket ground is now called the AMP Oval, both named after their sponsors. A motor sports team may advertise the names of the suppliers contributing to the working of the team. In the year 2001 there were over 230 sponsors for Formula One (F1), ranging from engineering and oil companies to food and fashion businesses.

The UEFA Champions League logo and sponsors.

The bigger the club, the bigger the sponsorship deal. As a result, smaller clubs unable to land support from national or international businesses seek **sponsorship** from local businesses. The expenditure of a smaller club is moderate and so the business can make a suitable and affordable contribution, still linking its name with sport and having its name advertised in the locality.

Certain sponsors supply their product for the benefit of the team free of charge. The Coca Cola Company, who produce the isotonic sports drink 'powerade' have deals with The Football League and was the official sponsor of The FIFA World Cup in Germany, 2006. The product, at such events, was made readily available to all teams in turn for large audiences watching the positive image of their heroes satisfying themselves with the drink.

Advantages for sport and the events

Some sports are seen to be so popular and an excellent advertising medium, both nationally and internationally, that larger companies will sponsor the whole sport. This gives the sport/event financial security for the future in that improvements can be made to its facilities and administration. The increase of money attracts the best performers, which in turn improves the standard and appeal of the sport/event. In return for the company having exclusive rights on advertising, the organisers, clubs and players benefit from the financial input.

▶ Active Challenge

Look in your P.E. department for the names of companies helping sport. Look at award schemes, adverts for sports events, books and any local sponsors linked to school.

Disadvantages for the sponsor

Sponsorship does not automatically guarantee success; the sponsor takes a risk if backing new talent. The sponsor speculates on the performer reaching the top of their chosen field. One of the risks with sportspeople is injury, which may stall, shorten or even finish a career. The sponsor takes on this risk knowing that there may be limited return for their investment if an athlete is out of action.

Disadvantages for the performer

A **sponsorship** deal, while it lasts, can be a great benefit, but many are only short-term contracts, making the financial situation insecure. The power of the sponsor can sometimes be too great. They can expect the performer to wear a certain brand of clothing whether playing or not, resulting in the athlete feeling demotivated and used by the sponsor. A contract may also include a number of duties that the player is committed to outside sport. In the 1998 World Cup there was controversy with the Brazilian team and its sponsors Nike. Despite their major player, Ronaldo, being ill, the sponsors allegedly demanded that he take part in the final.

Negative long-term effects of sponsorship

After a long period of sponsorship to a club or league, the money put forward is relied upon to keep the club functioning. Should the sponsor withdraw its backing from a sporting body that has relied too heavily on this assistance, it may well be left in financial difficulties.

Sky paid £1.024 billion for the exclusive rights to broadcast the Premier football matches until 2007. After this time a second bidder must be allowed to have rights to a substantial contract from 2007–2010. The Irish company Setanta are main contenders. Many clubs are concerned about the financial implications and worry that a deal with a smaller company will not be as lucrative for them. Less money will have a massive impact on buying new players in and fulfilling existing contracts they have with established players already in the club. For a large club like Manchester United the Sky rights amount to a third of its total income. Smaller clubs, with less ability to market themselves, rely more heavily on the TV rights.

In extreme cases, the sports become reliant on the sponsors for a major part of their financial existence. When ITV Digital bought the rights to broadcast Nationwide League football games and then the company collapsed, this caused financial concerns for clubs with some, such as Bradford City, being forced into administration.

Some **sponsorship** may, for some reason, get bad publicity. Negative publicity may well reflect badly on the club and tarnish its image.

In some cases the sponsors become too powerful. As the company holds the purse strings it can dictate its terms over the sporting organisation and control how it is run. Changes are often to do with making money or projecting the product and may well ignore the traditions and considerations of players and supporters alike.

If the sponsors get too much control over the sport then they begin to take charge of events and not the specialised sports bodies themselves. To make a game more marketable the rules of the sport can change due to the sponsor's demands. Cricket is a prime example of this. Rather than follow the traditional rules of the game and wear whites as their kit, each county team wear a different coloured kit for one-day games. In some cricket competitions the number of overs in the game has changed in order to make it more appealing to the television audience.

The coloured kits of the different counties give identity to the teams. Keen followers will want to buy a replica.

Sponsors can also control the timing of the events. Traditionally football matches used to start at 3:00 on Saturday afternoons. After BSkyB made an exclusive deal to broadcast live Premiership football, it influenced a change so that matches are played on Sundays, have various starting times and later kick-offs for midweek matches. The sponsors have demanded the changes in order to capture the primetime viewing slots for the television coverage. For international matches similar changes to starting times have been made to suit viewing audiences. Although the changes are good for the audiences they are not always in the best interests of the performers.

Sponsors are attracted to the major sports and the most successful performers as they want their product to be linked with success. This creates an imbalance not only in sports coverage in the media but also in competition, where the best-financed performers have more resources to compete and win at the highest level. For the less popular sports, it is difficult to get sponsorship despite the sports being worthy in their own right.

The government have in place a funding scheme called **Sportsmatch**. It is there to support grassroots sport in the community. Any non-profit making organisation, able to improve the basic skills of their activity and increase participation for the young in their local area, may apply. Any sponsorship money put forward to the organisation for this cause will be matched pound for pound by the government.

Rugby league, in the month of March 2006 alone, benefited by £43 1000 (half by **sponsorship**, half by Sportsmatch). This will help 33 500 young people playing rugby for the first time.

Many sponsors will only put money into a high profile sport, as this is the easiest way of getting the best return. Ten years ago, many athletes found it difficult to get sufficient sponsorship to compete at the highest level. It is only recently, now that the image of athletics has risen, due to the personalities in the sport and increased television coverage creating an international appeal, that sponsors are more willing to direct money towards this activity. For some, the importance of making money for the sponsor spoils the enjoyment of the sport.

Acceptable and unacceptable types of sponsorship

Generally when sports seek sponsorship they do so from companies that have an appropriately healthy, positive and wholesome image. However, some products traditionally linked with sports in today's society are losing their credibility. Two prime examples are alcohol and tobacco.

These products, although continuing to have a link with sport, have restrictions on them so that they can only have a link with adult events. Tobacco companies are a major sponsor of F1 racing and have been so for many years. The link to cigarettes is now so controversial, as smoking is increasingly associated with poor health conditions, that the sponsorship is scheduled to stop in 2006.

Michael Schumacher's suit advertises cigarette companies. Tobacco is clearly linked with poor health, so Formula One ended tobacco sponsorship in 2006.

What to do:

1. Make a list of the advantages and disadvantages of sponsorship. Answer from both the performer's and sponsor's viewpoints.

2. From what you have read in this section write your opinions on why some sponsorship is seen to be unacceptable and others acceptable.

Key Terms:

Advertising	► displaying a product, name or logo in public
Goodwill	► supporting a performer or sport financially without any monetary return
Institute of Sports Sponsorship (ISS)	► promotes best practice in sponsorship, working closely with sports bodies, government and the media
Sponsorship	► backing performers financially in return for advertising a product
Sportsmatch	► government scheme encouraging grass roots sport in the community

Summary

In most sponsorship deals, both the company and the performer gain from the partnership. For the performer, having financial backing relieves the stress of how a training and competitive programme is funded. This gives the performer freedom to choose the best methods in order to challenge the top sportspeople in the world. For the company, they are seen to support a particular sport, putting them in a favourable light with the public whilst advertising their product nationally or internationally.

The sponsor may feel that the more money they provide, the greater their influence in the running of the sport. This, at times, has a detrimental effect on the performers and can change the traditions of the sport itself. Some sponsors who care about the sport with which they are involved can ensure the standards of the sport are maintained and developed in the future.

Types of media

Sport uses all the different forms of media to bring itself to the widest audience. In each newspaper there are the sports columns; there are programmes and whole channels on TV and radio devoted to sport; and information technology (IT) provides access to many websites devoted to a particular sport.

The different forms of the media include TV, radio, press (magazines/specialist publications) and information technology.

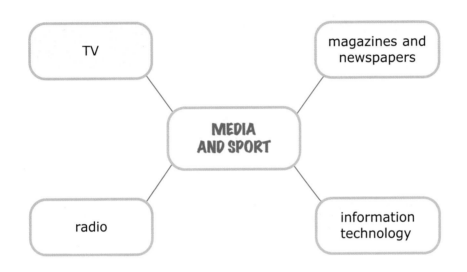

Task 6

What to do:

1. Copy the spidergram shown above.
2. Add to each category names of TV channels, newspapers, magazines and websites that have connections with sport.

Types of television broadcast

Terrestrial television includes BBC1, BBC2, ITV, Channel 4 and Channel 5. All televisions can receive these channels providing they have an aerial to pick up the signal. The BBC programmes are financed by revenue from TV licence sales, whilst the independent channels pay their way by advertisements between and at the end of programmes shown. Certain programmes may even be sponsored by particular products, which are seen at the beginning, end and intervals of the programme.

The competition between terrestrial and **satellite television** companies is such that the Independent Television Commission (ITC) has to organise the allocation of sporting broadcasts between them as they feel that some sporting events are of major importance and should be available to everybody. This prevents the wealthier satellite companies buying up all the best sporting events. As a result, there are some sporting events which are protected by the ITC so that terrestrial TV can broadcast them. These sporting events make up two groups, 'A' and 'B'. Events on the category 'A' list are legally bound to have the rights of their live coverage on the free TV channels. The 'B' list can be shown on satellite or digital TV as long as there is provision made for highlights and delayed coverage for terrestrial TV. There are strict guidelines for 'B' list events concerning regulations on the length of the highlight coverage and how long after the live event it should be transmitted. Protecting the events in this way guarantees the traditional events are available in some way to the 'free to air' broadcasters.

2006 A and B listed sporting events protected by the Broadcasting Act

Category 'A' events

FIFA World Cup

FA Cup

Scottish Cup Final (applies to Scotland only)

The Grand National

The Epsom Derby

Wimbledon Finals

The European Football Championship Finals

Rugby League Challenge Cup Finals

Rugby World Cup Final

Category 'B' events

Cricket Test matches played in England

Non-finals matches at Wimbledon

The Rugby World Cup (not the final)

Six Nations Championships (matches involving home countries)

The Commonwealth Games

The IAAF World Athletic Championships

The Cricket World Cup (limited to the final, semi-final and any matches involving UK teams)

The Ryder Cup

The Open Championship in Golf

●●●● ▶ Active Challenge

With a partner decide on changes to the 'A' and 'B' list you would make so that sports of your choice could be seen on terrestrial television.

Satellite television and sport

Subscription television was first transmitted into homes by BSkyB (British Sky Broadcasting Group PLC) in 1989 and has completely changed the way broadcasting operates. The main companies for this type of transmission are BSkyB, Cable TV and Freeview.

For companies to gain the right to broadcast particular events, not on the A list, each have to make a bid for the rights to do so. The successful bid, which is largely based on the amount of money offered, earns exclusive rights to that sporting event. The more popular the sport the more expensive it is to buy the rights. Although winning the bid costs multi-millions of pounds, by selling the coverage the companies make their money back.

There are several specialist sports channels provided by BSkyB, broadcasting a wide variety of sports for all tastes. Eurosport is a sports channel showing a variety of events taking place in Europe. The coverage is of a wide variety of activities, including those that have yet to make their mark in Britain. This broadens the number of sports shown and so giving people the chance to see a sport for the first time and possibly be interested enough to participate in it.

Viewers can watch sports events interactively. This facility allows viewers a variety of choices when watching sport, which include different matches to watch, a choice of commentary, access to player profiles and the ability to view the match using a different camera angle. The new options provide greater freedom and give detailed information to the viewers, which can increase their interest and knowledge in the sport.

Pay per view

If a person subscribes to BSkyB they are eligible to watch sporting events that are broadcast on neither terrestrial nor BSkyB channels. These are **pay per view** events – the customer pays a certain amount of money to receive the event. Boxing is one of the main sports that are broadcast in this way. Here the companies feel that there will be such a demand to see the event that they can make money by showing it in this way.

What to do:

1. Write a paragraph on how 'free to air' and subscription television differs.

How the media helps the understanding of sport

The various methods of the media help improve people's understanding of sport and current affairs, popularise personalities and provide sports' entertainment. Each form of media employs a series of experts (past players, pundits, presenters and journalists) to give their judgements, opinions and views on the sport in question.

Types of coverage

There are several different types of sporting broadcast, each with a different way of presenting the subject. For each event the director has an influence on how the information comes across: what and how it is said and particular points to be discussed. Therefore, the public see and hear what the director decides. Presenters may put their own slant on what they say during a broadcast, as long as it is within stated boundaries, or a script may be used and read off an autocue.

Television programmes can be classified as informative, educational, instructive and entertaining. This reflects the general content and aims of the programme. Many programmes contain different elements.

Informative programmes

News, news bulletins and sport update programmes, together with Ceefax and Teletext services, are all in the informative programme group. They are based on facts, intending to give the viewer more information about a sport, event, club or performer. They are designed to give the public updates on results, future events and current issues regarding a sport or activity.

Educational programmes

Educational, schools and skills programmes are productions dealing with coaching and helping people learn about the skills, tactics and strategies of a game or activity. Sometimes, school programmes will suggest ways for further development and give information of where to take up an activity in the area. Some broadcasts are documentary-based and so are concerned with the facts about an event or activity, like the history of a sport for example. For some people, knowing more about a sport is interesting, increases their understanding of the game and can increase its popularity.

On the spot interviews after a match capture the emotion of the moment, making them entertaining.

Instructive programmes

This type of coverage is closely linked with educational programmes, but is mainly interested in teaching the viewer about a specific sport. They appeal to a specialist market interested in a particular activity. Some programmes mix the type of coverage shown. The broadcasting of the cricket test matches, largely under the heading of entertainment, have in the lunch break a 'master/super class' section, where experts and coaches relay coaching points, instructing young players on how to improve their technique. This part of the programme would fall under the informative title.

Entertaining programmes

These programmes are designed for enjoyment. They can include coverage of live matches and special events, highlight programmes and celebrity quiz shows. The drama of a game, for some, can be entertainment enough, but the addition of the commentary gives greater information and insight and can enhance the appeal even more. To add to the entertainment, a series of presenters, pundits and experts are employed to give their opinion on the event. Expert commentators, who have often competed at the highest level themselves, give in-depth views that are accurate and factual. Those currently involved in the sport can give up-to-date information on the issues relevant at the time. Live coverage matches are cheap to produce and attract large audiences even when broadcast in off-peak viewing time.

Highlight programmes

Highlight programmes, showing the events of the day, pick out the best of the action in the time they have available. Here the audience sees exactly what the director wants them to see. This is usually the best of the action and any contentious moments too (particularly in football). These isolated incidents can be over-sensationalised by the panel of experts, becoming more talked about than the play itself.

Sports quiz shows

Sports quiz shows have high ratings on television. This is due to the popular personalities on the show attracting the audiences. The quiz seems secondary to the antics of the personalities. The appeal to the public may be that they see respected sportspeople having fun and making people laugh. Guest appearances of current, popular sportspeople can attract a bigger audience, as people want to know more about and have greater access to their sporting role models.

Manchester United has such a following that it produces its own programmes broadcast on its own channel. This gives fans up-to-date information on players, club and fixtures.

What to do:

1. Write two sentences on each of the four types of television broadcast.

Radio, press, IT and sport

Radio

Radio broadcasts regularly produce specialist sports programmes. These include coverage of live matches, discussion programmes and informative programmes. There is little rivalry between radio and television, as television regards itself as far more popular. Radio is therefore allowed to broadcast all sporting events live. There are several channels devoted solely to sport and news including Five Live, Talksport and BBC Radio Four's coverage of the cricket test matches. Cricket enthusiasts take their radios to the matches so that they can hear a commentary whilst they are watching the match live. Some people watch an event on television with the sound down, whilst listening to the radio commentary.

Press

The back pages of most newspapers are devoted to current sporting news. Each newspaper employs journalists and photographers to gather up-to-the-minute information about the matches and events for publication in the morning press. With this form of media the reader sees the match through the eyes of the journalists who are able to put their opinions forward and influence the reader.

Sports magazines devoted to the specialised reader are a large expanding market, the most popular subjects being football and golf. These publications contain entertaining, instructive and informative articles.

Title	Sport	Average issue readership	Total average net circulation per issue
Golf Monthly	golf	73 589	661 000
442	football	82 539	554 000
Golf World	golf	70 019	449 000
Rugby World	rugby	36 926	405 000
Angling Times	fishing	60 487	370 000
Match	football	70 398	300 000
Shoot!	football	30 222	219 000
Total Football	football	24 954	188 000
Yachting Monthly	yachting	37 516	175 000

Circulation of leading sports magazines in 2003.

IT

This is the newest and quickest-developing form of media. IT provides a way to access up-to-date information about sports, events and personalities in sport for those with access to an on-line computer. (It is worth remembering that some websites remain unchanged for a long time, so they may not be that current, but generally there is a note at the end of the website saying when it was last updated.) Many sports governing bodies, major clubs and smaller teams provide a website for those interested to learn more about them. The Internet also provides an advertising vehicle for retailers. Goods can be bought and sold quickly and easily using this service.

The impact of television coverage of sport has been both positive and negative. Terrestrial TV has had its share of sport reduced by Sky as it cannot pay the same amount of money to buy the rights to broadcast particular events. Both types of broadcast still have a major influence to make.

Terrestrial TV

Positive effects of coverage

- Keeps people informed of current trends and players
- More exposure of the sport and of a better quality

Live coverage brings sport to the majority of people.

- Increased technology aids decision making
- Pundits (education/informative/opinions from experience increases appreciation)
- BBC license fee (funding)
- New events can be seen
- Development of role models
- Enhances development of sport
- Seeing the sport on television may encourage participation
- The more it is seen on TV then the more supporters it may attract
- The more coverage of a sport the easier it may be to attract sponsors making more money available to that sport
- People become familiar with the sports personalities and, hopefully, become positive role models
- Money from broadcast bids goes direct to the sport.

Negative effects of coverage

- Major sports have most of the coverage to the detriment of the minority sports
- Can discourage watching live (sit in comfort of own home)
- Small incidents on the field of play can often be exaggerated and sensationalised
- The director of viewing controls what is watched
- Director controls how the sport is put across
- Can put the channel's own slant on a subject
- Excessive coverage can affect interest
- Subtle rule changes to sports may occur to increase the appeal to TV spectators – such as the tie-break rule in tennis
- Replays can undermine the officials/umpires
- Puts extra pressure on sports stars on both performance and demands for interviews
- Demand to see the personalities affects their privacy.

Task 9

What to do:

1. Choose six of the above points.
2. Put them into full sentences with examples.

Cable and satellite TV

Cable and satellite broadcasts have had a major influence on watching sport. Although there is greater air time and a wider variety of sports, it is only available to those who can pay a monthly subscription. With any network they have positive and negative influences on many aspects of sport.

Positive effects of coverage

- Greater coverage of minority sports (Sky's 'Extreme Sports'. Channel broadcasts on average 18 minority sports per week)
- Makes a variety of sports more accessible
- Increases the funding for sport

Financial Constraints

- Heightens the profile of sport and so can attract interest and sponsorship
- Increased depth of coverage for major sports – some football clubs have their own channels such as Manchester United and Celtic
- Impact on participation (can encourage greater participation by stimulating interest, thereby encouraging people to take part themselves)
- More live sport can be seen.

Negative effects of coverage

- Some networks may always have the traditional gender pundits and presenters matched with a sport. Reinforcing stereotypes in this way may give the impression that the sport is unavailable to certain sections of people and therefore reduce participation
- Matches can be rescheduled due to the best broadcast day for the network – this often happens to the premiership coverage.
- The start time of a match can change so it goes out at the optimum time for the network.
- Traditional events have gone to sky – only subscribers can see Welsh soccer and live test cricket matches from 2006.
- Sport can suffer from over exposure as people tire of the saturation coverage.

Sometimes the influence of TV coverage is not so black and white. A person may see an event on TV and as a result be so motivated that they go see it live; on the other hand they may think why go out of the home when TV gives the best view and they can watch it in the comfort of their own surroundings?

Key Terms:

Pay per view	►	extra sporting events, bought individually by the viewer and available only to subscription viewers
Satellite TV	►	extra programmes available to those who purchase a receiver and pay a subscription
Terrestrial	►	programmes available to everyone with a television and an aerial

Summary

Sport is such a popular and marketable commodity that all forms of media devote time, space and money to it. There are several successful television channels specifically devoted to sport. The influence of the director of the programme or columnist of the paper is massive on the viewer or reader, enough to persuade them to think in a certain way. Although there are many advantages of the media's involvement in sport, there are also disadvantages as well; for the benefit of sport, getting the right balance is important.

Government Policies, Funding and Target Groups

What you will learn about in this section

1. Government Policies
2. Funding for Sport
3. Target Groups

1 Government Policies

Policies

The central government of the UK has seen a great need to promote public health as a major policy. UK Sport and each country's sports council are responsible for implementing government directives and are funded by the Lottery. In general terms the sports councils are concerned with the following:

Acquisition young acquiring the basic skills as part of P.E. at school.

Participation all having the opportunity to join in sport and recreation of their choice.

Performance encouragement and opportunity given to anyone wishing to improve their personal standards of performance.

Excellence encouragement and opportunity provided to those with outstanding ability including professionals as well as top amateurs to reach national representation.

In turn each country has devised the most suitable way forward to promote and apply healthier living to their people. Each government has worked closely with their Sports Council to create a workable way of increasing the amount of exercise people take.

sports council wales
cyngor chwaraeon cymru

Role of the Sports Council for Wales

1. Deliver the Welsh Assembly Government's strategy for sport and physical activity set out in the document 'Climbing Higher'.
2. Work to develop and improve education, knowledge, practice and training in sport and Physical Education for the welfare of the people and to encourage the attainment of high standards.
3. Cultivate, encourage and support the provision of facilities for sport and physical recreation.
4. Help, support and advise individuals and teams taking part in sport and physical activity for the benefit of their health and social well-being.

Climbing higher

The Welsh Assembly Government drew up the Climbing Higher document for the good of the Welsh people in the long term. It sets out a strategy for sport and physical activity for the next 20 years and taps the nations' passion for culture and sport. Within the document, specific plans link physical activity with health, the economy, culture, society, the environment and the world stage.

A focus on health

Climbing Higher sets out a strategy that will help people in Wales become fitter, more active and healthier by making physical activity a part of their everyday lives.

Here is a résumé of the document's target for health:

Wales will meet the best global standards set out for sport and physical activity, which is that adults take part in physical activity (PA) for 30 minutes, 5 times per week.

- Primary age range:

  Children in primary school will take part in PA for 60 minutes five times per week. Primary schools provide a minimum of two hours of curriculum based sport and PA per week.

- Secondary age range:

  At least 90% of boys and girls will take part in sport and physical activity for 60 minutes, five times per week.
  Schools will provide a minimum of two hours of curriculum based and 1 hour of extra-curricular sport and physical activity per week.

In the long term the government wants to make participation in physical activity a legacy for the future. It aims to take barriers away preventing people from taking part, especially for women, girls, ethnic minorities and people living in deprived areas. At the same time, with the help of the Sports Council of Wales, develop sporting talent, support schemes for Wales and increase access to top-class sports coaching for those with aptitude.

One of the largest investments in health made by the Welsh Assembly Government is their provision of free swimming for children, young people and the over 60s. Such is the commitment to a healthier population that £10 million has been put aside to fund this initiative. It is key to the Health Challenge Wales directive and is the first of its kind in Europe.

In 2004/05 the playground scheme 'In the Zone' was developed and launched in primary schools. This scheme, funded by the Welsh Assembly Government aims to keep children more active during lunch times. Support and training are given to the lunch time supervisors, encouraging children to take part in the more traditional games like hopscotch and skipping. The project will make a major contribution in helping the children meet the 60 minutes of physical activity, 5 times per week recommendation.

What to do:

1. The Welsh Assembly Government sees a need for the country's population to be healthier. What policies, directives and programmes show this?

2. Find more information on the Internet to help with your answer.

2 Funding for Sport

Funding for sport can come from many different groups. As well as TV rights, Sports Councils, merchandising and gate receipts, private organisations, trusts and specific governing bodies of sports can contribute financially. Each group has its own criteria for providing financial support to a sporting cause, which must be met on application. Some of the ways to fund sport are shown below:

Talented Athlete Scholarship Scheme (TASS) This is a government funded scheme managed on behalf of UK Sport, forming a partnership between sport and further and higher education. It aims to support sportspeople in their endeavour to reach world-class levels. Scholarships are worth up to £3 000 a year and are granted to able and disabled athletes.

Sports Aid Foundation This is a voluntary organisation.

Awards for all This award is designed to help clubs or sports organisations applying for £500–£5 000 of Lottery funding. The money is aimed to help with: coaching or training courses, equipment, start up costs, publicity materials and volunteers' expenses.

Football foundation The trust will help football at any level. The FA Premier league, national stadia and grass-roots football all have access to their financial help.

Sportsmatch This is a government run initiative. It aims to encourage businesses to sponsor sport at a grass-roots level, ultimately increasing the amount of money they contribute to sport at the junior stage. New money put up by businesses in this way (a minimum of £1 000), can be matched on a pound for pound basis.

Foundation for sports and the arts This group distributes about £650 million a year to a wide variety of projects applied for by sport and arts organisations.

Princes Trust The Trust aims to help young, disadvantaged people between the ages of 18–30. It will also help with training costs for sportspeople with disabilities, providing them with low interest loans and grants.

National governing bodies Many governing bodies have their own grant schemes helping to promote their own sport. If no such schemes exist then they often know of and can direct groups to other funding sources.

Sports Aid This is a voluntary organisation offering grants to elite sportspeople who have reached international standard in their sport. Financial assistance is given to help meet the costs of training, travel and coaching at a time when the athlete is preparing for competition.

The Sports Aid Charitable Trust This is a sister group to Sports Aid. This trust offers financial aid to young people who are developing their talents and to sportspeople with a disability.

National Lottery A wide variety of sporting groups can apply for Lottery funding. The fund will support a range of projects from local to international level, with priority given to those benefiting the whole community. Money from this fund is available to elite sportsmen and women to help with training, coaching, travel and other related expenses.

Summary

Groups offering the potential for financial support to sport, clubs or individuals, have a series of criteria set out that the applicant must meet. Certain trusts and foundations, not specifically set up for sport, can also award money to these groups as long as their criteria are met. Such groups include European Funding, Rural Funding and New Deal. Other groups like Commercial Sponsorship will assist with clothing and equipment or similar rather than a money award. Each nation sets aside money to help promote a healthier lifestyle for its people. Often this money is spent locally according to an area's specific needs.

What to do:

1. What ways of funding, as a direct effect of government policy, is there in your local area?

2. Write your findings down in sentences.

3 Target Groups

Several groups of people are targeted to improve their access to sport. Each government aims to make sport and physical exercise available to all their population. Research highlights the problem groups, policy then sets out the plan to improve the problem and finally the implementation of initiatives removes the barriers so more people are involved.

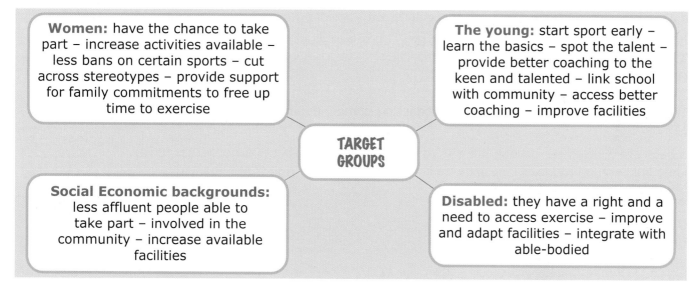

Women: have the chance to take part – increase activities available – less bans on certain sports – cut across stereotypes – provide support for family commitments to free up time to exercise

The young: start sport early – learn the basics – spot the talent – provide better coaching to the keen and talented – link school with community – access better coaching – improve facilities

TARGET GROUPS

Social Economic backgrounds: less affluent people able to take part – involved in the community – increase available facilities

Disabled: they have a right and a need to access exercise – improve and adapt facilities – integrate with able-bodied

In 2000, the P.E. and School Sport (PESS) Project was set up, as a result of a task force report outlining key actions required in order to make physical activity appealing to young school children and raise standards of P.E. in schools. The PESS project is managed by the Sports Council for Wales on behalf of the Welsh Assembly Government. ESTYN is commissioned by the Welsh Assembly to evaluate progress made by the PESS project and commented in its evaluation of work in 2005–6, '*There is increasing evidence to show that the PESS initiative is meeting its aim of raising standards in physical education across Wales.*'

In addition to this, a programme called 5 × 60 was launched in September 2006, to increase extracurricular opportunities in secondary schools. Funded by the Welsh Assembly Government and managed by the Sports Council for Wales, 5 × 60 deploys fully trained officers into secondary schools to extend the extracurricular programme and arrange activities to take place before and after school, at lunch times and weekends. It is hoped that all schools in Wales will be involved in the programme by 2009.

Dragon Sport

Dragon Sport is a scheme funded by the National Lottery to encourage participation in sport for 7–11 year olds, providing sporting opportunities that are fun, enjoyable and safe. It introduces children to coaching, skill development and appropriate competition, using versions of the adult game, modified to meet their needs and skill levels. Liaising closely with schools and community sports clubs, Dragon Sport is making a dramatic impact on sports participation by encouraging children to become involved in a variety of organised sporting activities.

Whilst the primary focus of Dragon Sport is improving sports provision for 7–11 year olds across Wales, it also focuses on recruiting parents and other volunteers as helpers to support the development of after school and community sports clubs.

The scheme targets 8 sports: Athletics, tennis, cricket, netball, football, rugby, hockey and golf.

For schools engaging in the scheme, Dragon Sport provides equipment for taking part. A sports bag containing modified equipment for use with primary school children and resource cards to help with playing the activity are given on application.

The activity cards were developed in association with the sport's governing body and are especially designed in the following ways:

- All children can use them
- Games are easy to set up
- They are curriculum compatible
- They give hints to organisers on safety, adapting games, equipment and follow-up games.

Two bags are allowed per school, but a third can be made available to schools that have made a link with a local club. The scheme is open to schools in Wales and England.

The activities focus on basic skills:

- Use adapted equipment
- Use simplified rules
- Prepares for the full game
- Each activity resembles the sport it is based on
- They are safe but challenging.

To qualify as a volunteer, potential staff must be or have one of the following:

- Qualified teacher
- Community sports leader
- Recognised play leader qualification
- Qualified youth worker
- Recognised current governing body coach award.

All volunteers go through a series of training sessions over a four hour period. Each session specifically trains the delivery of the Dragon Sport scheme with its unique nature.

Active Schools England

The schools initiative in England is called Active Schools. This is divided into two sections – 'Activemark' for the primary sector and 'Sportsmark' for the secondary level. The general aim of the initiatives intends to let children get the best possible start in sport. The initiative is produced in association with The British Heart Foundation, who produces the Active School Resource Pack showing how to plan all-round physical activity.

Activemark

Activemark was designed to respond to the decline of time spent on P.E. in schools due to pressure to deliver other subjects in the National Curriculum. When schools achieve the award it shows that there is good practice taking place in the P.E. department. The department will be well-organised and actively promote the benefits of physical activity.

There are two levels to achieve - 'Activemark' and 'Activemark Gold'. Each award lasts for three years then schools reapply.

Sportsmark

Achieving Sportsmark relies on good practice in place in the secondary schools' P.E. department.

- Develop sports partnerships with community
- Leadership training
- Opportunities for students to extend leadership skills
- Continuous development for teachers
- Support for talented performers
- Development for targets for physical education and school sport
- Opportunities for competition in and out of school
- **SPORTSMARK**
- Planned core time
- Opportunities to extend outside school core curriculum with other organisations
- Opportunities to extend outside school core curriculum in clubs
- Encourages positive sporting attitudes
- Breadth and balance of P.E. curriculum
- Promotion of fair play

Key Terms:

Sports councils	▶ led by UK Sport, distributes lottery money promoting sport in their country
Target groups	▶ a section of people singled out for attention
Dragon Sport	▶ Sports programme for the young resulting from Welsh Assembly initiatives
TOPS Programme	▶ Sportscotland programme designed to promote physical activity in schools and the community
Sportscotland Active schools	▶ initiative ensuring the delivery of the TOPS programme
Sport England Active schools	▶ divided into 'Activemark' and 'Sportsmark' are designed to give children the best start in sport

School, Community and Resources

What you will learn about in this section

1. School and Community Links
2. Provision of Community Resources

1 School and Community Links

Government initiatives actively encourage schools linking with the community. Schools can tap into local specialist human resources and facilities for the good of their children's progress. By making these connections children become familiar with local experts and clubs, perhaps giving them the confidence and interest to continue taking part when they leave school.

A good example of a scheme linking school with the community is the Active Sports Programme.

Active Sports Programme

Helps to develop and keep players active from all backgrounds and abilities. It is a five year development programme targeting ten sports. Local clubs are at the heart of the scheme and provide the key to good quality coaching, competition and opportunities for participation. The scheme links together the sports governing body, local authority, education services, local clubs, community and schools.

Active Sports encourages participation and progression in the chosen sport.

Netball example

Sport England worked with 45 sporting partnerships to find the sports most likely to keep people active. One of the ten sports chosen, in England, was netball. The programme aims to enhance the skills of the game and give opportunities to young people to keep in the sport and progress as far as they can.

The programme is financed by Lottery funding with clubs drawing up their action plan and applying for finance to implement their schemes.

Stage one – Local Schemes

The programme aims to enhance basic skills, usually learnt in schools, of youngsters who want to progress and continue with their chosen sport. They go to local skills awards days targeting 10–11 year olds who are not yet in a club. This could lead to training over a period of two years at a local coaching centre.

Stage two – Club Development

Regular coaching is provided for youngsters aged 11–16 years using accredited clubs. At this stage children work towards their England Netball Bronze cap. For this they have to satisfy the Active Sports minimum standards of safe play and equal opportunities.

Stage three – Assessment

Here the players hoping to continue participation are assessed as a continuous process with coaches and teachers recommending players to the higher level.

Stage four – Development Squads

Those players identified and selected go on to Satellite Academies. 12–14 year olds receive 40 hours more training. The 14–16 age group receives performance enhancing and fitness training with 80 hours of support per year.

This scheme helps to attract more people to the game of netball. A team of trained development officers ensures the netball action groups have all they need to bring the sport successfully into the community. Active Sports aims to improve the quality of coaching available for young people, encouraging them to sustain their interest as a foundation for lifelong involvement.

2   Provision of Community Resources

Public funding for sport in the UK

UK Sport and Sports Councils access the Lottery fund and use the money for the best results and benefit of their respective communities.

Local government may operate on a parish (village and rural communities), town, city or district council level. The facilities can be run by the councils themselves or a private company can be contracted by the council, with the aim of running the centre at a profit within stated guidelines. If a centre cannot finance itself then the local council can help by meeting any shortfall. Such subsidies help to keep the centre open.

In the UK, the government filters money for local sport through to the local councils. In turn, local government has elected councillors who have the responsibility of making provision for leisure in their locality.

The Department of Culture, Media and Sport (DCMS), created in 1992, influences sport in Britain. Since 1994, it has been responsible for the distribution of the National Lottery (Lotto) fund, including that allocated for use in sport. The DCMS provides grants to the sport councils of each country.

Collectively, the sports councils have over £1billion per year allocated to them by the government for sport. The government also provides guidelines to the councils affecting the building of facilities and the amount of land available for sport use at a local level. With UK trends moving away from participating in team games and more toward individual gym and general health pursuits, policies drawn up by the politicians change accordingly.

Each county council has a designated officer for sport. They create a link between local, regional and national sports bodies. Their local knowledge and interest recognise where there is most need for improvement. The general aim is to encourage and enable sporting prospects for all.

Local authorities provide 1 600 public leisure centres in the UK. These offer a wide range of sports and activities with sports halls, swimming pools and outside facilities. These facilities make sport available to all members of the community at a reasonable cost. There are subsidies made for particular users and time slots reserved for certain groups, to attract as many types of people as possible.

What to do:

1. State the connection between local and national government provision for sport in the community.

Private provision for sport

Sport centres come under three categories – commercial sports centres, private clubs and employee sports centres. The demand is so great for gyms and health clubs that private provision has had to increase in this area in order to meet the demand. In 2002, there were over 3 500 private health clubs in the UK, with the number still growing. There are many small business providers for this type of leisure pursuit, but there are seven main companies sharing a million members.

Company	Main club boards	No. of members in UK	No. of UK sites
Whitbread	Marriott	300 000	110
Fitness First	Fitness First	210 000	90
Esporta	Esporta	167 000	37
Cannons	Cannons Courtney's	160 000	57
Holmes Place	Holmes Place	132 000	42
Hilton Group	Living Well	115 000	88
De Vere	Village & De Vere Greens	98 000	41

Leisure companies in the UK in 2001.

Source:
Leisure and hospitality business, fitness focus supplement, August 2001.

Commercial sports centres charge membership fees and sometimes a joining fee. They may also charge extra for particular activities or for the use of health and beauty treatments.

Private clubs usually offer one major sport, but can sometimes specialise in two areas successfully. Wimbledon is such a club offering two sports, its full name being Wimbledon Lawn Tennis and Croquet Club. Private clubs are self-financing through club membership and, in the case of Wimbledon, earn money from holding a showcase event annually.

An employer can also set up sporting provision for their employees by providing a sports centre. In some cases, a subsidised membership fee may be charged, or some companies provide the facility free of charge. By offering such facilities the company has a healthier work force, the extra provision may make employees more loyal to the company and for certain jobs, fitness may be necessary to do the job well, so the company can increase effectiveness of their workforce.

Role of Private and Public Sectors

What you will learn about in this section

1. Sports Clubs and Their Members
2. Private Clubs
3. Ways a Club can Encourage Young People's Participation

1 Sports Clubs and Their Members

In order to play many sports there is often a need to join a formal club. (Some activities, like swimming and rambling, are an exception.) These clubs are classed as voluntary organisations and many exist all over the country. Many of them offer the opportunity to compete not only with those in the club, but other teams too. There are millions of people who join clubs to improve their skills, compete against others and meet other people with similar interests.

Sport	No. of clubs	No. of members	Average no. of members per club
football	42000	1500 000	36
snooker	5300	1500 000	283
golf	2877	1126 000	391
tennis	2450	750 000	306
bowls	8600	500 000	58
sailing/yachting	1620	450 000	278
motor sports	750	420 000	560
rugby union	2026	284 000	140
martial arts	1000	175 000	175
athletics	1750	135 000	77
hockey	2000	90 000	45

Number of UK sports clubs and their members for selected sports.

Source: Sports associations/NTC Marketing pocket book/keynote.

The purpose of joining a club is to play a sport or participate in an activity. For this to happen there is much work and organising to do behind the scenes. Members often take on the various jobs involved in the running of a club voluntarily. These people form a committee, who meet regularly to discuss issues involving club matters and its development.

2 Private Clubs

Health clubs have increasingly become more popular in the last 20 years. The number has grown considerably due to demand.

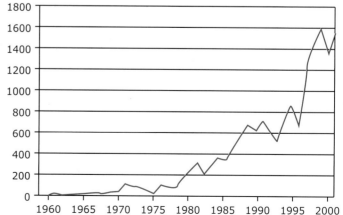

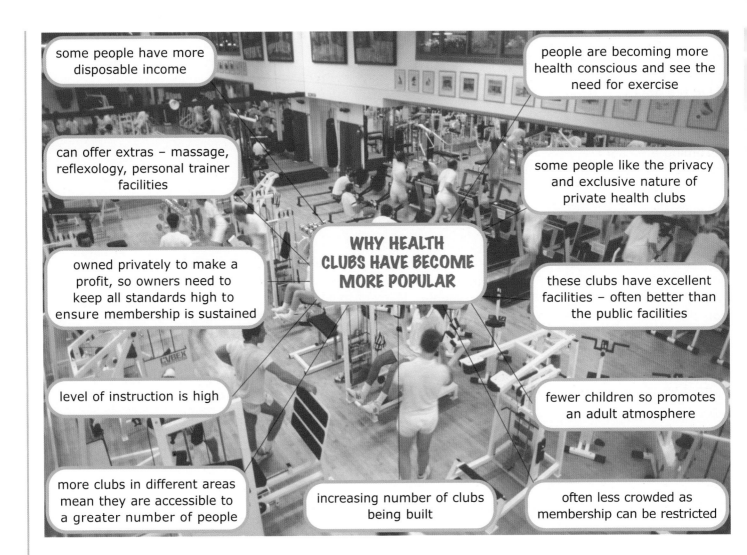

some people have more disposable income

people are becoming more health conscious and see the need for exercise

can offer extras – massage, reflexology, personal trainer facilities

some people like the privacy and exclusive nature of private health clubs

WHY HEALTH CLUBS HAVE BECOME MORE POPULAR

owned privately to make a profit, so owners need to keep all standards high to ensure membership is sustained

these clubs have excellent facilities – often better than the public facilities

level of instruction is high

fewer children so promotes an adult atmosphere

more clubs in different areas mean they are accessible to a greater number of people

increasing number of clubs being built

often less crowded as membership can be restricted

What to do:

1. From the information above make a spidergram for all the key points of why private gyms have become more popular.

Task 1

3   Ways a Club Can Encourage Young People's Participation

Clubs can play their part in the community in keeping people active, continuing the efforts started by the schools. For some young people, approaching any club, irrespective of size, can be a daunting prospect. Clubs can help by taking down some of the barriers young people might think exist.

By running special introductory courses for their sport, clubs are seen to recognise that there are people with basic skills and that they are welcome. It also demonstrates their willingness to open their doors to new people encouraging them into their ranks with a chance of making a team.

Similar introductory courses can be set up for school leavers bridging the gap between school and community sport. By setting up such courses before pupils leave, clubs can tap into a ready market and have a better chance of keeping this group physically active. It is important to bridge this gap, especially for girls, as statistically, once they have left school take several years to participate in sport again.

By readily opening its doors to the local population a club creates a link with the neighbourhood. This can be seen as a positive sign that the club recognises the community, wants to be a part of it and is willing to do something for those that live in the area.

When inviting prospective new members into the club they should ensure there is a warm and welcoming atmosphere. People, especially youths, are more likely to stay if they feel accepted and comfortable in a friendly club.

For sports that attract a wide age band, like bowls for instance, a club could benefit from having in place and promoting a youth programme, with a youth coordinator. A junior section of a club can gradually integrate youngsters into the mainstream game ensuring that the rules, etiquette and a certain skill level is understood and attained so that they can confidently move up the ranks.

Advertising the club well and promoting the merits of being a member can encourage greater participation. If the club also endorses the benefits to health and social well-being then continued involvement may ensue.

Successful clubs cater for all ages and abilities.

Some sports can benefit from separate boys and girls activities. Clubs recognising this may give the best chance of all to improve, succeed, become leaders and be effective in different roles in the activity.

Keeping costs low can encourage a larger membership more inclined to remain at the club. If the subscriptions are priced reasonably then the young players will become seniors, this not only keeps the club viable but creates a sense of continuation and tradition within its members too. Making discounts, concessions and helping with transport costs may make the prospects of joining more attractive. With more members there is a bigger pool of players to draw from and this could lead to greater success in competition.

What to do:

1. Using the information on ways clubs can encourage participation, create a spidergram of the key points.

Performance Pressures and Drugs

What you will learn about in this section

1. Pressure on Performance to Take Drugs
2. Positive and Negative Role Models

1 Pressure on Performance to Take Drugs

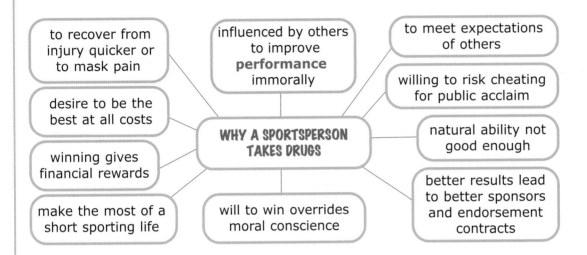

The rewards for winning can be great in sport. Some athletes are tempted to cheat in order to win. This undermines the integrity of the sport and so the governing bodies of different sports have clear drug-testing policies to try to keep their sport 'clean'.

Each sport has its own list of banned substances, which are published to make it clear to performers and their coaches what cannot be taken during training and competition. The effects of taking different drugs are wide and varied: some help to hide pain, like methadone (an opioid analgesic); others develop the body artificially, like anabolic steroids.

The governing bodies work to try to keep a good name for sports and look after the interests of the athletes. The International Olympic Committee (IOC) medical commission works to: 'protect the health of athletes ... ensure respect for both medical and sport ethics ... enforce equality for all competing athletes.'

Summary

Taking **drugs** has an effect on the body and mind of a person. Some of these effects are useless to the sportsperson. However, through research, some drugs are seen to have a beneficial effect on **performance**. Some sportspeople are tempted to break the rules of the governing bodies as they see only the rewards of their drug abuse. By taking drugs the health of the performer can be seriously endangered. Regulations and procedures are put in place by the governing bodies of each sport to help and guide the performer to make an ethical choice. The sporting authorities want athletes to be safe, sport to have a good name and competition to remain fair.

2 Positive and Negative Role Models

Why companies use sports stars

Companies will select sports stars to advertise their product very carefully. They will choose a star that has the correct qualities matching their product.

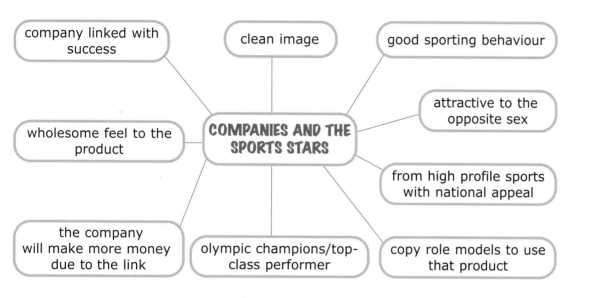

What to do:

1. Choose a sports star who advertises a product.

2. Give three reasons why you think they were particularly chosen by the company.

Put your ideas into logical sentences – consider the following:

Positive:

- How a sportsperson can positively affect young and their participation by displaying good sportsmanship
- Will to succeed
- Shows good lifestyle and morals
- Young emulate the stars and their skills
- Many stars succeed in a clean way – no drugs
- Seen as healthy and promoting a good way to live

Negative:

- Can challenge the referee/umpire
- Poor disciplinary record/attitude in stars sets poor example
- Encourages gamesmanship/cheating/trying to con ref – diving for penalties/feigning injury/to get opponent booked/sent off

Sports personalities are increasingly in the public eye and are therefore under constant scrutiny by the media and the public alike. The signals given off and the behaviour exhibited by sports stars can have a marked influence on culture and society.

Some successful players see it their duty to develop participation within their chosen field – the veteran Sir Bobby Charlton and more recently David Beckham have soccer schools to their name. Setting up such coaching schools shows a commitment to the sport and an interest in furthering the skills of youngster. This type of behaviour is positive, caring and a good example to follow.

At the other end of the scale some sports people underplay their responsibility of role models to others and exhibit less than acceptable conduct. The trappings of success, for some are too much to handle. Fast cars and a reckless lifestyle are all recorded and publicised by the media. The image of their hero/heroine committing drink/ driving offences for example, are readily accessible to the young. For fans who want to be like their star unlawful actions are wrongly seen as acceptable.

Key Terms:

Drugs	► substances (other than food) which have a physiological effect when taken into the body
Fatigue	► extreme tiredness resulting in the body's inability to complete a task
Performance-enhancing drugs	► substances that artificially improve personal characteristics and performance

Summary

Individual sportspeople who are regularly in the public eye are often copied by admiring fans. More women are now becoming role models as their sport is increasing in popularity and so earns them further coverage on the television.

The popularity of certain sports can vary from area to area and time to time. Seasonal sports have key times of the year attracting more participants. Some sports enjoy a short term of favour and then go out of fashion, making way for a new trend to take its place.

Assessment and Evaluation of Physical Fitness

What you will learn about in this section

1. What is Physical Fitness?
2. The Need to be Fit
3. Pulse as an Indicator of Physical Fitness
4. Factors Affecting Fitness
5. Why Physical Fitness Testing is Necessary
6. Definition of the Components of Physical Fitness (Health-related and Skill-related)
7. The Link between Physical Fitness, Fitness Components and Sporting Activities

1   What is Physical Fitness?

Fitness can be described as the body's ability to meet the demands of the environment. To be fit for sport is totally different to being fit for everyday life. The sporting environment can be much more demanding and rigorous. Also different sports require different levels and types of fitness. If you are fit for volleyball you may not necessarily be fit for squash.

2   The Need to be Fit

An athlete needs to be fit for their activity in order to cope with the intensity and duration that activity demands. A contact sport, like rugby, will require high levels of muscular strength to withstand the physicality of the game.

Being fit may reduce the incidence of injury. A well-developed muscle surrounding a bone may give protection to a player being tackled in football.

3   Pulse as an Indicator of Physical Fitness

The condition of the cardiovascular system can be a good indicator and the basis of fitness. There are three indicators linked with Heart Rate that usually show fitness in a performer:

- Lower Resting Heart Rate
- Takes longer for a fit person to reach their Maximum Heart Rate
- Recovery Rate is quicker back to Resting Heart Rate.

4   Factors Affecting Fitness

There are many factors influencing the fitness level of a person.

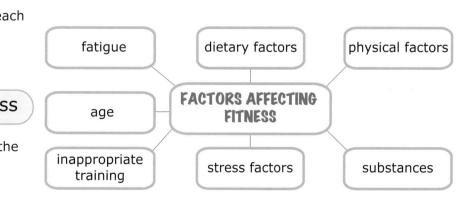

Fatigue

When the body tires it becomes less effective. A sportsperson, tiring in a game, will be unable to maintain the standard of play they started with. The aspects of skill-related fitness will become less effective: for example, passing a ball will be less accurate and tackles could be mistimed. As well as a decrease in the level of skill performance, the quality of decision making gets worse. Both of these combine to lower overall performance and increase the likelihood of dangerous play.

The body needs rests in order to recover. If a fatigued performer continues, then there is a possibility that they may have to stop completely. Any athlete at any level of sport can suffer the effects of fatigue. A player may know they should stop, but desire and determination keeps them going without realising their change in form. In these cases it is up to the coach or manager to be aware of the signs of fatigue and be prepared to stop training, stop the event or substitute a team member. By following a rigorous training programme the effects of fatigue can be offset.

What to do:

1. Fatigue affects the skill of a performer. Give four examples of different sports and the skills affected.

> Your answer should include: name of the sport, skill component and sporting action affected.

Dietary factors

Everyone needs a balance of the seven nutrients in their everyday diet. There are several ways diet can affect performance:

- The calorific intake should be adequate to sustain the amount of exercise undertaken
- The diet should match the needs of the sport
- The liquid intake should adapt to the type of exercise. Taking on liquids before and during the exercise will stave off the effects of dehydration. Drinking liquids after the event will also help to maintain the correct balance of liquids in the body aiding recovery.

Physical factors

There are weight guidelines for people depending on their height. Excess weight can affect fitness. Carrying extra weight can put increased strain on the cardiovascular system, making the heart work harder than it should. Extra weight can reduce effectiveness in performance:

- Carrying more weight often reduces speed
- Being a bigger size can prevent full flexibility
- Moving extra weight can create a lack of agility
- Putting on weight on different parts of the body can cause a lack of balance.

The physical size of a person can have an effect on levels of skill-related fitness. For example, tall people tend to have longer levers, which can affect their speed of movement. Their centre of gravity is also higher, affecting their ability to change direction quickly.

Substances

Any chemical consumed, inhaled or injected into the body is classed as a drug. Drugs can affect the physical or mental condition of the body. Different drugs have different effects (described in detail in p 92. Some drugs and their effects are briefly described below:

Cigarettes raises heart rate and blood pressure

Alcohol slow reaction – impairs judgement

Anabolic agents increase muscle mass – affect sexual characteristics and moods

Stimulants reduces feeling of tiredness – results in irritability, high blood pressure, increased heart rate

Opioid Analgesics helps pain relief – loss of coordination, balance and concentration

Beta Blockers slows heart rate – relaxes a person in tense situations

Stress factors

The feelings of stress, tension and pressure can all affect the performance of a player. However, experiencing these psychological feelings can have a positive effect by helping some players bring an edge to their performance. Often, the bigger the competition or game, the greater the effect on the individual or team.

Stress is similar to tension. Positive thinking sportspeople will turn what can be seen as a negative feeling into a positive one by declaring this as the 'buzz' they get. Being stressed can have the effect of making the performer more alert and able to react better to situations. Although, too much stress can lower levels of performance. For example, a tennis player may be so affected that they are unable to play successful shots, which in turn affects their confidence. A downward spiral of worse play can then follow.

Tension can happen at any time before an event: minutes, hours, days before it is scheduled. This may badly affect training or performance. Some players, however, need this tension in order to bring the best out of their play. When a lot is at stake, like the final of a major competition, the importance of the occasion may make or break a player's performance.

Pressure on a player may come about due to the particular game, the other team, the crowd or the particular play in the match. Keeping calm and being able to adapt to the pressure is a sign of a champion. It can give the edge to a player, making them more determined. Others may crack under the pressure, as it is just too much for them to handle. In a game example there may be little time left and a team needs to hold onto a 1–0 lead, so they are said to soak up the pressure of the other team's efforts.

Before a match, players feel tension; this can give an edge to their play.

How fitness can be seen in a practical setting

When players and performers compete there are ways their fitness can be identified. A performer who can last the distance and be as effective from the start to the finish of an event shows a high level of fitness. These levels directly relate to both health and skill-related fitness components and can be seen in the following:

Breathing

Working without becoming breathless allows the oxygen to keep being supplied to the working muscles.

Muscles

They will keep working effectively if provided with the correct supply of oxygen. The muscles, therefore, can keep working in the correct way and at the correct rate necessary for effectiveness without tiring for the whole of the match/event.

Skills

Skills required in that activity will be maintained at a high level throughout the proceedings. High levels of coordination, speed, balance, reactions, agility and strength show fitness. When a player, at the end of a game, can still place a ball accurately, control the direction of a shot, adapt easily to changes in play, perform actions smoothly, maintains the proper technique and keep their concentration, this indicates their good level of fitness.

Footballers need to be fit enough to play at the highest level throughout the match, plus the allotted time added on.

Task 4

What to do:

1. For each of the components of skill-related fitness:
   - choose one sporting event
   - choose a related skill in that game
   - give an instance, in a competitive situation, when good fitness benefits the player.

Example
Event – Football
Skill – Speed
Instance – Late in the game a poor back pass is made to the goalkeeper, the attacker outruns the defender to the ball, shoots and scores.

Measurements of the Effects of Training

What you will learn about in this section

1. Working Out Areas to Train
2. Linking Skill-related Fitness Components to Sport
3. How Tests Are Administered
4. Why It Is Important to Ensure Validity
5. Data Interpretation
6. Interpreting Different forms of Presentation

1 Working Out Areas to Train

For training to be effective it should meet the requirements of the activity and the individual. A coach will identify different aspects of the game and work out which systems are used to supply the energy:

- aerobic
- CP
- lactic acid – the training will concentrate on developing them.

The coach will work out the different energy requirements for each playing position, once again adapting the training for them. The skills of the positions will be a major factor on the training programme. In rugby, at times, the backs will train in a very different way to the forwards.

The individual needs of a player, based on their fitness levels, will be taken into account. All this knowledge determines the design of the training programme. So any programme design is affected by:

- game
- playing position
- player's individual fitness levels.

Strength – to tackle

Agility – to avoid a tackle

Endurance – to keep skills throughout a match

2 Linking Skill-related Fitness Components to Sport

The nature of any sport or activity is governed by the rules, equipment, playing surface, playing area, numbers involved, event duration and how to score and win in a competitive situation. All these factors determine the type of actions and strategies that are performed and so demand a particular mix of skill-related fitness components necessary for success in that activity.

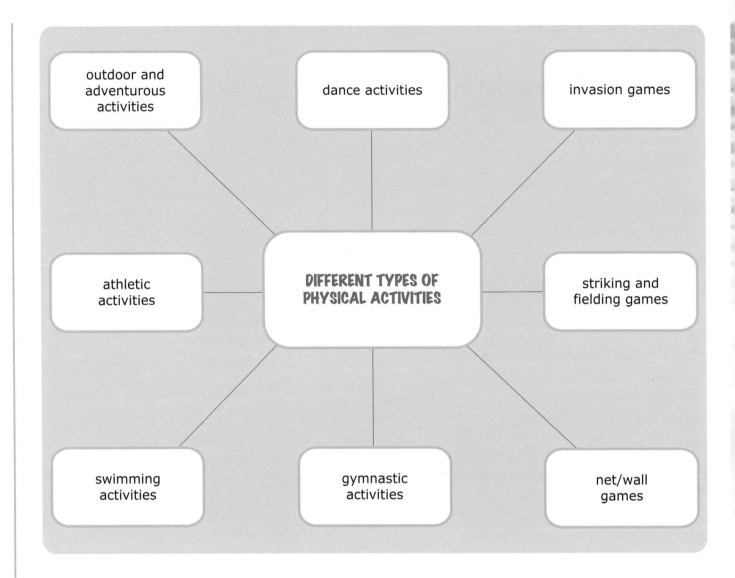

What to do:

1. Choose six sports and, for each, list the three most important components of skill-related fitness.
2. Put your ideas into sentences, one for each sporting example.
3. Link the correct definition with the component of skill.

Clues to help complete the task.

When working out the skill-related fitness components needed for an activity consider the following:

- Is there equipment involved?
- Is there a need to respond quickly to another stimulus?
- Is there a need to manoeuvre and change direction?
- Is power in the actions necessary?
- Does speed play an important part in the action?
- Is balance needed to complete an action?

What makes a successful shot putter?

Skill-related fitness

- **Strength** of the muscles to resist the force of the shot
- **Speed** combining with strength to make power
- **Balance** to start the action under control and giving a position to move effectively from
- **Agility** to cross the circle and shift the weight in a controlled way
- **Power** for a single, explosive action extending the arm (combining strength and speed)

Health-related fitness

- **Flexibility** needed at the hips to turn the body with forward momentum so the arm is moving forwards and upwards at release
- **Body composition** big build with large muscle and heavy weight
- **Muscular strength** able to perform a single maximum contraction to overcome resistance

Personal qualities

- ambition
- discipline
- determination
- self belief
- confidence
- single-mindedness
- good under pressure

Be able to identify the perfect model

The perfect model

This event is unique to other athletic activities. As a result it has certain skills, progressions and training methods linked with it. The knowledge of the event and the performer influences the coach to set out an individual programme, hopefully maximising success.

What makes a successful football player?

Skill-related fitness

- **Agility** to out-manoeuvre opponents
- **Speed** to move fast to avoid opponent/to mark opponent
- **Power** to combine strength and speed together for long kicks/shooting
- **Reaction time** to respond to opponents' movements or a quick passage of play

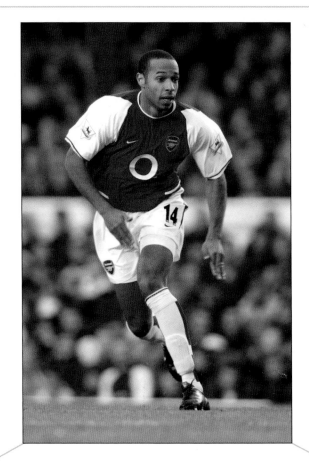

Health-related fitness

- **Muscular endurance** to maintain high-skill levels throughout the game
- **Flexibility** joints able to move into extreme positions without injury
- **Muscular strength** to compete physically with other players and produce powerful shots
- **Body composition** medium to large frame with muscle and little or no fat

Personal qualities

- competitiveness
- determination
- good under pressure
- contributor to team play
- confidence

Be able to identify the perfect model

The perfect model

Footballers need many skills and qualities to be successful. A midfield player needs to link the defence and the attack. This requires both aerobic and anaerobic fitness. They have to be good at tracking back to mark a player and tackle for the ball. Midfielders also need to be accurate passers, often starting the attack with a penetrating pass. The long pass is often used by midfield players. This pass can often split the defence and be the start of an attacking move for players running off the ball in the attacking third of the pitch.

What makes a successful netball player?

Skill-related fitness

- **Speed** to outpace the opponent whether marking or dodging
- **Agility** ability to change direction quickly without losing balance
- **Balance** to land from any direction and keep stable during the throw or shot and to hold a stretch over the ball when your opponent has posession
- **Reaction** to intercept the ball and mark a player

Health-related fitness

- **Muscular strength** for throwing, jumping and moving with explosive strength
- **Muscular endurance** stamina needed so player remains skilful and effective for the duration of the game
- **Flexibility** so the player can stretch the joints to their fullest extent without incurring injury when twisting, stretching and catching the ball awkwardly
- **Body composition** choosing the most suitable position according to build

Personal qualities

- competitiveness
- team player
- determination
- self-discipline
- concentration
- good under pressure
- ability to adapt to the circumstances

Be able to identify the perfect model

The perfect model

There are many skills required in netball that lead to effective play, each requiring specialised training. Shooting skills, if performed well, can boost the team's confidence as the players have worked hard to get the ball into the circle for the opportunity to add to their score. Both the goal attack and goal shooter are allowed to shoot. When taking a shot they will need to concentrate on the following phases of the action if they are to be successful:

How high levels of fitness can be identified in a sporting activity

A performer, training appropriately, should increase the levels of all physical fitness components. As training progresses, for example, they should therefore be quicker, stronger and more powerful.

A fit performer will remain injury free and be able to take part in most competitive matches. After a game/event they will also recover quickly with their body systems returning to resting condition.

Many players can begin an activity performing skills accurately and at the correct speed. However, a truly fit performer can maintain these high levels throughout the competition. The key to being fit is being able to last the distance and in some sports a little extra too – there may be cause to have extra time in a match for instance. During all the phases of the game high standards of skill, concentration and commitment should be maintained and reproduced when necessary.

Signs of a fit performer
Even towards the end of a competition, a fit performer should be able to:

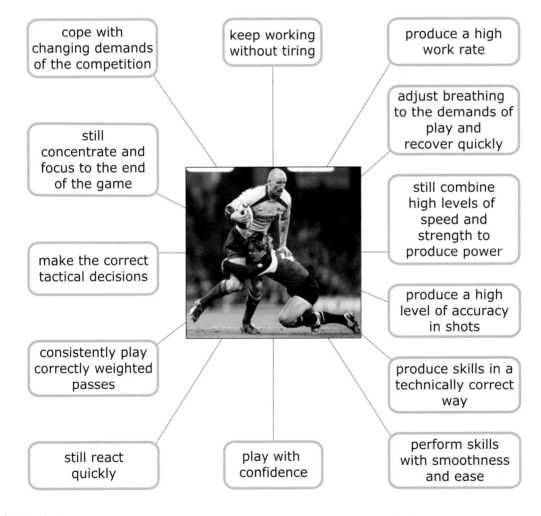

- cope with changing demands of the competition
- keep working without tiring
- produce a high work rate
- adjust breathing to the demands of play and recover quickly
- still concentrate and focus to the end of the game
- still combine high levels of speed and strength to produce power
- make the correct tactical decisions
- produce a high level of accuracy in shots
- consistently play correctly weighted passes
- produce skills in a technically correct way
- still react quickly
- play with confidence
- perform skills with smoothness and ease

What to do:

1. Choose a physical activity.
2. Give three examples from a game/competition carried out as part of your chosen activity of how a fit performer can be identified.

3 How Tests are Administered

When a person conducts a test it is important that they make it the same for all those who are being tested. This gives a level playing field so that no one has an advantage over anyone else. All instructions should be clear and easy to follow. The performer should be reassured and a check made as to whether they fully understand the procedure.

All performers should:

- know the course
- know what is expected of them
- recognise norms
- be warmed-up and prepared for the physical test.

The importance of following correct procedures has a bearing on **reliability**:

- Being consistent and following the correct procedures for all tests makes the test results reliable. This gives the chance for consistent results to be recorded, used in the future and compared with recognised norms.
- How motivated the performer is to do their best in the test?
- Is the performer tired?
- How long is it since the performer's last meal and the test?
- For tests taking place outside, the conditions should be the same each time the test is carried out. The weather and season could change the surface and temperature, which in turn will affect the results.

4 Why it is Important to Ensure Validity

Validity

If the results are to be used meaningfully then the test's **validity** must be ensured.

- Does the test measure what you want it to?
- Is it relevant to the competitive activity/event?
- Is it a true reflection of the performer's ability?
- Will it be recorded and set against recognised results tables?

Comparison

If carried out in the same way each time, then the results will be true and can be compared legitimately with recognised norms. These results may be compared with past results and those of other peers.

Safety

Safety is an important consideration when conducting any test. The following questions must be answered:

- Is the space correct, does it suit the test?
- Is the surface suitable?
- Is the correct clothing being worn by the performer?
- Is the correct equipment available for use?
- Are the lighting conditions suitable?

Be fully prepared and appropriately dressed for the test.

What to do:

1. For each of the following – reliability, validity, comparison and safety:

   Write a sentence on why that pointer is important when administering a test.

5 Data Interpretation

For any results to be used in identifying the performer's progress it is essential that the testing procedure is the same every time, this ensures the validity of the test.

The Evaluation Process Loop

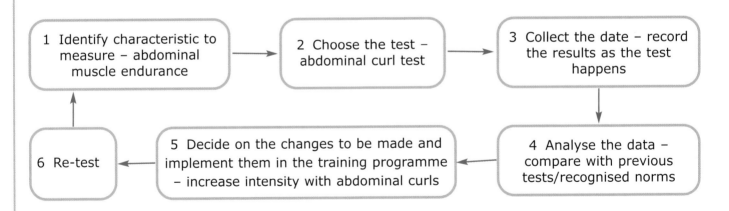

1 Identify characteristic to measure – abdominal muscle endurance → 2 Choose the test – abdominal curl test → 3 Collect the date – record the results as the test happens

6 Re-test ← 5 Decide on the changes to be made and implement them in the training programme – increase intensity with abdominal curls ← 4 Analyse the data – compare with previous tests/recognised norms

Analysing any **data** from the test needs close study. It may be that the results are presented in a variety of ways. How results are presented can depend on the test itself, what the results want to emphasise and to whom the results are being shown. Any result should be compared with recognised norms/percentile rankings, giving a clear reflection of the performer's fitness levels.

6 Interpreting Different Forms of Presentation

Graphs

Graphs can plot changes made to an individual over a period of time. This would clearly adapt to the changing heart rate of a performer over an exercise period. The number of heartbeats being recorded on the side of the graph in ascending degrees and the period of time of the exercise along the bottom in minutes. Multiple sets of readings can be plotted on the same graph in order that they can be compared with each other.

Sport	Adenosine Triphosphate and Creatine Phosphate or Creatine Phosphate System	Lactic Acid System-O2	O2
Basketball	60	20	20
Fencing	90	10	
Field events	90	10	
Golf swing	95	5	
Gymnastics	80	15	5
Hockey	50	20	30
Distance running	10	20	70
Rowing	20	30	50
Skiing	33	33	34
Soccer	50	20	30
Sprints	90	10	
Swimming 1500m	10	20	70
Tennis	70	20	10
Volleyball	80	5	15

Interpreting the example

The example shows the changing heart rate of the performer. It plots the heart rate, showing how it fluctuates as a result of the exercise intensity and duration. From the graph and using knowledge of fitness, judgements can be made as to the type of exercise being performed and the fitness level of the performer.

What to do:

1. Study the graph.
2. Answer the following questions:

   What is the resting heart rate?

   What is the highest heart rate?

   What type of exercise is being performed?

   At what times are the periods of greatest exercise intensity?

   How long does it take for the performer to go back to their resting heart rate?

Bar charts

These provide a visual and clear display of the information gathered. The chart has a series of bars; each bar could represent an individual, item or sport. Along the bottom could be a time period or target group.

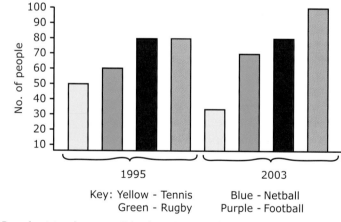

Bar chart to show possible changing trends in participation

What to do:

1. Study the bar chart and answer the following questions:

   What do the bars represent?

   Why are there different colours?

   Over what period does the chart cover?

   In what sport has the best improvement in participation been seen?

   Which sport shows the worst progression?

Pie charts

Pie charts are simple ways of showing, visually, a set of basic pieces of information. These charts can be colourful in order to distinguish between the different pieces of information.

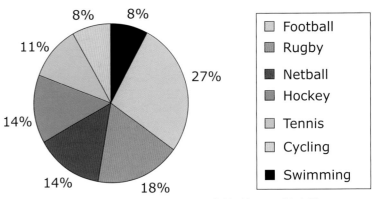

This Pie Chart shows possible percentage of 11–16-year-olds taking part in their Chosen Sport.

The whole pie is 100% of the subject being charted; this can represent for example a day, a timetable or a series of leisure pursuits. The whole pie is divided up, clearly showing how it is apportioned and the general amount of each.

A pie chart gives an immediate representation of the portions of the subject in question. The sections are often differently coloured to help distinguish between the sections. If only colour is used on the chart, there is often a key explaining what each portion signifies. Sometimes each section can contain writing, giving the title of what that portion represents.

What to do:

1. Using the pie chart example, create a pie chart of your own using test results as a theme.

Percentile rankings

Percentile rankings are constructed from a series of studied tests. The results of the tests are analysed and converted to a percentage relating to the overall performance of the test group. The resulting rankings show a graded range of performance scores for that group.

The target group is a cross section of individuals of a particular age or gender, for example. The individuals represent a wide variety of abilities for that target group. All members of the group are given the same test. Each time the test is performed it is done so under the same conditions so the results are reliable. After the tests have been completed the results are correlated and converted to a percentile rankings table. This table can then be used to compare a similar individual's performance of the same test showing where they are in relation to the whole group.

Age %-ile	14 years	15 years	16 years	17 years +
90	44	46	47	50
80	41	43	44	47
70	38	40	42	45
60	37	38	39	43
50	35	37	38	41
40	34	35	36	39
30	32	33	34	37
20	29	30	31	32
10	24	25	25	28

The example shows percentile norms (centimetres) for sit and reach: Boys

Task 6

Questionnaire

A questionnaire is a series of questions designed to find out a personal response to a given subject.

It is important to know exactly what you want to find out and to use questions that keep to these points. When the questionnaire is complete, careful study of the responses is necessary. This can take time as the writing may be difficult to read and the English may not be easy to understand.

When using a questionnaire certain factors have to be taken into consideration – is the questionnaire:

- easy to understand?
- in need of explanation before answers can be made?
- using the appropriate language for the person answering?
- better answered verbally by the performer and written down by someone else?

Completing a questionnaire takes a degree of concentration and therefore should be completed in an appropriate environment. The place should be quiet, free from distractions and there should be no pressure of time. Any of these mentioned factors could influence the responses given.

Example Questionnaire

NAME		FORM		DATE	

ACTIVITY

Please answer the questions in the spaces provided

PERSONAL ABILITY
1 What do you think is your main strength in the activity?_____
2 What do you think is your main weakness in the activity?_____
3 In the activity, which skill did you find the most difficult to perform?_____

TRAINING PROGRAMME
4 Did the training programme devised for you suit your ability?_____
5 What personal qualities did it take to complete the training programme?_____
6 Are there any changes, from your experience, you would make to a future training programme?
_____
7 Which area did the training programme improve most?_____

FEEDBACK
8 What kinds of feedback did you receive on your performance?_____
9 Was the feedback given clear?_____
10 How did you react to being given feedback on your performance?_____
11 Was the feedback relevant to your performance?_____

OVERALL REACTION
12 How has your understanding changed on the effectiveness of using a training programme?
_____
13 Does your play differ in any way from that before the training programme?
_____
14 What is the most significant thing you have learnt from completing the training programme?
_____

THANK YOU FOR COMPLETING THIS QUESTIONNAIRE

What to do:

1. Create your own questionnaire.
2. Use fitness testing as your theme.
3. Have ten questions.
4. Find out about the performer's reactions to a named fitness test.

Interpreting results

How?

- Look carefully at the results of the performer
- After careful scrutiny see how they fit in with recognised tables of results or tests made of the target group
- If it is a re-test note the changes in the results
- Assess how much change has been made
- By looking at the changes a coach can predict the rate of change based on previous data.

Why?

- Feedback is given to the performer on how rates are changing
- Shows the strengths and weaknesses in the components of fitness being tested
- Knowledge of the results can motivate a performer to work harder to improve more or at a higher rate
- Will indicate whether further increases are required
- Allows the performer to understand why there are changes to the programme being made
- Allows the performer to see if the training is working
- Changes can be explained and then carefully planned with the athlete to give an understanding of why the adjustments are being made
- A date can be within the plan for the next re-test so a mid-term goal can be set motivating the performer.

Key Terms:

Reliability of a test	► consistent results over a period of trials
Validity	► a recognised and appropriate test carried out in a prescribed way
Data	► information collected about a subject
Graph	► information set out to show its rise and fall
Bar chart	► information set out in blocks to show an amount over a period of time
Pie chart	► information set out to show the proportions of a whole subject
Percentile ranking	► data recorded from target groups showing percentage of success

Summary

The results of a test are what will influence the training programme. By examining the results and looking for trends, the coach will build up a picture of what changes are necessary for the future. It is important that the performer is kept motivated in all phases of the test and training cycle. When re-testing the performer should understand the need for 100% effort each time in order to produce meaningful results for comparison.

When the information has been collected it is important that the coach works closely with the athlete so that all concerned understand the way forward, know the results and what they mean and so see the reason and need for future changes.

Fitness Component Testing

What you will learn about in this section

1. Health-related Fitness Component Testing
2. Skill-related Components of Physical Fitness Testing

1 Health-related Fitness Component Testing

Endurance-related components of fitness testing

Cardiovascular endurance testing

Strong and efficient heart and lungs will help a player keep working hard throughout a game without losing breath and lowering performance. The bleep test can measure heart and lung efficiency reflecting the oxygen uptake (VO_2 the maximum amount of oxygen that can be transported to, and used by, the muscles during exercise in one minute). The Harvard Step-up test and the 12 Minute Cooper Run are two other methods of measuring cardiovascular endurance.

Multistage fitness test

This test uses VO_2 as an indicator of fitness.

How it works

- Athletes listen to the tape or CD
- The athletes run to a cone and return only on the beep
- If an athlete fails to reach the cone on the beep twice in a row, then they are out
- The level they reached at that point is recorded as 'their level'.

Equipment needed

- 20m length course set out between cones
- 4 cones
- tape or CD of the test
- cassette or CD player
- recorder and recording sheet.

CAUTION! These tests were originally designed for mature athletes; and are not suitable for all students. Serious injuries can occur if students push themselves too hard.

Other tests for cardiovascular endurance are the 12 Minute Cooper Run and Harvard Step-Test. These tests use pulse and requency rate as the indicators of fitness.

Multistage fitness test results table		
Level	**Shuttles**	**VO₂ max**
4	9	25.5
5	9	32.9
6	10	36.4
7	10	39.9
8	10	43.3
9	11	46.8
10	11	50.2
11	12	53.7
12	12	57.1
13	13	74.4
14	13	64
15	13	67.5
16	14	70.9
17	14	74.4
18	15	77.9
19	15	81.3
20	15	84.8

12 Minute Cooper Run

How it works

- Athletes run for twelve minutes
- They cover as much distance as they can
- Marker cones are placed around the track to aid in measuring the distance covered
- Walking is allowed but performers are encouraged to push themselves as hard as they can
- The distance covered is recorded for each athlete.

Results table for adult males	
Rating	**Distance (meters)**
excellent	>2700 m
good	2300–2700 m
average	1900–2300 m
below average	1500–1900 m
poor	<1500 m

CAUTION! These results are for adult males.

Equipment needed

- athletics track
- marker cones
- recording sheets
- pen stopwatch.

Harvard step-up test

How it works

- Athlete steps up onto gym bench once every 2 seconds for a period of 5 minutes (150 steps)
- Help with keeping to the pace may be necessary
- 1 minute after the test – take pulse and record = Pulse 1
- 2 minutes after test – take pulse and record = Pulse 2
- 3 minutes after test – take pulse and record = Pulse 3.

Calculate the result by applying the following equation:

30000 divided by the sum of the 3 pulse recordings

Equipment needed

- standard gym bench
- recording sheet
- pen
- stopwatch
- assistant.

Normative data for the Harvard Step-up Test

The following table is for 16 year old athletes.

Gender	Excellent	Above Average	Average	Below Average	Poor
Male	>90	80–90	65–79	55–64	<55
Female	>86	76–86	61–75	50–60	<50

Table Reference: McArdle W.D. et al; Essential of Exercise Physiology; 20000

 **Active Challenge**

Find the Cooper 12 minute run on the internet and then write out the protocol for administering the test.

What to do:

1. Choose a sport.
2. Write a sentence on:
   What is good cardiovascular endurance?
3. Give two examples of how good cardiovascular endurance improves the performance of the activity.

Task 1

Muscular endurance testing

Performers working for lengthy periods need muscular endurance so they can keep their skill level high throughout the game.

Abdominal curl-up test

How it works

- Performer lies on back
- Bends knees to a 90 degree angle
- Feet flat on floor
- Hands resting on thighs
- Head resting on back of partner's hands
- Curls up slowly (using abdominal muscles) sliding hand up thighs to knees
- Returns slowly to starting position (complete curl takes 3 seconds)
- Repeats as many curls as possible keeping to the same rate
- Record the number of curls made.

Equipment needed

- flat surface
- mat for safety
- partner
- stopwatch
- recorder and recording sheet.

Curl-up test results table		
Males		
Rating	Age <35	35–44	>45
Excellent	60	50	40
Good	45	40	25
Fair	30	25	15
Poor	15	10	5

Females		
Rating	Age <35	35–44	>45
Excellent	50	40	30
Good	40	25	15
Fair	25	15	10
Poor	10	6	4

CAUTION! All results are for adults.

Another test for muscular endurance is the Press-up Test.

◀●●●● ▶ Active Challenge

Find the Press-up Test on the internet and then write out the protocol for its administration.

NCF abdominal curl conditioning test

The NCF Abdominal Curl Conditioning Test CD or audio tape is available from 'Coachwise 1st4Sport'

How it works

- Athlete listens to tape and follows the instructions
- As many sit ups are performed as possible
- All sit ups are performed to the beat from the tape/CD

- The number of sit ups performed correctly are counted by the assistant
- The number of sit ups are recorded from the start of the test until
  - the athlete cannot keep in time with the beeps, or
  - the sit ups are not completed correctly.

Equipment needed

- the NCF Abdominal Curl Conditioning Test CD or audio tape
- tape recorder or CD player
- gym mat
- stop watch
- assistant
- recording sheets
- pen.

	Normative scores		
Stage	**Number of sit ups Cumulative**	**Standard Male**	**Standard Female**
1	20	Poor	Poor
2	42	Poor	Fair
3	64	Fair	Fair
4	89	Fair	Good
5	116	Good	Good
6	146	Good	Very Good
7	180	Excellent	Excellent
8	217	Excellent	Excellent

CAUTION! The athlete has to push themselves to the limit so beware of injury or illness before conducting the test.

Strength-related components of fitness testing

Muscular strength testing

Static strength

Muscular strength is the muscles' ability to apply force and overcome resistance.

Hand grip dynamometer test

The Grip Dynamometer measures the force generated by the performer's hand in one grip action. This is an easy test to administer used as a measurement of general strength.

How it works

- Adjust the Grip Dynamometer to the size of the performer's hand – This is important as the accuracy of the adjustment will affect the results
- Performer grips the dynamometer with dominant hand
- The arm hangs by the side with dynamometer in line with the forearm
- A maximum grip strength is applied without any swinging of the arm
- The performer has two attempts for each hand – record the best result
- Best results are added together and divided by two to reach a score.

Equipment needed

- hand grip dynamometer
- record sheet and pen.

Table of results		
Rating	Male	Female
Excellent	>64kg	>38kg
Very good	56–64	34–38
Above Average	52–56	30–34
Average	48–52	26–30
Below average	44–48	22–26
Poor	40–44	20–22
Very poor	<40	<20

Another test for muscular strength is 1 Repetition Maximum Test (1-RM).

1-RM tests (repetition maximum tests)

How it works

- Once warmed up, the athlete chooses an achievable weight to lift
- The athlete should rest for several minutes, then increase the weight and lift again
- The athlete repeats this sequence, increasing the weight each time, until only one correct, full lift of that weight has been achieved
- This should then be recorded.

Equipment needed

- free weights – either dumbbells or barbells – or other appropriate gym equipment.

Power/explosive strength testing

The Standing Vertical Jump Test measures explosive leg strength. There are other tests measuring arm and leg strength too. Explosive leg strength is vital to athletes and games players needing to jump whether it be for distance or height.

The Vertical Jump Test and the standing broad jump test measure leg strength. The Pull-Up Test measures arm strength. Games players need to be able to jump for a ball in a challenge or to play a shot.

Sargant jump test

How it works

- Performer stands sideways to a wall
- While standing with feet flat, performer reaches up with their arm nearest to the wall
- The height where the stretched fingers reach is measured
- Standing slightly away from the wall (for safety), the performer jumps vertically as high as possible using arms and legs for maximum height
- They touch the wall at the highest point possible (by chalking the fingers a clear mark is left to measure)
- The distance between the two measures is recorded
- The performer has three attempts.

Vertical jump test results table		
Rating	Male (cms)	Female (cms)
excellent	>70	>60
very good	61–70	51–60
above average	51–60	41–50
average	41–50	31–40
below average	31–40	21–30
poor	21–30	11–20
very poor	<21	<11

Equipment needed

- indoor area
- measuring tape
- chalk
- recorder and recording sheet.

The difference between muscular strength and endurance

Muscular strength and muscular endurance are similar, but not the same. Strength is the ability to shift a weight and muscular endurance is the ability to shift weight repeatedly, or over a long period of time. When an activity takes place over a long period it uses muscular endurance; for short, explosive events muscular strength is necessary. Team games use a combination of both types.

Standing long jump test

How it works

- The athlete positions themselves at the end of the sandpit
- The athlete should stand with both feet together and with feet up to the edge
- They then crouch, lean forward, swings their arms for momentum to jump as far horizontally into the sand pit as possible
- They land with both feet into the sand
- The start of the jump must be from a static position
- A measurement should be taken from the edge of the sand pit to the nearest point of contact into the sand.

Equipment needed

- long jump pit
- pen
- tape measure
- assistant recorder
- record sheet
- teacher/coach measures.

The following table is for 15 to 16 year old athletes:

Gender	Excellent	Above average	Average	Below average	Poor
Male	>2.01m	2.00–1.86m	1.85–1.76m	1.75–1.65m	<1.65m
Female	>1.66m	1.65–1.56m	1.55–1.46m	1.45–1.35m	<1.35cm

Source - "Brianmac"

Shoulder hyperextension test

How it works

- The athlete holds one end of a length of rope with the left hand
- With the right hand, the athlete holds the rope four inches from the left hand
- Both arms are extended in front of the chest and the arms rotated overhead and behind the neck, until the rope touches the back
- As resistance occurs, the right hand slides along the rope
- The distance is measured between the two thumbs, to the nearest $1/4$ of an inch
- The shoulder width from deltoid to deltoid is measured, to the nearest $1/4$ of an inch
- Subtract the shoulder width distance from the thumb distance
- The test is repeated three times and the best distance recorded.

Equipment needed

- length of rope
- tape measure
- recording sheets.

Flexibility-related components of fitness testing

Testing flexibility

Players need to move the joints to their full range without hurting themselves. In football, tackling effectively needs flexibility. The sit and reach test is the most common test for flexibility.

Sit and reach

How it works

- Person sits, straight legged, with feet touching the start of the measuring block
- They reach forward and place hands on the block to be measured
- If they reach as far as their toes this measures 0cm, beyond their toes it is +0cm and if it is not as far as their toes it is -0cm
- Recorder measures the distance along the block that the hands reach.

Equipment needed

Another test for flexibility is the Shoulder Hypertension Test.

- indoor area
- wooden block or bench
- measure

Sit and reach results table (cms)		
Rating	Male	Female
super	>+27	>+30
excellent	+17 to +27	+21 to +30
good	+6 to +16	+11 to +20
average	0 to +5	+1 to +10
fair	-8 to -1	-7 to 0
poor	-19 to -9	-14 to -8
very poor	<-19	<-14

What to do:

1. Choose either static strength or flexibility.
2. Write down how you would recognise accomplishment in your choice.
3. Choose a sport.
4. Give two examples of how your choice improves the skills/performance of the activity.

Health-related fitness component

Body composition

The percentage of muscle, fat and bone in the body can reflect the fitness of a person as it reflects their physical characteristics. The proportion of body fat to lean *mass*, however, will vary according to the type of diet and how much exercise is taken by the individual.

Skin-fold callipers test

How it works

There are four main areas to take a reading from:

- **Biceps** at the front of the upper arm
- **Triceps** at the back of the upper arm
- **Supra-iliac** at the front of the body above the hips
- **Subscapula** at the bottom point of the scapula (shoulder blade).

In all cases take care not to include muscle in the callipers. Prior to measurement muscles are tensed and then relaxed. Arm readings are taken with the arm by the performer's side. Readings should be taken after a normal breath out. Three measurements

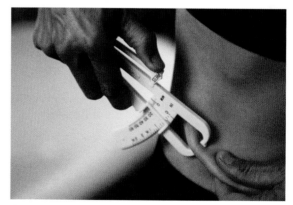

Skin-fold calliper being used to measure the amount of fat at the Supra-iliac area.

are taken at each site. The three measurements are added and divided by three to give the average in millimetres (mm). The sum of the four skin-fold measurements gives the body fat percentage.

A **skin-fold calliper** is an adjustable instrument that measures the amount of fat at different places on the body. The method is to place skin and underlying layers of fat between callipers, a dial gives the reading of the thickness of the flesh. There are four main measurements to take:

Equipment needed

- skin-fold calliper
- record sheet and pen.

Body Fat Percentage Overall Ratings Table				
Body Fat %	Men	Women	Male Athletes	Female Athletes
Lean	<12.0	<17	<7.0	<12.0
Average	12–20.9	17–27.0	7–14.0	12–24.9
Moderately	21–25.9	28–32.9	>15.0	>25.0
Overweight				
Overweight	>26	>33	N/A	N/A

Task 3

What to do:

1. Calculate your own Body Mass Index: $BMI = \dfrac{Man(kg)}{Height(M^2)}$
2. Record your calculations.

Calculating a person's Body Mass Index (BMI) is a measure of body weight and an indicator of health. Usually, the higher the BMI, the higher the % of body fat – BMI is therefore a general indicator of how fat someone is. Sportspeople with a high % of lean body mass will have a higher than average BMI because muscle weighs more than fat. So the BMI is not always the best indicator of health for these people.

Task 4

What to do:

1. Calculate your own Body Mass Index.
2. Write down your calculations.

Agility testing

Agility is the ability to change direction quickly and still keep the body under control. Its component of skill-related fitness is needed in most games, gymnastics and skiing.

Illinois agility test

How it works

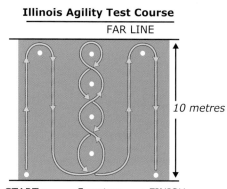

Illinois Agility Test Course

- The performer begins by lying face down on the floor at the starting point.
- On the whistle, the performer jumps to their feet and makes their way around the course to the finish.
- At the same time a stopwatch should be used to time how long it takes to the finish.

Equipment needed

- flat surface to set the course on approximately 15m x 8m
- 8 cones
- stopwatch
- recorder and recording sheet.

Results Table for 16 Year-olds					
Gender	Excellent	Above Average	Average	Below Average	Poor
Male	<15.9 secs	15.9–16.7 secs	16.8–17.6 secs	17.7–18.8 secs	>18.8 secs
Female	<17.5 secs	17.5–18.6 secs	18.7–22.4 secs	22.5–23.4 secs	>23.4 secs

Another test for agility is the T Drill test.

'T' Drill test

How it works

- Three cones are aligned 5m apart
- Cone four is placed 10m forward of the middle cone
- The cones form a 'T' shape.

The athlete

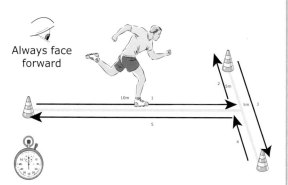

- Starts at the cone at the base of the 'T'
- On the command the athlete and the stopwatch start
- The athlete should run to the middle cone and touch it, then
- Sidestep to the cone on the left and touch it – 5m
  Sidesteps to the cone on the far right and touches it – 10m
  Sidesteps back to the middle cone and touches it – 5m
  Run backwards to base of the 'T' and touches it – 10m
  The teacher/coach stops thenwatch

Pupils perform the test, train for 3–4 weeks, then repeat the test, comparing the results.

Diagram of pathway

Equipment needed

- flat surface
- four cones
- stopwatch
- recording sheet
- pen
- assistant recorder
- teacher/coach timing.

Speed

Speed is the maximum rate a person can move their body over a certain distance. Most sports rely on a performer to move the whole body at speed, so tests for this type of speed are appropriate.

30m sprint test

How it works

- The 30m straight is measured out
- From a standing start
- Performer sets off as quickly as possible
- At the same time stopwatch starts
- Performer sprints to the finishing line as quickly as possible
- As performer crosses finishing point stopwatch is stopped
- Time recorded to 100th/sec.

Equipment needed

- flat, even running surface
- 30m tape measure
- 2 cones
- stopwatch
- recording sheet and pen.

The following are national norms for 16 to 19 year-olds. Results have been measured in seconds.

	Male	Female
Excellent	<4.1	<4.6
Above Average	4.3 - 4.1	4.7 - 4.6
Average	4.5 - 4.4	4.9 - 4.8
Below Average	4.7 - 4.6	5.1 - 4.10
Poor	>4.7	>5.1

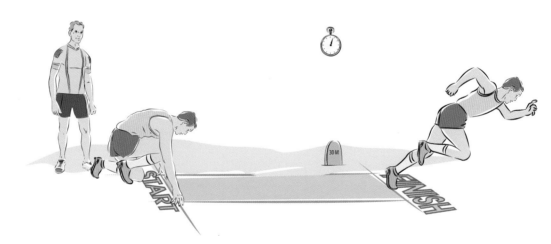

Task 5

What to do:

1. Choose either speed or strength.
2. Write down how you would recognise accomplishment in your choice.
3. Choose a sport.
4. Give two examples of how your choice improves the skills/performance of the activity.

Example
Agility
Netball
1 Wing Attack changing direction to dodge marker.
2 Goal Defence changing direction, turning and moving to recover shot off the netball post's ring.

50m sprint test

How it works

- Course marked out as follows – 10m – 30m – 10m
- Athletes use a standing start
- On command they run the course as quickly as possible
- An assistant times the athlete between the 10m line to the 40m line
- A recording is made of the 'flying start' 30m section.

Equipment needed

- 40m tape measure
- stop watch
- recording sheet
- pen
- assistant recorder
- assistant timer.

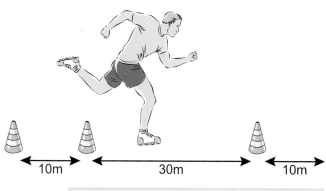

Time (secs) for 30m flying sprint		
Males	Females	Rating
<4.0	<4.5	Excellent
4.2–4.0	4.6–4.5	Good
4.4–4.3	4.8–4.7	Average
4.6–4.5	5.0–4.9	Fair
>4.6	>5.0	Poor

Reaction time

The time it takes for a performer to react to a stimulus = simple reaction time when a performer is presented with two stimuli, each requiring a different response, this is choice reaction time.

Ruler Drop Test

How it works

- The ruler is held by the assistant, with arm outstretched.
- The ruler is between the outstretched thumb and finger of dominant hand.
- The performer's thumb is level with the '0' on the ruler.
- The assistant instructs the performer to catch the ruler in thumb and finger as soon as the ruler is released.
- The assistant records distance between the bottom of the ruler and the top of the performer's thumb at the point of the catch.

Equipment needed

- one 1m ruler
- an assistant
- recording sheet and pen.

Table of results—national norms for 16 to 19 year-olds	
Excellent	<7.5cms
Above average	7.5–15.9cms
Average	15.9–20.4cms
Below average	20.4–28cms
Poor	>28cms

Balance

Balance is the ability to keep the body stable whether still, moving or in different shapes by keeping the centre of gravity over the base.

Stork stand test

How it works

- The performer stands upright on both feet in a comfortable position with their hands placed on their hips
- One leg is lifted and the toes of that foot are placed on the knee of the other leg
- When directed to do so the performer raises the heel of their standing foot and stands on their toes
- At the same time the stopwatch is started
- The performer balances for as long as possible without letting the heel off the ground or the other foot move away from the knee
- A record is made of how long the balance was held
- The test is repeated using the other leg.

Equipment needed

- any warm and dry space
- stopwatch
- recorder and recording sheet.

Results Table for 15–16 Year-olds				
Excellent	Above Average	Average	Below Average	Poor
>50 secs	40–49 secs	26–39 secs	11–25 secs	<11 secs

What to do:

1. Choose either reaction time or balance.
2. Write down how you would recognise accomplishment in your choice.
3. Choose a sport.
4. Give two examples of how your choice improves the skills/performance of the activity.

Example
- Reaction time

Football:

1 Attacker in the six yard box reacts to the keeper spilling the ball and moves quickly to kick the ball to score.
2 Keeper moving and diving quickly to save a power shot struck in the 18 yard box.

Task 6

Co-ordination

The ability to combine two or more body parts at the same time. It can also be defined as: the ability to carry out a series of movements smoothly and efficiently.

Alternate hand wall throw

How it works

- A 2m distance is measured from a smooth wall.
- The performer stands that distance away.
- The performer holds a tennis ball in dominant hand.
- The performer throws ball against wall.
- The performer catches ball in the other hand.
- The performer then throws ball from that hand.
- It is caught in the dominant hand.
- The performer should repeat the catch and throw as many times as possible in 30 seconds.

Equipment needed

- smooth wall
- 2m measure
- tennis ball
- stopwatch
- recording sheet and pen.

Results Table for 15–16 Year-olds	
High score	above 35
Above average	35–30
Average	29–25
Below average	24–20
Low score	below 20

What to do:

For coordination:

1. Write down how you would recognise accomplishment in your choice.
2. Choose a sport.
3. Give two examples of how your choice improves the skills/performance of the activity.
4. Work together in a small group (about 5–7 people.)
5. One person conducts the test, the rest take the test.
6. Collate your results.
7. Create a bar chart of your results.

Summary

For tests to be useful to the coach and the performer they should focus on the muscle groups and energy systems used in the activity for which the athlete is training. Each test should be carried out in the same way each time so that the results are reliable and can be compared to previous tests and recognised norms. The tester should be aware of the many variables which can affect the test results and measurements. Every attempt should be made to reconstruct the same conditions as for previous tests so the results are a true reflection of the performer's fitness.

Cardiovascular Response to Physical Exercise

What you will learn about in this section

1. Short-Term Effects of Exercise on the Body
2. Working Muscles Produce Heat
3. Long-term Effects of Exercise on the Circulatory System

At rest the heart rate slows down (decreases); this is due to the fact that it does not have to work so hard to circulate the blood to the resting muscles. **Resting heart rate** is on average about 72 beats per minute, although various factors change this such as gender and age. This rate is sufficient to supply the muscles with the necessary blood and nutrients. Exercise changes all of this.

1 Short-Term Effects of Exercise on the Body

Muscles need oxygen to work. As soon as the muscles begin to work harder than they normally do there is a need for greater supplies of oxygen to them. Oxygen combines with **haemoglobin** in the red blood cells to produce oxyhaemoglobin. The heart rate increases accordingly to transfer this oxygenated blood to the working muscles.

The increase in the heart rate depends on the type and intensity of the exercise. With low impact work the rate will increase slightly, but with a workload of greater intensity the rate rises more dramatically. With exercise the rate and volume of the heart change. An area in the brain called the 'cardiac centre' controls and regulates how hard the heart works.

2 Working Muscles Produce Heat

As well as producing movement when they are working, muscles also produce heat. Too much heat is bad for the body and can cause **heat exhaustion**. To prevent the body temperature rising, blood vessels at the surface of the skin open (**dilate**) and heat is transported away from the body. More waste products are made during exercise. These can interfere with the effective running of the body. Salt and water are such waste products. These exit the body via the pores and capillaries at the surface of the skin.

During exercise, there is a greater need for more blood to circulate around the body. The arteries automatically adapt to this demand. Their internal diameter, called the **endothelium**, automatically widens to let more blood through.

Immediate effects of exercise

oxygen inhaled regularly for aerobic respiration; tidal volume increases

the skin reddens as blood moves to the surface of the skin helping heat loss

body becomes sweaty – water evaporates at the surface to cool the body

cardiac output increases as demand for O_2 in the working muscles increases

air exhaled to stop the build-up of carbon dioxide and rid moisture

gaseous exchange in alveoli – with training the gaseous exchange becomes more efficient as more alveoli are prepared to take on the exchange of oxygen and carbon dioxide

breathing rate increases and becomes deeper and more regular = aerobic respiration

blood moved to the skin surface for heat regulation

waste water released from the body as sweat on the surface of the skin

heart beat increases supplying the demand for more oxygen in the working muscles

shunting of blood to working muscles

salt loss helps rid sweating from the body

glucose – glycogen is stored in muscles and the liver and released as glucose to allow the muscles to work

stroke volume increases as the heart sends out more blood per beat

fatigue and ache in muscles, as the ability to use oxygen for the production of energy becomes less efficient

adrenalin (a hormone) released preparing the body for action

blood flow reduced to areas not in use, like the digestive system

the performer may become stressed

the performer may suffer an injury

The effects of exercise and the link between the circulatory and respiratory systems.

3   Long-term Effects of Exercise on the Circulatory System

Endurance training, commonly known as aerobic training, helps strengthen the heart. This type of training is progressive over time. With training the general size of the heart gets bigger, the walls become thicker, stronger and more robust. The resting **stroke volume** increases and so does the cardiac output.

Whilst everything else is increasing, the heart rate does the opposite. A useful indicator of good fitness is the **resting heart rate**. The slower it is per minute, the more efficient the heart is. It can pump the required amount of blood with fewer beats. Therefore, the slower the resting heartbeat, the fitter the person. With good aerobic fitness, a person will usually be able to keep working efficiently without tiring or losing skill.

Task 2

What to do:

1. Taking regular exercise affects the body in many ways. Using the two headings 'Immediate Effects of Exercise' and 'Long-term Effects of Exercise', make a list of the different changes that happen to the body.

Key Terms:

Cardiac output	► the amount of blood pumped by the heart in one minute
Dilate	► open up or become wider
Endothelium	► internal space of the blood vessels; in arteries this changes according to the amount of blood transported
Endurance	► the ability to keep working over a period without tiring or losing skill
Haemoglobin	► found in red blood cells, transports oxygen to body tissue
Heat exhaustion	► fatigue brought on by the body temperature rising
Maximum heart rate	► calculated as 220 minus age
Recovery rate	► the time it takes for the heart to return to resting rate after exercise
Resting heart rate	► number of heart beats per minute when the body is at rest
Stroke volume	► the amount of blood pumped by the heart in one beat

Summary

The contents of blood keep the body alive: the circulation of blood to different parts of the body is vital. Oxygen, nutrients and hormones give the tissues of the body what they need to work. Waste products such as salt, heat, water, carbon dioxide and urea are all removed from the body so it is not poisoned.

When a person exercises, the circulatory system needs to work faster as there is greater demand by the muscles for oxygen. With regular exercise, the body can be trained to make these adjustments quickly and efficiently.

A properly planned training programme should meet the demands of the individual and their chosen activity. It should gradually increase in intensity as the body adapts to the new stresses and demands made of it. This gradual increase helps to avoid injury and will not place excessive stress on the circulatory system.

Cardiorespiratory Responses to Exercise

What you will learn about in this section

1. Effects of Oxygen Uptake
2. Breathing Frequency and the Effect on Vital Capacity
3. More Efficient Oxygen and Carbon Dioxide Diffusion
4. Improved Delivery of Oxygen to Working Muscles
5. Increased Stroke Volume

The function of the respiratory system is to get oxygen into the body and carbon dioxide and other waste products out. This happens through the act of breathing. Breathing in (inhalation) gets the oxygen in, so it can be used by the body to release energy. Breathing out (exhalation) removes carbon dioxide (and other waste products) so it does not build up and poison the body.

Air's journey to the lungs

The exchange of gases takes place in the lungs. From the nose or mouth, air enters the trachea and moves towards the lungs. It divides into two branches called 'bronchi'. These subdivide into smaller tubes called 'bronchioles'. At the end of these are alveoli. These are air sacs with many mini blood vessels called 'capillaries' running from them.

The respiration and circulation link

There has to be a link between the respiratory and circulatory systems. The oxygen has to go from the respiratory system to the circulatory system and back to the respiratory system again. It follows this order:

- The oxygen breathed in goes through the mouth or nose, down the trachea, into the lungs and into the alveoli (air sacs).
- The oxygen passes through the alveoli walls into the red blood cells, via the capillaries.
- The oxygen joins with haemoglobin to make oxyhaemoglobin.
- The oxyhaemoglobin is used by the working body and is transported by the circulatory system to cells needing to release energy.
- Carbon dioxide is produced as a waste product.
- This is converted into a gas and passes back through the alveoli walls, via the capillaries into the blood plasma.
- Blood takes it back to the capillaries in the lungs.
- The carbon dioxide passes through the capillary and alveoli walls into the alveoli (air sacs).
- It is then exhaled from the body.

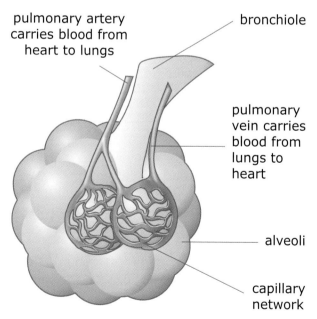

pulmonary artery carries blood from heart to lungs

bronchiole

pulmonary vein carries blood from lungs to heart

alveoli

capillary network

The exchange of gases is vital for our survival. With training, this exchange becomes more efficient as more alveoli are prepared to make the swap between oxygen (in) and carbon dioxide (out). Regular exercise conditions the lungs to excrete more of the poisonous carbon dioxide from the body. If too much carbon dioxide remained in the body, it would be fatal.

Task 1

What to do:

1. Write three key sentences about the passage of air and its importance using the following key terms: pathway taken, exchange of gases, effects of training.

1 Effects of Oxygen Uptake

During exercise the demand for more oxygen is increased in order to fuel the working muscles. There is also an increase in the production of carbon dioxide. This is converted into a gas and removed via capillaries, alveoli and lungs and exhaled. In prolonged exercise more oxygen is used from each delivery. The greater the oxygen uptake the longer the muscles can work without tiring.

2 Breathing Frequency and the Effect on Vital Capacity

At rest, on average, a person breathes about 15 times a minute. This rate adequately supplies the body systems with enough oxygen to keep them working and the subsequent removal of harmful substances under normal circumstances.

Behind the scenes breathing

We can feel our chest expand and fall as we breathe in and out. What we are not aware of is the change in the air going into and out of our body. The air we breathe in is different from the air that we breathe out. We now know why we breathe, so let's look at the changes in inhaled and exhaled air.

The parts that make up inhaled and exhaled air are called its 'composition'.

The lungs, at different stages of breathing, have varying amounts of air in them. **Tidal volume** is the amount of air breathed into and out of the body during normal breathing. During exercise, the volume is forced to change. Therefore, it is called **forced breathing**. **Vital capacity** is the largest amount or volume of air that can be exhaled (breathed out) after the largest possible inhalation (breathed in). **Residual volume** is the amount of air that, even after as much air as possible has been exhaled, is left in the lungs.

Composition of inhaled air

79% = nitrogen
20% = oxygen
trace = carbon dioxide

Composition of exhaled air

79% = nitrogen
16% = oxygen
4% = carbon diox

●●●● ▶ Active Challenge

Exhaled air has more moisture in it. This is because water is a waste product. Some water is removed from your body as you breathe out. Moisture in exhaled air is demonstrated by the mirror test.

Hold a mirror just below your lip and exhale. What do you see?

When you are exercising, how else is water removed from the body?

How exercise affects breathing

Breathing becomes heavier and quicker as a result. During exercise there is a greater need for more oxygen to supply the working muscles. This results in more waste products that need to be removed from the body. The rate of breathing rises therefore according to the new intensity workload. The rate of breathing can increase up to 50 breaths per minute during extreme exercise.

As a result the amount of oxygen a person needs to take in increases. There is a limit to the increase for each person called the 'VO$_2$ maximum'. During exercise, the vital capacity will increase because of the demand for a greater intake of air. Both the residual volume and the tidal volume increase but only slightly.

What to do:

1. Write a sentence on how an increase in exercise affects the following: tidal volume, forced breathing, vital capacity, residual volume.

3   More Efficient Oxygen and Carbon Dioxide Diffusion

During exercise the demand for oxygen increases. As the muscles use the oxygen they produce carbon dioxide. Carbon dioxide is a poison and needs to be quickly removed from the body. Therefore, there needs to be an exchange or diffusion of gases.

Diffusion can be said to be a movement of gases from an area where there is a high amount to an area where there is a low amount. The greater the difference in concentration of gases the greater the rate of diffusion.

Undertaking an exercise programme that improves the oxygen intake - VO$_2$ max, which is the maximum amount of oxygen the body can take in at one breath, means that more carbon dioxide can be removed.

This removal takes place in the alveoli via the capillaries. Increased fitness also increases the amount of capillaries and so improves the diffusion of the gases when exercising, breathing in through the nose moistens and warms the air. This prepares the air making it more conducive for the gaseous exchange. An efficient gaseous exchange allows the muscles to work for longer periods.

4   Improved Delivery of Oxygen to Working Muscles

As a person becomes fitter, the body's ability to breathe in more air for longer periods of time develops. This increases the amount of oxygen entering the body for use by the working muscles. A fit person also begins to increase the quantity and quality of their blood. More red blood cells are formed as a result. These provide more opportunity for oxyhaemoglobin to be delivered to their working muscles allowing them to work harder for longer.

Active Challenge

Count the number of breaths you make at rest for one minute.

Perform maximal exercise, such as step-ups, for one minute.

Again, count the number of breaths for one minute.

Time how long it takes breathing to return to rest.

Task 3

5 Increased Stroke Volume

Regular exercise at the right intensity will affect the efficiency of the heart. The heart is muscle and in the same way biceps and triceps develop so will the heart. It will increase in size and strength. With a bigger and more powerful heart the stroke volume will increase. Therefore there will be more blood pumped out of the heart by one ventricle at each contraction. This makes the heart more efficient – it will be able to deliver as much blood but with fewer contractions. That is why a fit person has a lower resting heart rate.

What to do:

1. Create a visual representation to show the difference between an unfit and a fit person's heart.

Key Terms:

Alveoli	► air sacs where gaseous exchange takes place
VO$_2$ Maximum	► (VO$_2$ max) the largest amount of oxygen that can be transported to and used by muscle in one minute
Diffusion	► the spreading of particles of gas from a region of high concentrate to a region of low concentrate
Expiration	► breathing out, exhalation
Forced breathing	► the change in breathing during exercise when requirements increase
Inspiration	► breathing in, inhalation
Residual volume	► the amount of air left in the lungs after a maximal exhalation
Tidal volume	► amount of air breathed in or out during normal breathing
Vital capacity	► amount of air that can be breathed out, after a deep breath in

Summary

A fit and healthy respiratory system is vital. It fuels the muscles and takes away poisonous carbon dioxide from the body. Aerobic and anaerobic systems are used at different times depending on the types of stress put on the body. The respiratory and circulatory systems are linked. The key is the link between the alveoli of the respiratory system and the capillaries of the circulatory system. Training improves the systems.

Redistribution of Blood during Exercise

What you will learn about in this section

1. Vascular Shunt
2. Cooling Down System – Sweating/Evaporation

When exercise commences there are many changes that take place in the body. The circulatory system plays a major part in making the necessary modifications to its usual routine.

1 Vascular Shunt

We know that muscles need oxygen to work and the way oxygen reaches the working muscles is via lungs, alveoli and capillaries in the process of diffusion into the blood stream. The blood plays its role as the carrier of oxygen to these working muscles.

During exercise the role of blood becomes vital to the body's well-being.

When exercising, the body needs more oxygen at the site of the working muscles. The distribution of blood around the body changes according to the demand allowing the working parts to be supplied with the necessary amounts of oxygen. This redistribution of the cardiac output is called the 'vascular shunt'.

Blood flow reduces to systems not in use. The digestive system, for instance, receives less oxygen during exercise, as its needs are negligible under such circumstances.

2 Cooling Down System - Sweating Evaporation

When exercising, the release of energy produces heat. If the body becomes too hot, it will not be able to keep functioning properly. The body has different ways of controlling temperature.

As the body temperature rises, blood is redistributed to the surface of the skin. As blood is 'shunted' to the surface, the blood vessels expand, allowing heat to be reduced quickly. The widening of the vessels under the skin is called vasolidation, allowing heat to be lost by radiation.

Another way to combat overheating is by sweating. During exercise sweat glands produce sweat. This is mainly water produced as a by-product of exercise. The heat from the body makes the water evaporate at the surface of the skin, which helps to cool the body. In intense, prolonged exercise it is important to replace water loss by regularly drinking fluids.

●●●● ▶ Active Challenge

You will need a watch for this challenge. Observe your partner exercising – jumping on the spot will be easy to do. Time how long it takes for the performer's cheeks to flush.

Summary

Interval training over short distances at fast speeds results in an oxygen debt. By continuing this training new capillaries are formed, heart muscle is strengthened and the delivery of oxygen is improved, which stops the build-up of lactic acid. The overall effect is called an 'oxygen debt tolerance', which the performer develops through this type of training.

Exercise Effects on the Body

What you will learn about in this section

1 Training (Aerobic) Threshold

2 Training Zones

3 Long-term Effects of Exercise through Training

Training thresholds and training zones are determined by heart rate. As the heart rate increases different zones of training are reached and passed. The effect of working in different zones affects and develops the body in different ways. Performers can regulate the intensity of their training if they know their **maximum heart rate**.

220 – age = maximum heart rate

1 Training (Aerobic) Threshold

The training threshold is the barrier to pass beyond for exercise to have any effect on the body. It is not until a performer's heart rate increases beyond this threshold that the exercise intensity is stressful enough to make it adapt and improve. Below this level the exercise will be too easy to make a difference.

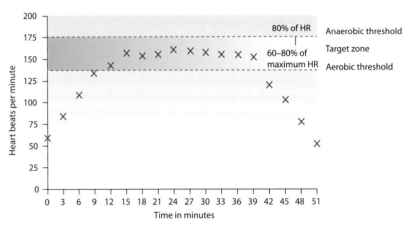

The pulse increase, when training in the target zone, of a 16 year-old

2 Training Zones

There are two zones affecting the body in different ways. They are determined by the heart rate and therefore the intensity of the exercise.

Target zone (aerobic)

This zone is reached when exercise makes the body work between 60–80% of the maximum heart rate. Training in this zone improves cardiovascular fitness. It can work at easy to moderate level for long periods of time.

Training in this zone will work as long as the FITT (Frequency, Intensity, Time and Type) rules are applied.

Training zone (anaerobic)

This zone is reached when the exercise intensity makes the body work above 80% of its maximum heart rate. The body works anaerobically in this zone. There will be a build-up of lactic acid as a result of working at this intensity. This will tire the body, making the training time shorter and the recovery time longer.

3 Long-term Effects of Exercise through Training

If an appropriate training programme is followed regularly it will cause the body to change and adapt to the different stresses asked of it. A training programme with the correct levels of frequency, intensity and duration applied to it will have a marked effect on the body in the long term.

bones become stronger

increased stroke volume

tendons become stronger

increased vital capacity

red blood cells increase – more oxyhaemoglobin for working muscles

increased cardiac output

able to breathe in more air and do so for longer

increased CV endurance as the respiration and circulatory systems improve

can cope with more lactic acid during exercise

heart becomes larger and stronger

increased VO$_2$ max

recovery rate improves

arteries larger and more elastic leads to blood pressure reduction

lower resting heart rate

general fitness level improves

increased capillarisation

depending on the type of training – specific fitness levels improve

more oxygen in and more carbon dioxide out

ligaments become more flexible

body uses more fat and less carbohydrates as a fuel for exercise – this will affect weight

quantity and quality of the blood improves

able to work closer to the VO$_2$ max

Long-term effects of aerobic exercise at the right intensity improves endurance.

What to do:

1. Rearrange each piece of information around the cyclist photo above, into the following groups: cardio, respiratory, general.

Key Terms:

Vascular shunt	▶	the redistribution of the cardiac output
Vasolidation	▶	widening of the vessels under the skin
Threshold of training	▶	level of intensity above which exercise begins to have an effect on the body
Target zone	▶	aerobic exercise level working heart between 60–80% of MHR
Training zone	▶	anaerobic exercise level working heart above 80% of MHR
Lactic acid	▶	chemical build-up in the muscles during anaerobic exercise

Summary

Endurance training, commonly referred to as aerobic training, helps strengthen the circulatory and respiratory systems. The effects of this training are that a performer can work at a higher intensity for longer periods of time.

Energy Systems

What you will learn about in this section

1. ATP-CP System or Creative Phosphate System
2. Lactic Acid System
3. Aerobic System
4. Aerobic and Anaerobic Activities
5. Application – Lactate Production

Different energy systems

The body converts fuel to energy and releases it into the body using different respiratory systems. These systems automatically kick in depending on the type, intensity and duration of the exercise performed.

1 ATP-CP System or Creative Phosphate System

ATP-CP stands for the chemicals – adenosine triphosphate and creatine phosphate.

When energy is produced anaerobically no oxygen is used in its initial release. Some sports wholly use anaerobic respiration. These are activities where there is a need for a single maximum burst of energy. Athletic field events are good examples of anaerobic exercise. In throwing and jumping events the actions used are explosive. They use one all-out burst of maximum effort to complete the event. The time it takes to complete the attempt is very short, so the energy is produced from the supplies already in the body.

The demand of the muscles for oxygen is so great that the cardiovascular systems do not have time to supply the demand. Energy is produced without the presence of oxygen by the chemical 'Adenosine Triphosphate' (ATP).

This system provides an immediate source of energy. It can only be sustained for up to 10 seconds. There are limited stores of ATP in the body and what there are, are used up quickly. As it does not need oxygen to provide the energy it is classed as anaerobic.

Many performers who need to use this energy system will train to build up muscle to contain more levels of ATP-CP. This will allow them to perform for longer periods at the highest possible intensity.

Athletic field events use ATP-CP system; Steve Backley demonstrates this in the men's javelin.

2 Lactic Acid System

This system provides energy to working muscles performing high intensity exercise, when oxygen is not readily available. This cannot be sustained for long. This system works between the periods of 10 seconds to three minutes. Therefore it is a short-term energy system, which is classed as anaerobic.

ATP can only supply the energy for a short time. If the demand for energy continues for over a minute then another system provides the energy, called the **lactic acid** system. This releases energy by breaking down carbohydrates. The side effect of the body using this system is that there is a build-up of lactic acid in the muscles. Lactic acid is a poison and causes cramp in the muscles.

No air = anaerobic   The formula is: glucose ➝ carbon dioxide, water, energy, lactic acid

You can tell when a player has just used their anaerobic system from their breathing pattern. After working very hard in the activity their breath may be shallow and gasping. This is an indication that there is an **oxygen debt**, a state in which the body needs more oxygen than it can supply.

This type of energy provision can only carry on for 45–60 seconds. After this, the lactic acid in the muscles becomes too high and prevents muscular contraction. The anaerobic system stops. The body then cannot keep running at its fastest speed or keep lifting heavy weights.

Lactic acid builds up in the body if oxygen is not present and can cause pain and cramp. The body cannot keep working the muscles without oxygen for any prolonged length of time. So thereafter the aerobic system begins to work.

Outfield games players will use all respiratory systems during the game.

3 Aerobic System

Energy released in aerobic activity needs a sufficient supply of oxygen to the tissues. With enough oxygen present the activity can go on for long periods, as long as the difficulty or intensity does not become too great. This aerobic fitness allows us to keep going at a moderate level. The aerobic system is used in moderate to hard continuous activities that usually take place over longer periods of time. The oxygen is breathed in and diffused into the circulatory system. In this type of activity, breathing becomes more regular and deeper. The muscles need oxygen to contract and in aerobic respiration this oxygen enters the body by the breathing process.

Extra air = aerobic   The formula for this is: glucose + oxygen ➝ carbon dioxide, water, energy

4 Aerobic and Anaerobic Activities

In all games a combination of all the systems is required. There will be times requiring high intensity work (anaerobic) and low intensity work (aerobic). A player while moving and positioning themselves correctly on the pitch, according to the play, is using aerobic respiration. This is aerobic because the intensity of the exercise is low/moderate and will continue throughout the game. When the player takes a shot, for example, one maximal contraction is used. For this action the ATP/CP system comes into operation.

Different sports use the systems to different degrees. Footballers use both systems, whilst squash players predominantly use the ATP/CP and lactic acid systems, as each stroke of the ball is one maximal effort.

Aerobic and anaerobic respiration is used in rugby.

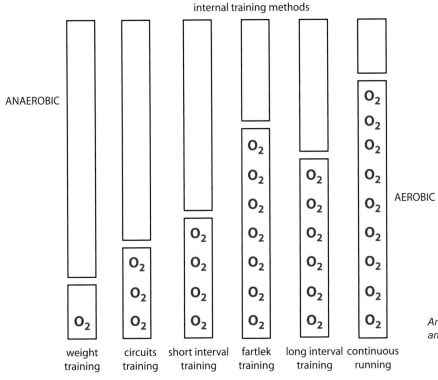

internal training methods

ANAEROBIC

AEROBIC

weight training | circuits training | short interval training | fartlek training | long interval training | continuous running

An approximate link between training methods and aerobic and anaerobic respiration.

What to do:

1. Link the following game situations below into ATP/CP, lactic acid and aerobic systems. Give at least one reason for your decision.

   a. Jogging to a new space in the game according to the play.

   b. Using a turn of pace to beat a defender over a short distance.

   c. An attacker having attempted an attack, but fails, sprints back to opposition defender to make a tackle.

Task 1

Lactic acid is produced after muscular action. If oxygen is not present it starts to build up. This stops the muscles from working properly, making them tire, ache and cramp up.

Athletes train to improve their alactic/lactic threshold. They do this by working just below the anaerobic threshold (or lactic threshold). This is called 'tempo training' and improves the ability to rid the body of lactic acid and so increase the resistance of muscles to tiring. Raising this threshold is essential for all endurance events.

Oxygen debt occurrence

During high intensity exercise using the **ATP/CP** and lactic acid systems the muscles need more oxygen to rid the body of the build-up of lactic acid. This extra oxygen is called the **oxygen debt.** The body pays off this debt by gulping air into the lungs. As a result the lactic acid is turned into carbon dioxide, water and a lactate component. So when you see a sportsperson panting and gulping for breath you know they have just used anaerobic respiration and they are trying to repay the oxygen debt and recover from it.

Endurance athletes, like the cross-country skier in the photo, have a high lactic threshold.

What to do:

1. Study the comments below on the changes in respiration to an athlete in a 400m race. Put them into the order in which the athlete would experience them.

   a. She breathes quickly and respires aerobically.
   b. The oxygen debt is repaid.
   c. Her muscles ache.
   d. Lactic acid forms in the muscles.
   e. She begins anaerobic respiration in her muscles.
   f. She breathes slowly and respires aerobically.

Key Terms:

ATP-CP system	► Anaerobic system providing energy for short maximal contractions up to 10 seconds
Lactic acid system	► Anaerobic system providing energy for high intensity exercise from 10 seconds to three minutes
Aerobic system	► energy system using oxygen to supply energy to working muscles
Lactic threshold	► the limit of the body's ability to remove lactic acid
Oxygen debt	► the way oxygen is paid back after anaerobic exercise

Summary

The energy systems fuelling the working muscles change according to the intensity and duration of the exercise undertaken. During a team game different passages of play can require a player to utilise each system in order to be effective.

Lactic acid is the performer's enemy as it can cause discomfort and muscle fatigue. Through training, the lactic threshold can be raised so greater amounts of lactic acid can be removed from the body. This allows the body to work at higher intensities for longer periods.

Factors Affecting Movement

What you will learn about in this section

1. The Definition of a Joint
2. Classification of Joints
3. Different Joint Locations in the Body
4. The Significance of Synovial Joints
5. In-depth Understanding of Synovial Joints
6. Functions of Different Parts of a Joint
7. The Importance of Cartilage, Tendons and Ligaments in Sport
8. Different Types of Synovial Joint

1 The Definition of a Joint

A **joint** is the place where two or more bones meet.

There does not have to be movement there.

The **fused** bones of the cranium are as much a joint as the meeting of the humerus and ulna at the elbow. The joints where there are movement are more significant to the actions of the sportsperson.

Some joints allow a large range of movements, such as the hip joint. Other joints, like the joint at the wrist, give much smaller and more restricted movement. This is owing to the size and arrangement of the bones. Although there are elements common to all joints, each type is formed in a different way and it is this arrangement that leads to the different ways we can move.

What to do:

1. Write out a definition of the word 'joint'.

Skiing involves a range of movements at different joints.

Task 1

2 Classification of Joints

In the body there are three types of joint. These are:

- non-movable
- slightly movable
- freely movable

They all differ according to how much movement they allow.

Non-movable joints are fixed: here there is no movement at the joint. Any place where the bones are fused together is a non-movable joint. These occur in the crown of the cranium and the coccyx, which lies at the base of the spine.

Slightly movable joints have gaps between the bones, which allow a small amount of movement. These gaps are usually filled with cartilage. The bones of the vertebral column and the joints of the ribs and the sternum are examples of slightly movable joints.

Freely movable are the most complex of the three types. They are designed for movement and have the most obvious relevance to physical activity.

3 Different Joint Locations in the Body

The following are all **synovial** joints. These joints allow the greatest movement. You only need to remember those in bold.

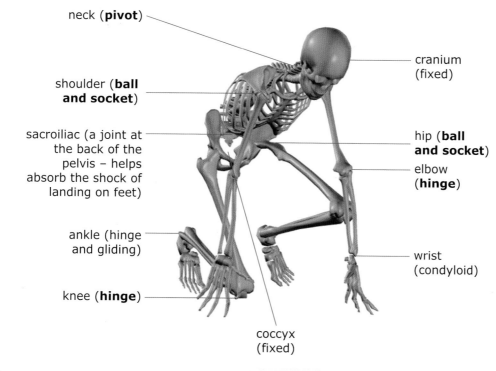

neck (**pivot**)

cranium (fixed)

shoulder (**ball and socket**)

sacroiliac (a joint at the back of the pelvis – helps absorb the shock of landing on feet)

hip (**ball and socket**)

elbow (**hinge**)

ankle (hinge and gliding)

wrist (condyloid)

knee (**hinge**)

coccyx (fixed)

What to do:

1. Make a table of the body's joints.
2. State where the joints are in the body. Use neck, knee, hip, elbow and shoulder as headings.
3. State the type of joint each is and the bones involved.

4 The Significance of Synovial Joints

Freely movable joints are common in the human body. The components of this type of joint have built-in safety factors to help guard against injury. These joints are designed to reduce wear and tear, absorb shock and reduce friction. These factors are especially important when performing skills at pace and with power.

5 In-depth Understanding of Synovial Joints

Knee joint

There are many parts to the knee joint. Its position demands that it can withstand hard pressure. This makes it a robust joint. The ligaments that hold the bones in place are called the 'cruciates'. When footballers have serious knee injuries it is these ligaments that are often damaged. Between the femur (thigh bone) and the tibia (shin bone) is the semi-lunar cartilage that helps lubricate the joint. This is also the damaged or torn tissue in knee-twisting injuries and cartilage problems.

knee
joint

6 Functions of Different Parts of a Joint

Cartilage covers the ends of the bones where they meet and stops the bones touching each other. This is called 'hyaline cartilage'. The cartilage acts as a cushion and creates a barrier, reducing the amount of **friction** that occurs when the bones are moving against each other. This stops the bones wearing each other away.

Synovial fluid lubricates the joint. Like oiling the chain of a bike or putting oil in the car, synovial fluid allows all the parts to move against each other smoothly. It also keeps the joint free from infection.

Synovial membrane lies inside the capsule. It is here where the synovial fluid is produced.

Synovial capsule is a tough fibre that surrounds the joint holding the fluid in place.

Ligaments surround the sides of the joint. Ligaments are made of tough elastic fibres. It is the ligaments that hold the bones in place, so keeping the joint together. The stability of the joint relies on the strength of the ligaments and on the muscles supporting the joint.

Tendons are not strictly part of the joint, although they play an important part in the joint's movement. Their job is to attach muscle to bone. Without tendons muscle would float around the bone and movement would be impossible. It is this attachment that creates an anchor for muscles to shorten and bring about different actions. Tendons are very strong because great exertion is required for some actions. As the muscle needs to be held firm, the tendons act as a non-elastic anchor.

What to do:

1. Link the matching words. Each word can be used only once.

elastic   hyaline   lubricate

barrier between the bones   synovial fluid

reduces friction   tough fibre   ligaments

stabilise   tough   acts as a cushion

attach bone to bone   helps move freely

synovial capsule   cartilage

surrounds the joint

Joints are used in every movement.

●●●● ▶ **Active Challenge**

With a partner say what built-in safety factors there are in a synovial joint

Key Terms:

Cartilage	► tough, flexible tissue; can be found at the end of bones
Friction	► action of two surfaces rubbing together creating heat
Fused	► two or more bones knitted together so no movement occurs
Joint	► the point where two or more bones meet
Ligament	► tough, rounded, elastic fibre attaching bone to bone at a joint
Synovial capsule	► tough fibre surrounding the synovial joint
Synovial fluid	► fluid; found in synovial joint
Synovial joints	► lubricating freely movable joints with ends covered in cartilage
Synovial membrane	► lining inside joint capsule where synovial fluid is produced
Tendons	► strong, non-elastic tissue attaching bone to muscle

7   The Importance of Cartilage, Tendons and Ligaments in Sport

Cartilage is a shock absorber. When running, the knee takes a lot of pounding. It is the cartilage that acts as a cushion so that the bones do not rub together and wear away. If the cartilage were not there, pain would occur at the joint due to the friction of the bones rubbing together. This is especially important in activities like long distance running, where there is continued use of the joint. Cartilage damage is common in sportspeople. A frayed cartilage decreases the efficiency of the joint and is extremely painful.

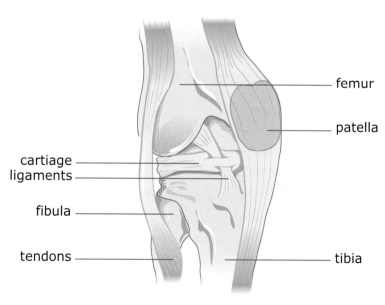

Cross-section of a knee joint showing cartilage, tendons and ligaments.

Ligaments attach bone to bone. As there is much movement of bones, ligaments have to be strong and elastic. If there were no ligaments the joint would be unstable. Running, stopping and changing direction all put pressure on the joint. When changing direction at speed it is the ligaments that keep the bones in the right place. If the ligaments are stretched too far then they tear and the joint **dislocates**. After tearing it is unlikely that the ligaments will return to their former strength.

Tendons attach muscle to bone. Without tendons muscle would float around the bone and movement would be impossible. It is this attachment that creates an anchor for muscles to shorten and bring about different actions. Great exertion is required for some actions; therefore tendons are strong and non-elastic. If a muscle is large, or pulls in more than one direction, more than one tendon may be needed to anchor it. A weightlifter moving a maximum weight needs their tendons to hold firm and keep still. That is why they are non-elastic, just like a pole-vaulter pulling on the pole after take-off in order to clear the bar.

What to do:

1. Copy the table below. Use the headings: cartilage, tendons and ligaments.

2. Put the words from the word bank into the correct column. Words can only be used once.

Task 5

cartilage	tendons	ligaments

Word bank

flexible   at end of bone

elastic   sturdy   strong

attaches bone to muscle

made of many fibres

size changes depending on the size of the muscle

attaches bone to bone

cushions   non-elastic   tough

anchor   stabilise

8 Different Types of Synovial Joint

Each type of synovial joint is different. This is due to where it is in the body, how many bones are located at the joint and the variety of movement it allows.

Whenever a sportsperson is involved in an activity they are relying on the joints of the body to help the action.

In cricket the bowlers rely on the joints of the fingers to move forward and spin the ball.

Playing a forehand drive in tennis involves the shoulder rotating as the racket is swung forward.

Volleyball players rely on the joints of the leg to cushion their landing after performing a smash.

Pivot – neck – rotate and tilt the head – assisting rotation of body

Hinge – knee – extends and flexes – tuck knees for style and aerodynamics (also allows slight rotation as swimming – in breaststroke legs)

Ball and socket – full range of movement – shoulder – throwing ball

Ball and socket – full range of movement – hip – movement to avoid tackle/base to aid throw

Gliding – ankle – forward and back with slight sideways – base footballer passing the ball

Condyloid/gliding – wrist – forward backwards with some slight sideways movement – golfer at 'wrist break' phase of swing

Hinge – fingers – flexing and extending to grip the racket

Hinge – arm – flexing and extending with a slight amount of rotation to swing and apply topspin on the ball

What to do:

1. Give the correct joint type found at the following areas:

   hip, shoulder, knee, elbow, neck.

2. Order the joints from the greatest amount of movement to the least.

3. Link a sporting movement with each joint.

Summary

A joint is a meeting of two or more bones. There may or may not be movement there. The synovial type of joint is the most important to the sportsperson as the different types give the range of movements to complete all sporting actions.

It is the different sizes of bones and the way in which they are arranged that give them their joint type. In synovial joints there are parts that specialise in helping to prevent injury and ensuring smooth action at the joint. These include cartilage, synovial fluid and ligaments. The sportsperson can perform all the movements required for success as long as each joint is kept healthy and strong.

Movement at the Joints

What you will learn about in this section

1. Prime Movers/Fixators/Synergists Muscles
2. The Range of Movement at a Joint
3. How Joints Help the Sportsperson
4. The Effects of Age on Flexibility of the Joints
5. Voluntary Muscle
6. Antagonistic Muscle Action
7. Tendons and Ligaments

Movement occurs when muscles contract, move the bone and in turn change the angle of the joint. This can only happen because the muscles contracting are attached to the bone. They are fixed to the bones via tendons. The point where the working muscle is attached to the bone is called the Origin. At the point where the muscle attaches to the moving bone is called the 'insertion.'

The types of muscles connected to the skeleton are called voluntary muscles. Muscles can only pull. When muscles contract they shorten to pull bone and change angle at the joint. When trained, voluntary muscle can perform complex and controlled movement. Muscles also stabilise the body during movement.

They also have a secondary job of creating a layer around the bone to protect it from impact.

1 Prime Movers/Fixators/Synergists Muscles

Muscles are normally matched up – one at the front of the bone with another on the other side. Muscles usually work in pairs due to the fact that they can only pull.

Prime mover The prime mover (agonist) muscle is responsible for the action taking place. It contracts and pulls the bone creating the movement at the joint.

Antagonists Whilst the prime mover contracts, the antagonist muscle on the other side of the bone relaxes, allowing movement.

Synergists Other muscles are also involved indirectly with the action. Synergists hold the body position so that the prime mover can operate. These are known as guiding muscles stopping any unwanted movement of the prime mover.

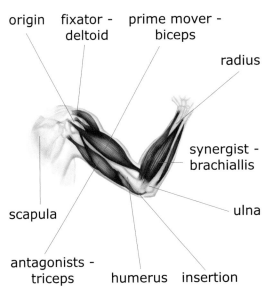

origin   fixator - deltoid   prime mover - biceps   radius   synergist - brachiallis   ulna   scapula   antagonists - triceps   humerus   insertion

Fixators Some muscles contract statically, they are called fixators. Their role is to stabilise and maintain a correct position. They provide a firm base for movement to occur. They stabilise the attachment of the origin to the prime mover so only the 'insertion bone' will move.

Origin Point where muscle attaches to bone.

Insertion Point where muscle attaches to the bone it moves.

If the centre of the body is where all movement comes from, then working out the different types of movement becomes simpler.

Adduction this movement brings part of the body towards the centre. In the butterfly arm action, adduction is when the arms pull to the sides in the 's' shape. **Add**uction is **add**ing it to the body.

Abduction this is the opposite action to adduction. The limbs are abducted from the centre. A goalkeeper abducts their arms when reaching to make a save. A badminton player abducts their arm when preparing for an overhead clear. A way to remember this is that when someone is kidnapped, they are abducted, for example, taken away.

Adduction as arms go back to torso.

Flexion closing the angle at a joint. When preparing to throw a ball the angle at the elbow decreases. This movement of flexion gives the arm space to create power in the throw. Catching a ball and bringing it to the body is flexion at the wrist, elbow and shoulder joints. Recovery phase of the sprint leg action is flexion at the knee.

Extension this is the opposite of flexion. It is when the angle increases between the bones at a joint. In the run-up for a jump the long jumper takes off and extends the take-off leg to generate as much upward lift as possible. This is an example of extension at the hips. Striding the leg forward to take a pace is extension at the knee.

Abduction as arm stretches to save.

Rotation the angles do not change but the joint moves in a circular motion. The throwing action of the service in tennis and the bowling action in cricket or rounders demonstrates this type of movement.

Rotation of shoulder to serve.

Flexion as angle at elbow decreases in preparation to bowl.

Extension of leg in long jump.

●●●● ▶ **Active Challenge**

Point to a joint on your own body for your partner to tell you:
- the name of the joint
- what movement happens there
- the type of joint
- an example of the joint's use in sport.

3 How Joints Help the Sportsperson

Joints work with muscles to create all movements in daily life and to complete sporting challenges. From the large strides of a long jumper to the small adjustments of the gymnast on the beam, it is joints that allow the range of movement seen. The agility required to dodge around an opponent and keep upright requires many frequent and minor adjustments from the tarsals, metatarsals and phalanges of the feet where they flex and extend to keep balanced. Striding, landing and taking weight could damage the bones if it were not for the cartilage that sits between them absorbing the shock.

In order that joints can achieve their full range they have to be prepared, trained and movements practised. To rotate the arm in the delivery of a javelin throw, a thorough warm-up is necessary, as well as all the previous training and conditioning. These make the joints more flexible, allowing a greater reach in the preparation and follow-through phases of a throw. The extra range leads to more leverage and the possibility of achieving a greater distance.

Example

Kicking a football = knee = hinge joint = lower leg moves forward to straighten the leg after contact = extension.

What to do:

Task 1

1. Link types of movement, joints and sporting actions together.

   Two types of movement are given to help you:
   - swimmer performing front crawl arm action
   - arm action required when shooting in netball or basketball.

4 The Effects of Age on Flexibility of the Joints

At different ages the body is capable of different movements. When the young gymnast performing on the asymmetric bars changes her grip from overhand to underhand to swing around the bar, she **dislocates** her shoulders. This relies on the **flexibility** and the softness of the tissues at the joint. As performers get older, tissues become less elastic and therefore their joints become less flexible and incapable of such adaptability. A warm-up that may have taken 15 minutes for a young teenager may take 30 minutes when they are in their early twenties.

If practised in the correct way, flexibility can be increased. To achieve the same standards becomes harder as a person gets older. The less flexible a person is, the more prone to injury they are. The joints will be unable to withstand the shock of forceful contact with the ground. The amount of muscle strength reduces with age, which can lead to instability around joints and a lack of mobility. Later in life arthritis can begin. There is some evidence that arthritis is hereditary. It can also come about because of the rigours of a strenuous sporting life.

Key Terms:

Abduction	► moving a limb or bone away from the body
Adduction	► moving a limb or bone towards the body
Dislocate	► move bones out of their usual joint arrangement
Extension	► increasing the angle at a joint
Flexibility	► degree of movement around a joint
Flexion	► decreasing the angle at a joint
Rotation	► bone movement in a circular or part circular direction

5 Voluntary Muscle

In the body there are three types of muscle: cardiac (only found in the heart), involuntary (working urinary organs, blood vessels and intestines of body automatically) and voluntary muscle, which is attached to the skeleton. It is the voluntary muscle that the sportsperson trains and develops in order to improve performance. There are about 600 individual muscles making up 40% of a person's total body weight.

Voluntary muscles also known as skeletal or striated muscles, are the most common muscle type in the body. These muscles attach to the skeleton and provide a person's shape. We can consciously control these muscles and dictate how they move. Their movement happens like this:

- a defender sees an attacker moving into a space
- a message goes through the defender's nervous system to the brain
- a decision is made through experience and training as to which muscles will be used in order to mark the opposition
- the brain sends messages to the appropriate muscles
- the action takes place.

All of this happens in a fraction of a second and this demonstrates why an attacker has a slight advantage over a defender. The defender can compensate for this by learning to read the game and to prepare for the most likely course of action from the attacker.

Link Muscles to Sporting Actions

Voluntary muscle (also called skeletal muscle) is the type that flexes when performing a sporting action, such as pulling quads to extend at the knee to kick a ball.

What to do:

1. Use all of the muscles listed below.
2. Link them with a sporting action.
3. Use the sporting example on the previous page to help you.

   biceps, triceps, deltoids, pectorals, trapezius, abdominals, latissimus dorsi, gluteals, quadriceps, hamstrings, gastrocnemius

> **Example**
> Abdominals, raise knee so flexing at the hips, used prior to take-off in high jump.

Muscles' Relation to Bone

Voluntary muscle is attached to the bone by tendons. The muscle, at the point where it moves, is the **insertion** and the point where it is fixed is the **origin**. When the arm flexes at the elbow the movement is at the elbow, so the fixed point in this example is the shoulder.

Location and functions of major muscles

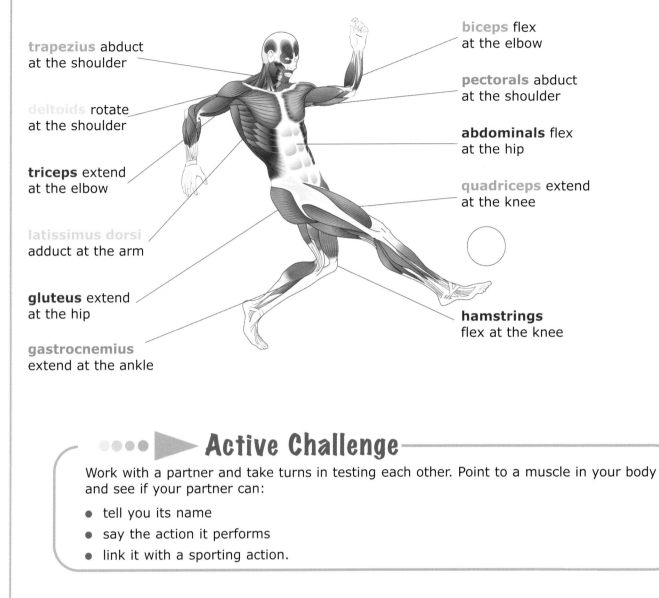

trapezius abduct at the shoulder

deltoids rotate at the shoulder

triceps extend at the elbow

latissimus dorsi adduct at the arm

gluteus extend at the hip

gastrocnemius extend at the ankle

biceps flex at the elbow

pectorals abduct at the shoulder

abdominals flex at the hip

quadriceps extend at the knee

hamstrings flex at the knee

●●●● ▶ Active Challenge

Work with a partner and take turns in testing each other. Point to a muscle in your body and see if your partner can:

- tell you its name
- say the action it performs
- link it with a sporting action.

6 Antagonistic Muscle Action

A definition of a lever is:

a simple machine that can be regarded as a rigid bar that can turn about a pivot. The relative positions of load, effort and pivot determine the type of lever.

Our limbs and joints consist of a series of levers. Levers enable a weight to be shifted. A small amount of effort enables a larger load to be lifted or moved. In any movement in the body there is always:

- the load = the weight to be moved or resistance
- the force to move the weight = provided by the effort of muscles
- the fulcrum or pivot point = the fixed point around which the movement occurs.

Although there are three ways in which weight can be moved we are concerned only with 'third order levers'.

Third order levers

In this order the fulcrum is at the opposite end to the resistance with effort in the middle.

This is common in many actions in sport. When performing the front crawl arm action the swimmer's shoulder joint is the pivot point, the muscle at the shoulder is the effort and the resistance is the water. The tennis shot is also an example of this order of levers. Here the player uses the racket as an extension of the arm in order to generate more speed. The rower's oars also increase the length of the lever in order to make the boat travel quicker through the water by covering more distance with each stroke. This order helps to generate increased speed and distance.

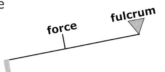

The action of rowing shows third order lever.

What to do:

1. Draw a simple diagram of a sporting action.
2. Label the action with load, force and fulcrum.
3. Write which order lever it is.

Example

Person kicking a football.
Load – football; force – muscles of the leg kicking; fulcrum – standing foot. Third order levers.

7 Tendons and Ligaments

Tendons

Muscles contract and move bone only because tendons are attaching them to each other. Tendons are strong; they have to be able to withstand the application of great effort with some actions from time to time. They are also non-elastic allowing them to hold a muscle firm, anchoring it so the movement can occur.

Ligaments

They attach bone to bone. They are strong, stabilising and together with muscles, support the joint. Ligaments have to be elastic so they can stretch at the site of a freely movable joint. Once stretched too far, however, ligaments rarely achieve their passed strength.

What to do:

1. Create a table showing the qualities of both tendons and ligaments.

Muscle and Movement

What you will learn about in this section

1. Types of Muscular Contraction: Isotonic/Isometric/Isokinetic
2. Development of Strength
3. Speed of Movement: Fast/Slow Twitch Muscle Fibres

1 Types of Muscular Contraction

Muscles can contract in different ways. The type of activity will demand that the muscles vary the way they contract as a range of situations arise. Some activities require only a small variety of types of contraction, others need a whole range. Training muscles in the most appropriate way to fit the activity is therefore vital to the sportsperson.

Isotonic

This type of contraction occurs whenever there is movement of the body. The ends of the muscles move closer to make the action. This is the most frequently used type of contraction in games play. As a muscle contracts (shortens and fattens), it causes concentric movement. When it relaxes to its first shape, it is an eccentric movement (lengthens and flattens). The eccentric action is the most efficient of the two types.

An easy way to remember the difference between concentric and eccentric is to think about using the stairs at home. When walking upstairs, it is a concentric contraction, as the muscles are shortening to step up. When walking downstairs, it is an eccentric contraction, as the leg has to lengthen and stretch to the next step down.

Working the muscles isotonically improves dynamic (moving) strength. This is especially good for games players. It develops cardiovascular and cardiorespiratory systems and increases power and endurance. As isotonic muscular contractions come about through movement, there may be a greater possibility of injury than with isometric muscular contractions.

The advantages of isotonic muscular contractions:
- the contraction strengthens the muscle throughout the range of movement
- when training a performer can choose isotonic exercises to match their activity.

The disadvantage of isotonic muscular contraction:
- due to the stress of the muscles lengthening to move, soreness may result.

Memory hints

An easy way to remember isotonic muscular contraction is that it occurs when there is movement of the body – isoTOnic – to – going TO somewhere = movement.

Isometric

This type of contraction takes place when the muscle length stays the same. It is used for stabilising parts of the body and holding the body steady so that movement can take place elsewhere. Isometric muscular contraction improves static strength. It is easy to perform and needs little or no equipment. However, it does not develop power or muscular endurance. The cardiovascular and cardiorespiratory systems are not improved. Few sports require this type of contraction alone.

The advantages of isometric muscular contraction:

- static strength improved so muscles can push, pull and hold up heavy objects
- these contractions are quick to perform
- they can be performed without the need of expensive equipment
- they can be performed anywhere.

The disadvantage of Isometric muscular contraction:

- muscle strength only gained at the angle the exercise is performed.

During isometric exercises the:

- blood pressure rises
- blood flow to the muscle stops
- there is a decrease of blood flowing back to the heart.

So this way of exercising could be dangerous for someone with a heart condition.

Isometric

Isokinetic

These muscular contractions are performed at a constant speed.

Isotonic contractions are different to isokinetic as they are usually slowest to start.

When training in this way specialised equipment is needed. The performer's muscle contractions are monitored and if they speed up then the load is increased to slow them down. The development is made automatically by the machine.

The advantages of isokinetic muscular contraction:

- all of the muscle gains strength throughout the range of movement
- this type of contraction is the fastest way to increase the strength of the muscle.

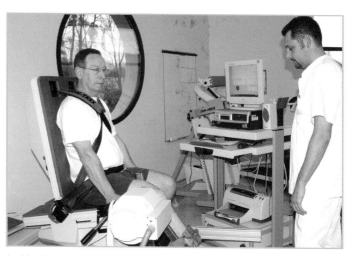

Isokinetic

Disadvantages of isokinetic muscular contraction:

- the specialised equipment is very expensive, so few gyms have them.

What to do:

1. Choose six sporting examples and link them with isotonic, isometric and isokinetic muscular contractions.

Key Terms:

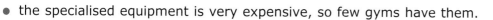

Isotonic muscular contraction	► contraction with movement
Isometric muscular contraction	► contraction with no movement
Isokinetic muscular contraction	► contractions at a constant speed

Summary

When training the performer needs to access the type of muscular contractions their sport requires and make use of them. They need to train in the most appropriate way, as near to the action and speed of performance required in competition, as possible. If training is not performed at competition pace then in a match or event the speed required will be inadequate. Most sports require isotonic muscular contractions and many training exercises can be adapted to the sport.

Isometric training alone is not enough. Due to its adverse effect on the heart this kind of training should be combined with isotonic work.

2   Development of Strength

Strength can be defined as the maximum weight lifted or moved in one try. By repeating strength exercises the size and strength of the muscle increases. A person who would take advantage of an increase in muscle size would be a rugby player in the scrum or an activity where bulk is an advantage, like a weight lifter. The advantage to the rugby player is that having a heavy and strong body allows them to tackle hard and withstand forceful tackles on themselves. As part of their regime weight training plays an important role.

Example of static strength.

An experienced athlete may use 'pyramid sets' as part of their training programme. This involves lifting increasingly heavier weights. The session may have six sections, starting with 10 repetitions of a lighter weight, working up to one repetition of the heaviest weight.

The strength of tendons, ligaments and bones will increase too. Weight training is a method used to improve muscular strength. To do this an athlete would have to lift heavy weights for few repetitions.

When the muscles increase in size they hypertrophy. If the training stops then muscles lose their size, the muscle is said to atrophy. If muscles are overworked they cannot contract. This happens if the muscles are expected to work for too long and fatigue sets in.

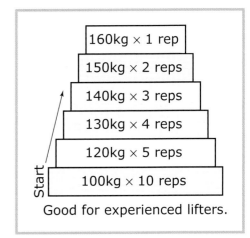

Good for experienced lifters.

160kg × 1 rep
150kg × 2 reps
140kg × 3 reps
130kg × 4 reps
120kg × 5 reps
100kg × 10 reps
Start

Development of static strength

A sportsperson will develop static strength by having weight training as part of their training programme. Development of this strength type will help in the following actions:

- holding firm in a scrum
- holding a balance in gymnastics
- holding weight steady above the head in weight lifting
- holding weight in judo holds.

Development of explosive strength (power)

Weights are also used to develop explosive strength. Jumpers and throwers will use weight training as part of their full training programme to help develop strength for a maximal contraction.

Development of dynamic strength

Weight machines are adapted to help develop dynamic strength. Rowers and swimmers are just two examples of sportspeople that take advantage of these.

Developing strength safely

In order to develop strength safely and appropriately, an understanding and knowledge of the performer and their needs is essential. Any development should relate to the activity being trained for and the level of fitness of the sportsperson.

A training programme should follow the principles of SPORT (Specificity, Progression, Overload, Reversibility and Tedium explained in detail in section 5.1 Physical Fitness).

A performer can be confident that training following these principles is appropriate and minimises the risk of injury.

The importance of FITT

The training programme will need developing as the performer's body adapts to the stresses and demands made on it. Therefore FITT (Frequency, Intensity, Time and Type) is varied within the programme.

The variations are made after re-testing and analysing the strength of the performer. The changes are made in the following ways:

Frequency the number of sessions undertaken

Intensity how difficult the sessions are

Time the length of the session

Type varying the exercises in the session so that interest is maintained

If FITT is applied properly, with the individual's ability in mind, then progress will be gradual and safe. It is important to remember that for a training programme to work it should work in parallel with an appropriate diet.

What to do:

1. Select a sport.
2. Give an example of the type of strength they need to perform.
3. Say three ways they could increase the intensity of a training session.

There are two different types of fibre in muscles. There are **fast twitch muscle fibres** (FTMF) and **slow twitch muscle fibres** (STMF). Each type is better suited to different activities. Every person has a natural combination of both in their body. This amount cannot be changed, although with the correct training improvements can be made to the efficiency of each type. Games and racket sport players will have a fairly even distribution but some will have a higher percentage of fast twitch muscle fibres.

Fast twitch muscle fibres

When the nervous system decides that an event requires short bursts of energy, the fast twitch muscle fibres are used. These are used for more explosive, powerful events and activities, which need quick reactions. FTMF contract fast and produce a powerful action. They work without the use of oxygen and so tire very quickly. Under a microscope they are white in colour. They are best used for speed events, throwing and jumping.

Slow twitch muscle fibres

The nervous system can detect when an event is slow and prolonged and will activate the slow twitch muscle fibres. These are more suited to endurance events. These fibres contract slowly and with little force. Due to the speed and force of the contractions they can contract many times and stay efficient over long periods. They have a good oxygen supply providing them with energy. Under a microscope they are red in colour. STMF are suited to events that take a long time to complete, such as long distance running, cycling and swimming.

What to do:

1. Read the paragraphs on the types of fibres in the muscles.
2. Make two columns headed FTMF and STMF.
3. List four main points for each type of fibre.

●●●● ▶ **Active Challenge**

In pairs, take turns in naming a sport. Your partner should say whether it needs fast or slow twitch muscle fibres for greatest success.

Key Terms:

Antagonist	▶ relaxing muscle allowing movement
Fast twitch muscle fibres	▶ muscle fibres used in events requiring quick reactions and power
Prime mover	▶ contracting muscle causing movement
Slow twitch muscle fibres	▶ muscle fibres required in endurance events

Summary

There are two different type of muscle fibres used in muscular contraction. When sudden bursts of energy are needed, fast twitch muscle fibres are used. When moderate effort over a long period is required, then slow twitch muscle fibres come into operation. Exercising for endurance will help an athlete perform long distance events. This type of exercise requires moderate effort and takes a long time to complete – here slow twitch muscle fibres are used.

Task 3

The Basic Concepts Regarding Eating for Exercise

What you will learn about in this section

1. Balanced Diets – Nutrients/Water/Fibre
2. BMR – Energy Balance/Equation
3. Dietary Needs – Carbohydrate Loading/High Protein Diet/Water
4. Diet and Hydration Before, During and After Exercise
5. Relationship between Exercise and Weight Levels

Increasingly many people have more opportunity for leisure pursuits due to more leisure time. Physical activity is a popular choice in filling this gap. As a result people are becoming more aware of what is needed for a healthy lifestyle.

The public's awareness and understanding of a healthier lifestyle is increased due to popular advertising in the media showing how to follow and maintain such a way of life.

Governments are playing their part too. The Welsh Assembly have published their 'Climbing higher' document. This is a plan for the next 20 years. In this time it aims to involve the majority of the Welsh Nation in healthy activities and so meet guidelines set out globally.

Many strive to achieve a healthier lifestyle. In order to achieve this, attitudes to health, exercise, fitness and diet need to be linked together. Each on their own is not enough, but adapting and refining knowledge and putting into practice all areas will go towards improving a person's quality of life.

1 Balanced Diets – Nutrients/Water/Fibre

The food we eat fuels our body just like petrol fuels a car. As the human body is more complex than a car engine, there are different types of food to keep the various parts of the body functioning properly. Food does the following:

- provides energy
- helps our bodies grow
- repairs injured tissue
- contributes to good general health.

It is important to have a balance of all of the seven types of food. Eating the correct quantities and combinations of food will keep the body system functioning properly, keep hair and skin in good condition and reduce the chances of obesity.

In general, a **balanced diet** is important, but, by changing the amounts of each nutrient eaten, a diet can be adapted to have a specific result for a sportsperson training for a particular event.

Seven parts to a balanced diet

Therefore a balanced diet is twofold:

1 It should have the right mix of nutrients, fibre and water.
2 The amount taken in should match the energy requirements.

food types	about the food	aid to the sportsperson
Carbohydrates (sugars and starch) 1	Fruit, cakes, beer, sweets, granulated sugar, bread, pasta, rice and potatoes. Stored in the liver and muscles as glycogen. Converts to glucose and used as energy for muscles of the body, brain and other organs. Excess converted and stored as fat. Should provide over 47% of daily energy requirements and if a person is training hard this should rise to 65–70%.	Provides a ready source of energy when the muscles require it. Carbohydrates in the highly processed form of sugars provide us with energy but no other nutrients so it is better to eat more starches. Athletes training hard use carbohydrates quickly, so diets should be high in this food type.
2 **Proteins**	Meat, fish, pulses (chick peas, lentils and beans), nuts, eggs and poultry. Builds body muscle, repairs tissue, enzymes and hormones. Proteins are broken down in the body as amino acids; 21 types are needed for our bodies to work properly. Our body can produce 13 types (non-essential amino acids) but the other eight (essential amino acids) come from protein foods. Excess is converted and stored as fat.	Builds muscle and repairs tissue within the body. Essential after an injury to heal quickly. Sportspeople who need large muscle size need extra proteins.
3 **Fats**	Milk, cheese, butter, oils, chocolate, fatty meats, soya beans and corn. Provider of energy – recommended daily intake 30% of a combination of saturated, polyunsaturated and monounsaturated fatty acids. Can be stored in the body.	Increase size and weight of body. Important for performers who benefit from having extra bulk, shot putters for instance. Unnecessary weight can inhibit performance and lead to high cholesterol levels. Fats are a form of stored energy, released slowly when there is a lack of carbohydrates.
4 **Vitamins**	Fruit (vitamin C), liver and carrots (vitamin A), whole grains and nuts (vitamin B1) and vegetable oil (vitamin E). Help with the general health of vision, skin condition, forming of red blood cells and blood clotting, and the good condition of bones and teeth.	The general health of athletes is important if they are to perform well. When training hard, vitamins from the B group are used more and so need to be replenished. This can be done by eating more of that food type or using supplements.

food types	about the food	aid to the sportsperson
5 Minerals	Milk and saltwater fish (iodine), red meat, liver and green vegetables (iron), milk, cheese and cereals (calcium). Calcium helps growth of bones, iron helps the making of red blood cells and the way oxygen is carried in the body by the haemoglobin. The more a person exercises the greater the intake needed, provided by a varied diet or supplements. Excessive amounts of the mineral salt can lead to high blood pressure.	Increase efficiency of carrying oxygen to the working muscles of the body. Iodine aids normal growth, essential for the athlete to help energy production. Iron helps produce red blood cells and so carry more oxygen round the body helping to prevent **fatigue**. Calcium helps blood to clot, aiding recovery from injury, and strengthens bones and muscles.
6 Fibre	Leaves, seed cases, cereals and whole grains. Fibre, or roughage, helps digestion but contains no nutrients. There are two types: insoluble – this adds bulk to our food, helping it to keep moving through the digestive system and so preventing constipation, and soluble – helps to reduce cholesterol, keeping the heart healthy.	Less cholesterol in the body makes the heart more efficient. By keeping the digestive system functioning regularly the body retains less waste.
7 Water	Fluids and food. Two-thirds of the body is made up of water. We need regular intakes to replenish what is lost in urine, sweat and condensation as we breathe.	Water allows the blood to flow more easily around the body. This is extremely important when exercising, as the body demands more oxygen, nutrients, heat control and waste removal. In endurance events, or when exercising in hot weather, water is lost quickly; this can lead to dehydration and heatstroke if not replenished.

What to do:

1. What is the major role in human diet of:
   - carbohydrates? • proteins? • fats? • vitamins?
2. Give three examples of foods that are good sources of:
   - vitamins • carbohydrates • proteins.
3. What two types of carbohydrates are there and in what form are they stored in the body?
4. How does the sportsperson use the following:
   - carbohydrates? • proteins? • water? • fats?

2   BMR – Energy Balance/Equation

How energy is calculated

The body needs energy all the time, even when sleeping. This is because the body is still functioning – the heart is beating, blood is circulating, the body is breathing. This lowest form of energy requirement is called the **basal metabolic rate** (BMR).

Each food type has an energy value which can be calculated in two ways:

- Joules are calculated by a moving force = energy needed when 1kg is moved by 1m by a force of 1 **newton**.
- Calories are calculated by a rise in temperature = amount of energy needed to raise temperature of 1g of water by 1°C.

The main ways we understand the above calculations are as kilojoules (kj) and kilocalories (kcal). This is because diets and nutritional information on food packaging deal in large quantities and so the equation is multiplied by 1000 to make the figures more manageable. A food with a low kilojoule or kilocalorie value will have to be eaten in a larger quantity than one with a high value to do the same job.

Individual energy requirements

There are many factors that change the energy requirements of people. At different stages of life greater or lesser levels of energy are needed. Teenagers need more than adults. Women, on average, need less energy than men as they have a smaller build. As people get older their pace of life slows down and their energy requirements reduce. Even same age, same gender people rarely have the same energy needs owing to variations in their lifestyles and build. These factors are out of our control but what does dramatically change our energy requirements and is in our control is the amount of activity we undertake.

Below is an approximate calculation of the daily intake requirements for people of different ages.

Boys 15 years old	11 500kj (2700kcal approx.)
Girls 15 years old	8800kj (2100kcal approx.)
Adult men	10 500kj (2500kcal approx.)
Adult women	8400kj (2000kcal approx.)
Older men	8800kj (2100kcal approx.)
Older women	8000kj (1900kcal approx.)

> ●●●● ► **Active Challenge**
>
> Discuss with a partner the reasons why people have different energy requirements. Think of four different reasons.

Factors affecting energy requirements

- Each sport has a different energy requirement.
- Length of activity.
- Intensity of activity.
- Level of opponent – easy game/lower level opponent.

Energy per hour needed for different activities:

Activity	Approx. energy (kj)	Activity	Approx. energy (kj)
Sleeping	252	Cycling	1280
Studying	420	Swimming	1300
Housework	798	Volleyball	1440
Walking	840	Tennis	1740
Golf	1080	Disco dancing	2100
Gardening	1260	Marathon running	4158

Special diets for sport

An increase in demands on the body from exercise means an increase in energy requirements. This should result in a change of diet to compensate for the new demand. The general diet for an athlete is high in carbohydrates, low in fat, with a high fluid intake, including **energy drinks** and/or water. This provides energy and keeps the fluid levels balanced.

Diets can be organised around an exercise programme. This will involve timing when meals are taken, the content of the meal depending on the activity and the quantity of food to be eaten. A top-class athlete acquires knowledge of how to use the different types of food to their best advantage. Each sportsperson's diet will vary due to individual differences of build, demands of the sport, position played in the team and any injury incurred.

Diet plays an important part in an athlete's performance. It is seen to be so important that many sportspeople are guided by specialist dieticians and follow strict eating habits. The dietician will play their part in the performer's success just as the coach does. There are crucial times when a sportsperson can adapt their diet to help performance.

By adapting their diet over the following periods the athlete can get the best results:

- the week before the event
- during the event
- the day of the event
- after the event.

Carbohydrate loading

Traditionally, **carbohydrate loading** is linked with long-distance events but other competitors can benefit too. Swimmers can use this diet effectively for their event. Carbohydrates are important to an athlete, as they are easy to digest and provide an instant source of energy. By eating more carbohydrates, a store of glycogen is built up in the body. In competition this store will reduce levels of fatigue and so help to maintain a standard of performance.

High protein diet

This diet requires the intake of a large amount of protein. Weightlifters and athletes, needing a loss of weight over a fairly short period of weeks, can adopt this diet. High protein diets can also be used in a rehabilitation programme after injury for the repair of damaged tissue.

A bodybuilder or a rugby player will use this type of diet to burn fat and increase muscle size. Taking creatine (a form of protein) supplements increases the effect. A rugby league player can eat as many as six meals a day taking in mainly proteins, some carbohydrates, but little or no fat. Throughout the day, they are encouraged to drink plenty of fluids and eat fruit as well as the prescribed meals. The protein will build up the muscle; carbohydrate will provide energy and fluids will keep the body hydrated.

Eating a high protein diet has the effect of reducing the storage of fat in the body. Some performers, who need to lose weight quite quickly, can use this type of diet. However, there is now evidence of long-term problems with this type of diet.

Problems with the diet

There are long-term effects of using high protein diets. When a bodybuilder takes in a high level of animal proteins this raises the cholesterol levels in the body, leading to a possibility of heart disease, diabetes, stroke and cancer. The performer using a high protein diet to control their weight can develop kidney damage in the long term.

Water

Water is essential, and especially to athletes when the balance in their body is changing due to the extra stresses put on them through the demands of the event. An increase of exercise raising the temperature of the body will cause sweating. The loss of water and salt in this way must be replaced to stop dehydration.

Dehydration will especially occur in hot conditions and in long-distance events.

If a sportsperson becomes dehydrated it will make them weak and disorientated.

4 Diet and Hydration Before, During and After Exercise

Diet for a long-distance athlete

Pre-event

The week before an event a runner's training routine and diet change. Due to the excesses of previous training, carbohydrates are low in the body while proteins are high. This combination is not appropriate for a long-distance athlete. So, four or five days before the race, many more carbohydrates are eaten in order to build up these energy stores for the event.

The training programme is now tapered so fewer miles are covered, allowing energy levels to build up and the speed of the shorter runs increases, preparing for a burst of speed during the race. By taking in extra carbohydrates and fewer fats, together with reducing the intensity of the training programme, the body is able to store these nutrients, as glycogen, for use in the race.

The usefulness of carbohydrates is so widely recognised by the long-distance athlete that 'pasta parties' are organised for the athletes two days before the London Marathon. Eating foods such as noodles, rice, potatoes and even beans on toast will have a similar effect.

Day of event

On the day of the event athletes will choose, from preference and experience, either a large meal three to four hours before the race, or a lighter one up to two hours before the race. This is the final chance, before the competition, to make sure that carbohydrates are stocked up and fluid levels are high.

During event

The prolonged, moderate to hard intensity of a long-distance race reduces the amount of water in the body. Low water levels reduce performance and prevent correct circulation and temperature control. Regular water intake is essential to the athlete to prevent dehydration. Energy drinks help the body to work hard for longer by using the carbohydrates in them.

Taking fluids during an endurance event is essential.

After event

An athlete must continue to drink fluids and energy drinks to replace the fluids and carbohydrates lost. High energy food can be eaten immediately after the race. Depending on the training programme following the event, a sensible meal including various carbohydrates is usual.

What to do:

1. Make a ten-point list about carbohydrate loading and the procedure for food and fluid intake for a long-distance event.

> Include ideas on the week before, day of race, during race and after race.

5 Relationship between Exercise and Weight Levels

There is clear link between the amount of calories taken in, the amount of exercise undertaken and weight levels. If there are more calories taken in than exercise taken then an increase of weight can be expected.

By regularly exercising:

- the appetite can reduce
- the basal metabolic rate (BMR) increases (this uses fat up even at rest)
- the body uses stored fat faster when extra energy is needed when exercising
- a balanced diet is important but carbohydrates are the fuel provider
- the more exercise taken then the more water needed as the body heats up and sweats, to stop dehydration
- eating more but not increasing exercise will store the extra as glycogen and fat in the body
- as muscle weighs heavier than fat, weight may increase.

The effects of over and under eating

How to lose weight:

- more exercise
- less calorie intake.

How to gain weight:

- make calorie intake exceed energy expended.

How to maintain weight:

- balance calorie intake with energy used.

Changing their diet to make a weight or to keep slim can have major consequences on a sportsperson.

make calorie intake
exceed energy expended

balance calorie intake
with energy used

less calorie intake,
more exercise taken

Weight problems affecting performance

Each athlete has an **optimum weight** at which they perform at their best. This depends on the correct balance of height, gender, bone structure and muscle girth (measurement around the flexed muscle).

Some athletes can keep to their optimum weight easily, whilst others constantly have to check what they eat. Some sports, like boxing and horse racing, demand a certain weight restriction; so for the boxer and the jockey, diets and quick weight loss are sometimes vital for them to compete. It is the fluids in the body that are lost when an athlete needs to make the weight category in a short period of time. The consequences of losing weight quickly can be that the body becomes dehydrated and the level of performance is reduced, making the competitor less effective. Some athletes will appear to be overweight; their large muscle girth will give a reading that is misleading. If a sportsperson is overweight it can have a bad effect on their performance as well as a poor effect on their health.

The demands of some sports for an athlete to be the optimum weight are essential for the greatest success. The effect of having too much fat can restrict the flexibility of the joints and so the athlete cannot move appropriately to execute the correct technique. Carrying too much weight will decrease the speed of movement, slowing a player down in a game. A performer will tire quickly because of the extra effort needed to carry more weight. In some sports, like archery and bowls, where speed is not a necessity, then being overweight is not a problem. It may even make the person more stable and so help accuracy.

Height to weight chart for adult men and women

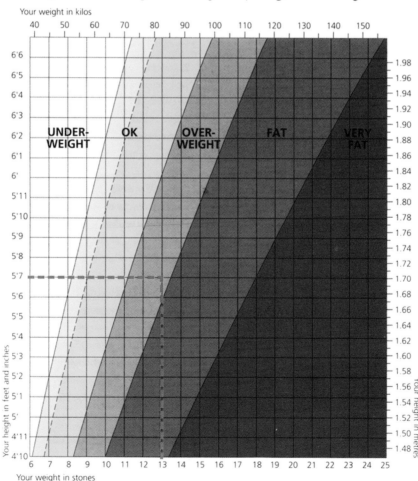

This chart is issued by the Food Standards Agency in the UK. The chart provides a guideline to adults showing what the correct weight of a person should be dependent on their height.

Degrees of being overweight

An **overweight** person can be said to be heavier than the average person of that gender, height and build. (See height to weight chart on the previous page.) The extra weight, however, is not necessarily a threat to the person's health (sometimes a lot of it is muscle).

Being **overfat** can have a direct effect on a person's health. In this category a person will have a high level of fat in comparison with their total body composition. Having this amount of fat can lead to obesity related disease: problems may include high blood pressure, strokes, cancer and heart attacks.

When a person reaches the stage of being **obese**, they are abnormally fat (more than 20% over the standard weight for their height). At this stage the health risks become more dangerous and can include diabetes, high blood pressure, heart disease, osteoarthritis and early mortality.

Being overweight is a problem of the twenty-first century. Many nations now record more than 20% of their population as clinically obese and well over half the population as overweight. This trend has increased throughout the world as fast food chains reach various areas. In the USA 60% of the population is overweight giving America the nickname 'the fat capital of the world'.

Possible dietary problems

In an effort to look like role models seen in the media, people put pressure on themselves about their weight, which can sometimes lead to eating disorders. Athletes may also do the same in an attempt to reach and maintain a low body weight ideal for their sport, but unnatural for themselves.

There are two main eating disorders:

Anorexia a person does not eat, they see themselves as fat; the problem is the obsessive state of mind. This condition leads to excessive weight loss.

Bulimia a person eats a lot and then forces themselves to vomit. This has the effect of weight loss.

Both eating disorders lead to bouts of depression and many severe medical problems, including kidney and liver damage, and even death.

What to do:

1. Choose five different types of sportsperson.
2. Write a sentence on what they may say about their diet and how it affects them.

> Include ideas on:
> energy needs of the activity, weight problems and how training changes, natural food preferences.

Task 3

Key Terms:

Balanced diet	▶ daily intake of food containing right amounts and types of nutrients
Basal metabolic rate	▶ the level at which energy is used without exercise
Carbohydrate loading	▶ building up carbohydrates in the body to use in endurance events
Energy drinks	▶ fluids containing carbohydrates
Fatigue	▶ the body's inability to complete a task
Newton	▶ a unit of force
Obese	▶ a person who is extremely overweight (more than 20% over the standard weight for their height); this condition can lead to many health problems
Optimum weight	▶ ideal weight for a person, giving them the best chance of success in an activity
Overfat	▶ a person having more body fat than is recommended for their gender and height
Overweight	▶ a person carrying more weight than is recommended for their gender and height

Summary

For general health, a balance of all seven nutrients in the daily diet is important.

Different types of food provide these nutrients helping the body to function properly. It is important to eat a variety of foods within a day so that all the body systems can function properly. In general, there needs to be a balance of all seven nutrients for everyday healthy living.

Each food has a different energy value. A person who strikes the correct balance between food intake and energy output according to activity levels will maintain a constant weight. The performer pursuing high-energy activities will have to increase the amount of food eaten to cope with the energy demand. When athletes understand the different qualities of food, they can use food to their best advantage. Once the requirements of the sport have been identified, the sportsperson can choose a special diet containing foods to help their performance. For example, a weightlifter needs to increase muscle size and strength so a high protein diet is appropriate. Whereas a long distance athlete needs a slow release of energy lasting the whole of the race, therefore a high carbohydrate loading diet suits them.

Combining training with eating certain foods in definite quantities can help an athlete to become more effective in their event. The following changes may then occur:

- change to their natural shape (changing the fat ratio and muscle size)
- improve their energy levels
- reduce their recovery periods.

Certain shapes of performer are suited to particular activities. This can be a natural body shape or a person can use diet to achieve the shape they want. Whether a heavier or lighter weight is pursued, both can result in health problems. In sports where weight is required heart disease, high blood pressure and diabetes can result; in sports where lighter weight is more suitable, eating disorders can result.

Health, Fitness and Exercise: Health Reasons For Participating in Physical Exercise

What you will learn about in this section

1. Personal Health Reasons for Participating in Physical Activity
2. Links with Health-related Physical Components of Fitness
3. Understanding the Difference and Relationship between Health and Fitness
4. The Effects of Lack of Exercise on Physical Performance
5. Lifestyle and Exercise for Improvement and Maintenance of Health and Fitness

1 Personal Health Reasons for Participating in Physical Activity

There are many reasons for taking part in sport. A person will choose a type of activity according to the benefits they want from physical exercise and which suits their personality. A person may choose exercise because they enjoy the activity, but other positive changes may result as well. General health (both physical and mental) and social behaviour (how people mix with others) may improve, whether planned for or not. In some cases people can gain employment in an area linked with their sporting interests. Owing to the wide range of rewards from exercise, most people can benefit whether the activity is strenuous or not. It is the health and fitness rewards that make exercising special in comparison with other leisure pursuits.

Taking part in physical exercise will help both a person's health and fitness. Remember the two definitions:

Health

State of complete physical, mental and social well-being, and not merely the absence of illness or disease.

Fitness

The ability to meet the demands of the environment.

physical well-being • social well-being • mental well-being • **EXERCISE HELPS A PERSON'S HEALTH**

●●●● ▶ Active Challenge

Choose five reasons why you participate in sport and discuss them with a partner.

Physical effects of exercise

In order for any involvement in physical activity to be of any value to a person's physical development, it must meet the FITT requirements:

Frequency taking part in physical activity at least four times per week

Intensity during these four sessions the heart rate must be raised to above 60% of its maximum

Time the heart rate should be raised to this level for no less than 20 minutes

Type the type of exercise should suit the sport and individual.

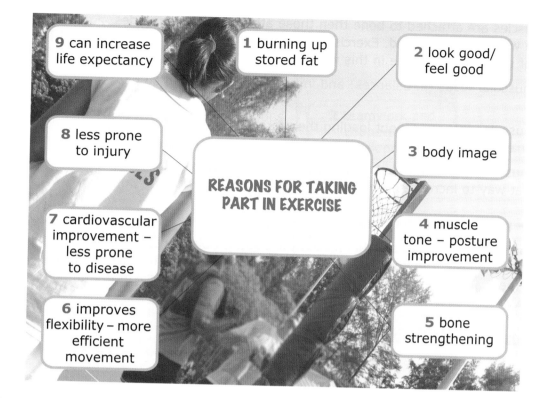

9 can increase life expectancy

1 burning up stored fat

2 look good/ feel good

8 less prone to injury

REASONS FOR TAKING PART IN EXERCISE

3 body image

7 cardiovascular improvement – less prone to disease

4 muscle tone – posture improvement

6 improves flexibility – more efficient movement

5 bone strengthening

1 Burning up stored fat

Exercise will put extra demands on the body. In turn body fat will be burnt ultimately changing the shape of the person. Exercise at the correct level burns calories and as long as the dietary intake remains the same, a person may lose weight with the extra activity.

2 Look good/feel good

The effect of fat burning and the improvement it has on the shape of the body can in turn make that person feel good about themselves.

3 Body image

The change to the body shape and condition will not only change the person's feelings towards themselves but will affect the opinions of others towards them too.

4 Muscle tone – posture improvement

With regular exercise the muscles become toned: this is a tightening of the muscles in a state of readiness to work. As a result, the more muscles are toned each can do their job properly, so improving posture. Depending on the type of training programme, the shape and size of the muscle will begin to develop. Many people want greater muscle definition. 'Dynamic posture' can directly relate to the athlete in action and the application of correct technique.

5 Bone strengthening

Vigorous physical exercise stimulates the uptake of calcium to the bones. In young people this helps to build bone mass and in older people reduces the loss of bone mass. Bone mass density (BMD) is important as it reduces the risk of osteoporosis. Regularly exercising can strengthen the bones as long as the effort exceeds that of normal. There are two ways this can happen by:

Impact – through the gravitational force of weight bearing – exercises like vigorous walking and jogging at the point of 'footstrike' apply here.

4 Challenge

A person may start a sport as a novice performer, happy to learn new skills. As their ability develops their confidence may grow in such a way that they desire competition and are confident to enter competition in the club. This may further develop so they want to compete against other clubs too.

For some individuals clearly set out goals and targets lead the performer through to higher levels of competition. Some have the ability, desire and application to represent their area, county and ultimately their country in their chosen sport.

5 Increase of self-worth – good performance can lead to respect of peers

As a person learns, develops and applies their knowledge in an activity personal confidence increases. Fellow players and peers also see this development: a good performance may earn respect for such achievements and further increase feelings of self-worth.

6 Chance to meet new people and make friends

Joining a group, club or society enables a person to increase the amount of people they know and so increase the possibility of friendships being made. With many sports there often is a social side, where groups stay after a game in the clubhouse, by regularly attending these social events friendships can be formed. Through sporting experiences a person can become more outgoing and confident in the company of others.

7 Mix with people with similar interests

When in a team or a group for a particular activity there is a common interest in the membership. This provides an opportunity to share and develop ideas on a common theme in a social environment.

8 Cooperation on many levels

If a person joins a club they may not only get the benefit of the physical activity but also in the general running of the club too. For example, fixtures have to be arranged, finances have to balance and facilities maintained. By working together for the good of the club, a person can be a player/organiser/helper, cooperating with fellow members for maximum success.

What to do:

1. Write out what you would say to a friend to encourage them to join a sports club. Include at least four different ideas.

Task 1

Mental effects of exercise

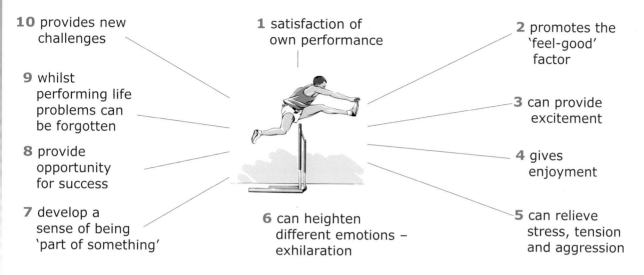

10 provides new challenges

9 whilst performing life problems can be forgotten

8 provide opportunity for success

7 develop a sense of being 'part of something'

1 satisfaction of own performance

6 can heighten different emotions – exhilaration

2 promotes the 'feel-good' factor

3 can provide excitement

4 gives enjoyment

5 can relieve stress, tension and aggression

1 Satisfaction of own performance

A person may take up physical exercise later in life for the first time since school or be a long-term regular exerciser. Whatever the circumstances, targets for development can be set so progress can be made. The satisfaction of reaching a higher standard through hard work, determination and effort can be the feeling that keeps that person continuing with exercise.

2 Promotes the 'feel-good' factor

The improvement to general body shape and posture can result in people feeling more positive about themselves. The fact that they have worked hard and got results increases the feeling of self-worth.

3 Can provide excitement

Some activities are attractive because they are exciting to perform. Skiing, climbing, skate-boarding and BMX track racing are all examples of sports that attract people because of the thrill and adrenalin rush they provide.

4 Gives enjoyment

There are various reasons why a person enjoys an activity: it can be the physical challenge, the tactical battle to outwit the opponent or the fun of playing as a team to achieve success. There is a sport suitable for everyone and those who seek exercise can usually find one they enjoy that satisfies them.

5 Can relieve stress, tension and aggression

Some activities are extremely competitive. These activities can act as a release valve for aggressive behaviour possibly making a person's general life calmer.

6 Can heighten different emotions – exhilaration

Some people are attracted to certain activities because they find them exhilarating. Skiing, windsurfing, sailing and white water canoeing are all examples of activities, which heighten the senses. It is these special feelings experienced when pursuing extreme sports certain people crave.

7 Develop a sense of being 'part of something'

Many people look for physical activities which are team, society or club based. By doing so they automatically become integral members of a group and so part of that unit. A sense of belonging follows, satisfying the personal needs of the individual.

8 Provide opportunity for success

The challenging situations set by physical exercise can be the draw for a person's participation. Reaching a goal or winning an event can have a positive effect on a person which encourages future participation. Many clubs arrange internal and/or external competitions. The competitive approach needed in some sports can link qualities needed in everyday life. In the relatively safe environment of sport, a competitive, personal characteristic may develop that could help effectiveness at work.

9 Whilst performing life problems can be forgotten

Having a hobby, especially one which is physically demanding, is something to look forward to and when taking part in a sport or activity a person deals with a new set of challenges; this can take their mind off problems from daily life.

10 Provides new challenges

Starting a new interest can extend the knowledge of the individual. New tactics, skills, strategies and safety factors may have to be learned. Technical terms and protocols may be necessary – as the knowledge and skills develop, personal pride in mastering the new achievements is felt and so pleasure and satisfaction result.

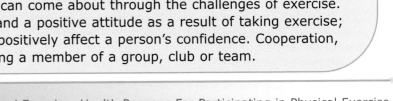

What to do:

1. Link each sentence on 'Health reason for participating in physical activity' below with one of the following headings – physical, social and mental.

   a. My skills have improved in basketball and I have made the area team; this makes me proud of my achievements.

   b. Despite my training sessions getting harder, I seem to be able to keep working for longer without tiring.

   c. Having joined a club I have met many new people.

   d. My pulse rate per minute is reducing; this means my heart is becoming more efficient.

   e. The rush of skiing my maximum speed downhill is what I really enjoy.

   f. I play right defender in the team – to be effective I need to work especially well with the right midfield player.

Summary

There are many advantages in taking physical activity. A person in the habit of regular exercise could benefit from their healthy lifestyle. Physically, the body and its systems can increase in fitness and be able to meet the pressures of a more demanding environment. A stronger body and its systems could increase life expectancy. Personal development can come about through the challenges of exercise. A person may develop determination, courage and a positive attitude as a result of taking exercise; in turn this may spill over into general life and positively affect a person's confidence. Cooperation, teamwork and friendship may develop from being a member of a group, club or team.

Task 2

2 Links with Health-related Physical Components of Fitness

A quick reminder of the health-related physical fitness components

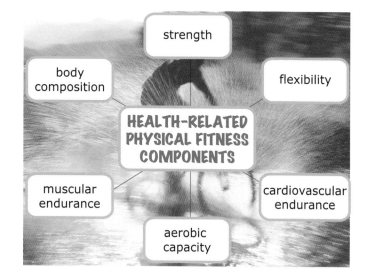

Regular physical activity, which is planned, at the correct level and adapted as the body adjusts will help the above components of health-related physical fitness to achieve general fitness.

If a person is training for a specific sport then the exercises will become more specialised and the levels of frequency, intensity, time will have to rise. This greater intensity takes fitness to a different level.

Links between the components

All the components are interlinked and the condition of one will affect the ability of one or more of the others.

What to do:

1. Use what you have learnt to write a sentence on the effects of one health-related fitness components on the other and how it could affect sporting performance:

   a. Strength on body composition.

   b. Cardiovascular endurance on aerobic capacity.

   c. Aerobic capacity on muscular endurance.

   d. Body composition on flexibility.

Blood pressure

With regular exercise at the right intensity and duration the heart will strengthen and become more efficient. Blood pressure is a useful way of measuring the efficiency of the heart.

Blood pressure is the amount of force the blood applies on the sides of the blood vessels. It is used as an indicator of how fit the circulatory system is. A sphygmomanometer is the instrument that measures blood pressure. The reading is given in units of millimetres of mercury (mmHg). One reading is the systolic pressure, the other is the diastolic pressure. On average, the systolic pressure for an adult will range between 100–140mmHg and the diastolic between 60–90mmHg.

The sphygmomanometer aims to check how well the heart (pump) and the blood vessels (pipes) are working. The higher the numbers on the reading the harder the heart is having to work due to the restrictions in the blood vessels. The harder the heart has to work, the sooner it could wear out.

Blood pressure is at its greatest when the blood is forced into the arteries by the contraction of the left ventricle. This reading gives the systolic pressure. Blood enters the ventricle from the atrium and then the left ventricle relaxes, the pressure reduces thus giving the diastolic pressure reading.

Blood pressure reading is shown in the following way:

$$\frac{\text{Systolic pressure}}{\text{Diastolic pressure}}$$

What affects blood pressure?

There are many circumstances affecting blood pressure.

Exercise will make the systolic pressure rise in order to meet the new demands for blood to transport the extra oxygen to the working muscles. When a person is sleeping the pressure will drop as there is a reduced demand.

Age in the young it tends to be low. As a person becomes older it becomes higher. Children's blood pressure will vary according to their gender, age and height. Older arteries are less elastic, which means they cannot expand to allow the greater amounts of blood needing to be moved. This is called hardening of the arteries.

Gender Men usually have a higher reading than women.

Personal circumstances If a person is tired, stressed or even at a different altitude their blood pressure will change. The last circumstance is important to the distance athlete.

How blood pressure can be reduced

There are several ways to control blood pressure:

- keep within the guidelines of body weight recommendations
- do not smoke as it makes the blood pressure rise and reduces the efficiency of the heart and blood vessels
- avoid too much alcohol

- eat less salt
- avoid stresses and worrying situations
- exercise regularly as it will relieve stress, keep the body systems working properly and help to keep your blood pressure within normal boundaries.

3 Understanding the Difference and Relationship between Health and Fitness

In order to be healthy you have to be fit. This is because health involves all social, mental and physical components. The development of all three components makes a person healthy.

Fitness is to do with the physical so your body may be functioning at a peak but the other aspects of health may not be present. Social and mental aspects of life may be lacking and underdeveloped. This means a person can be fit but not healthy.

So in order to be healthy a person has to be socially and mentally well adjusted but they also have to exercise in a general way so the physical aspect is developed. Exercise, therefore is the link between health and fitness.

General health is the basis on which to train harder. A person who trains specifically for a sport, then, has to 'raise the bar' of their state of good health and go beyond this level.

Training helps 'raise the bar'.

4 The Effects of Lack of Exercise on Physical Performance

Increase weight   If more calories are taken in than are burned then the result is weight gain. Following the guidelines for calorie intake can help a person keep the right balance. The effect on performance is that extra weight can increase fatigue, as there is more to shift. The extra bulk, as fat takes up more space than muscle, may also get in the way and restrict flexibility.

Muscle weighs more than fat so there may be an increase in overall body weight. For a performer who does not have a tendency to put on muscle and is relying on weight in their sport, such as forwards in rugby, this can be a disadvantage.

Less flexibility   If the joints are not regularly moved to their full range then the ability to move them to their fullest extent will be lost. This could inhibit a person rotating the arm in a tennis serve or kicking a ball in rugby or football.

Become breathless sooner   The body loses the ability to work for long periods without becoming breathless. A person will reach anaerobic capacity (VO$_2$ max) sooner.

Aerobic capacity reduced   The body's ability to exchange gases efficiently reduces. A person will find that lack of exercise prevents the body from working for long periods without tiring. As a result not enough oxygen reaches the working muscles and so fatigue sets in. This is due to the insufficient transportation of oxygen to the working muscles making the muscles tire, reducing skill levels and eventually preventing muscle contraction.

Loss of strength   Reduced stress on muscles allows them to become flaccid and weak. This gives rise to the saying 'use it or lose it'.

What to do:

1. For each of the headings above give a detrimental effect it would have on a sporting example. Choose a different sport for each heading.

For a person to be classed as healthy they have to develop all the following components:

- physical well-being
- mental well-being
- social well-being.

A person cannot truly be seen to be healthy unless they are physically fit. This means exercise provides the link and is crucial to a person's health.

To maintain a level of general fitness a person should try to exercise to following degree each week:

- Take exercise four times
- Raise the heart rate above 60% of maximum
- Keep the heart rate raised for no less than 20 minutes each session.

As the lifestyle changes people who exercise and are more active will require more energy. Those who are less active need less energy. This will have a direct bearing on the dietary requirements of the individual.

Summary

People, in general find they have more leisure time to use and are increasingly turning to physical activity to fill this gap. The media and governments are helping to educate and encourage the public into what is required for and the benefits of a healthy lifestyle. Trends towards making facilities more available to a wider group of people can only benefit the population as a whole.

As long as physical activity is undertaken throughout life then it will have a long-term bearing on a person's health. The key to a healthy lifestyle is consideration to all mental, social and physical well-being.

Physical well-being.　　*Social well-being.*　　*Mental well-being.*

Safe Practice: Assessing and Appreciating the Risks Involved in Chosen Practical Activities

What you will learn about in this section

1. Aspects of Safety
2. Appropriate Warm up Routines
3. Appropriate Cool Down Routines

1 Aspects of Safety

With any game, competitive activity or adventurous pursuit, there are potential dangers. Participants should be prepared properly for the event and trained for skill, strength and tactics. Coaching, training and experience build up knowledge and an awareness of the sport makes the game safer to play. Some dangers are easier to spot than others. In body contact sports, the risk of injury is plain to see. In racket sports there are dangers too. In squash, for example, the confined area could lead to collisions with the opposition and a squash ball just fits in the eye socket!

There are many safety precautions a player, coach, teacher, pupil or any officiator can take to safeguard against injury and mishap. There are common procedures for all and some specific to the individual and the event. Those common to all should be adapted to suit the sport and applied appropriately.

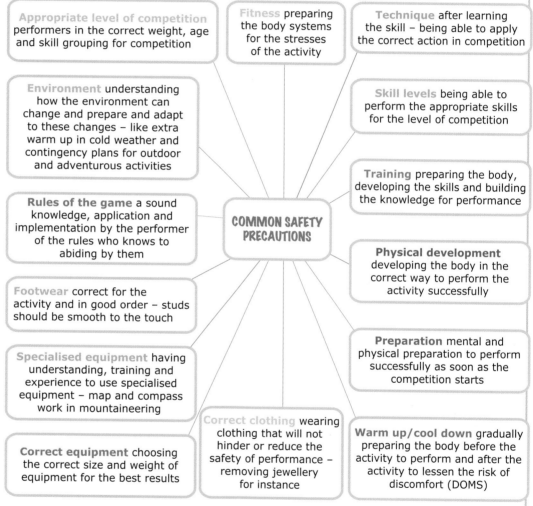

Appropriate level of competition performers in the correct weight, age and skill grouping for competition

Fitness preparing the body systems for the stresses of the activity

Technique after learning the skill – being able to apply the correct action in competition

Environment understanding how the environment can change and prepare and adapt to these changes – like extra warm up in cold weather and contingency plans for outdoor and adventurous activities

Skill levels being able to perform the appropriate skills for the level of competition

Rules of the game a sound knowledge, application and implementation by the performer of the rules who knows to abiding by them

COMMON SAFETY PRECAUTIONS

Training preparing the body, developing the skills and building the knowledge for performance

Physical development developing the body in the correct way to perform the activity successfully

Footwear correct for the activity and in good order – studs should be smooth to the touch

Specialised equipment having understanding, training and experience to use specialised equipment – map and compass work in mountaineering

Preparation mental and physical preparation to perform successfully as soon as the competition starts

Correct equipment choosing the correct size and weight of equipment for the best results

Correct clothing wearing clothing that will not hinder or reduce the safety of performance – removing jewellery for instance

Warm up/cool down gradually preparing the body before the activity to perform and after the activity to lessen the risk of discomfort (DOMS)

2 Appropriate Warm up Routines

A warm up should precede any physical activity whether training or competing. Although there are definite phases to all warm ups they should be relevant and appropriate to the sport in question. Sport-specific warm ups are essential as each has its own skills, techniques, actions – so appropriate parts of the body and muscles need to prepare for hard work.

Reasons for warm up

1 Gradually increase the heart rate to nearer working rate.
2 Gradually increase body temperature to nearer the working rate.
3 Gradually move the muscles and joints in ways that will be used in the competition.
4 Introduce skills to be used in the competition.
5 Increase the intensity so that body is prepared for competitive speed.
6 Systematically working through the routine will prepare the performer's mind for the competition – this may give them a better start than the opposition.
7 Allows players to work in small groups in the way they will in the game.

Warm up precedes all intensive work whether training or competition.

Order of a warm up

There are three phases to a warm up:

1 **Aerobic phase** – to start heart and lungs and begin to raise temperature – jogging – side stepping – skipping.
2 **Stretch and flexibility phase** – ease the muscles and joints into positions appropriate to the activity.
3 **Static** – slow stretching of muscles beyond normal position and held for short periods of time.

PNF stretching

PNF stretching – PNF stands for proprioceptive neuromuscular facilitation. These stretches are performed with a partner or trainer. They use isometric and concentric muscle contractions allowing the muscle to reach a state of relaxation. This allows the muscle to be further stretched and achieve a greater range of movement at the joint.

This type of exercise uses alternating contracting and relaxation of the muscles. This is how these stretches work:

Partner takes the stretch to maximum and that position is held between 10 and 30 seconds.

Performer then opposes the position with a 5–10 second isometric contraction, pushing against the partner.

The performer relaxes and breathes normally.

Partner then takes the relaxed muscle to the new maximum and holds again.

This is repeated 2/3 times if stretch is held for 10 seconds – make one repetition if stretch is held for 30 seconds.

Dynamic – slow flexing, swinging, lifting, lowering or rotating of body parts around the joint.

3 Skills and intensive exercise phase – increased pace more like that used in the competition, greater intensity, increased speed – sprinting, dribbling, passing, shooting.

What to do:

1. Create a table to include the key points of a warm up. Use the following headings:
    ● phase of warm up
    ● how the phase prepares the body
    ● exercises used in the phase

Task 1

Although the phases of the warm up remain the same the content of the exercises used differs greatly according to the chosen sport/event.

The following are three examples of warm ups that could be appropriate in athletics
• throwing event – shot-put • football • netball.

•••• ► **Active Challenge**

With a partner recap all the reasons why warming up is important to the sportsperson.

Athletic warm up example

Static Stretches

In brief this is the order a warm up should take:

Aerobic phase (5–10 minutes) – jogging or sidestepping to increase body temperature.

Flexibility phase (5–10 minutes) – **static stretches** to reduce muscle stiffness.

Stretch phase (5–10 minutes) – **dynamic (moving) stretches** to reduce muscle stiffness.

Skill phase (10–15 minutes) – specific drills for the sport – upper body/lower body/technique drills, for example:

• holding the shot in both hands in front of the body, lifting the shot up and out
• pushing the shot out like a basketball chest pass
• pushing the shot from the put position using only the wrist (to warm up the wrist).

Increased intensity phase (2 minutes) – working on technique with greater intensity, imitating the action used in the event now performed at speed:

• lighter weighted shot substitutes can be used
• practise full speed glide action without the shot.

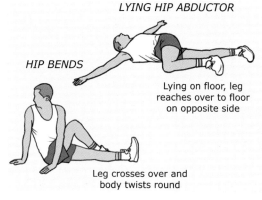

LYING HIP ABDUCTOR

HIP BENDS

Lying on floor, leg reaches over to floor on opposite side

Leg crosses over and body twists round

Flexibility exercises help to loosen up the muscles around the joints.

Dynamic Stretches

Flexing, relaxing, lifting, lowering and rotating parts make up this phase.

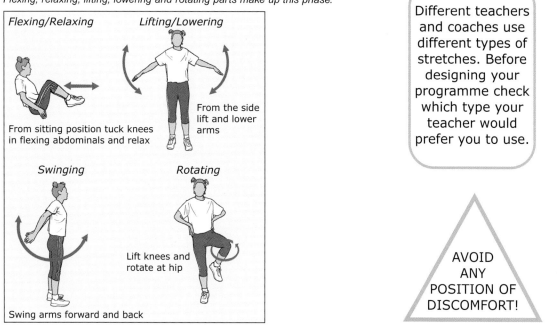

Flexing/Relaxing

From sitting position tuck knees in flexing abdominals and relax

Lifting/Lowering

From the side lift and lower arms

Swinging

Swing arms forward and back

Rotating

Lift knees and rotate at hip

Different teachers and coaches use different types of stretches. Before designing your programme check which type your teacher would prefer you to use.

AVOID ANY POSITION OF DISCOMFORT!

Football warm up example

Psychologically, the warm up will focus the mind of the performer and will help him or her prepare mentally for the game.

In brief, this is the order a warm up should take:

Aerobic phase (5–10 minutes) – Jogging or sidestepping to increase body temperature.

Task 2

What to do:

1. Give three different exercises other than those stated in the text that could be included in the aerobic phase of the warm up.

Flexibility phase (5–10 minutes) – **static stretches** to reduce muscle stiffness. Concentration can include work on hips, knees, ankles back, shoulders and neck joints.

Stretch phase (5–10 minutes) – **dynamic (moving) stretches** to reduce muscle stiffness. Concentration can include work on hamstrings, quadriceps, gastrocnemius and deltoids.

Skill phase (10–15 minutes) – specific drills for the sport such as passing, give and go or jumping to head the ball.

Increased intensity phase (2 minutes) – working on technique with greater intensity imitating the action used in the event now performed at speed. This phase can include shooting, sprinting and changing direction.

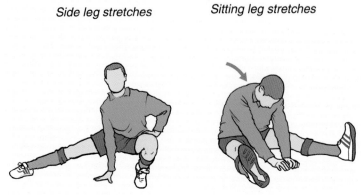

Side leg stretches   *Sitting leg stretches*

Flexibility exercises help to loosen the muscles around the joint.

Different teachers and coaches use different types of stretches. Before designing your programme check which type your teacher would prefer you to use.

DYNAMIC STRETCHES

Leg Stretches   *Groin Stretches*   *Hip Rotation*   *Waist Twists*

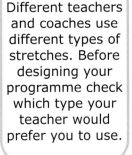

Gently raise and lower, stretching at the groin

Knees lift and lower, stretching at the groin

Standing on one leg lift knee and make large circles

On one leg - arms twist to right - right leg lifts and crosses to the opposite side

AVOID ANY POSITION OF DISCOMFORT!

Flexing, relaxing, swinging, lifting, lowering and rotating body parts make up this phase

●●●● ▶ Active Challenge

With a partner agree on three examples of dynamic stretches that would exercise arms and waist. Decide which muscles and joints would be used and say what sport they could link with.

Netball warm up example

Aerobic phase (5–10 minutes)

1 Jog freely around the court – on the whistle, change direction.

2 Jog freely around two courts – jump into the air when a line is reached.

3 Jog freely around the court – on the whistle, jump, land, step and stop.

4 Group divided into four teams each with different coloured bibs. On command, a colour is called out and that team tags the others. If tagged, they continue by hopping or skipping whilst the game continues until the next whistle change and a new tag team is chosen.

Flexibility phase (5–10 minutes) – **static stretches** to reduce muscle stiffness. This phase ensures the muscles around the joint are prepared for full extension.

> Different teachers and coaches use different types of stretches. Before designing your programme check which type your teacher would prefer you to use.

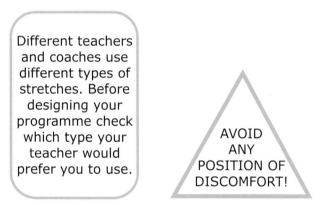

AVOID ANY POSITION OF DISCOMFORT!

Flexing, relaxing, swinging, lifting, lowering and rotating body parts make up this phase.

Static Stretches

Stretch phase (5–10 minutes) – **dynamic (moving) stretches** to reduce muscle stiffness. Areas for special attention are the muscles of:

a) the lower body – gastrocnemius, hamstrings, gluteals and abdominals

b) the torso – latissimus dorsi, pectorals and deltoids

c) upper body – biceps, triceps and trapezium.

Dynamic Stretches

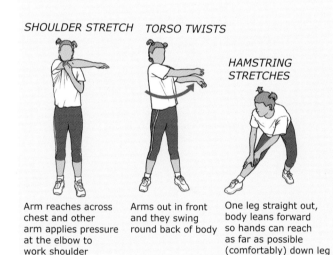

SHOULDER STRETCH   TORSO TWISTS

HAMSTRING STRETCHES

Arm reaches across chest and other arm applies pressure at the elbow to work shoulder

Arms out in front and they swing round back of body

One leg straight out, body leans forward so hands can reach as far as possible (comfortably) down leg

Flexibility Exercises help to loosen the muscles around the joint.

Skill phase (10–15 minutes) – specific drills for the sport; gradually the muscles are exercised closer to the manner needed in the game by incorporating the skills needed for play.

Passing drill

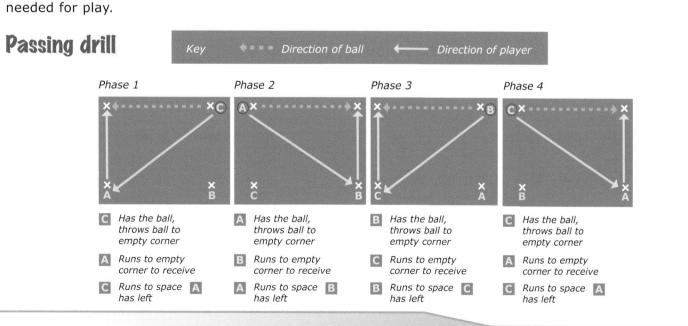

Key   ◄- - - Direction of ball   ◄—— Direction of player

Phase 1

C Has the ball, throws ball to empty corner
A Runs to empty corner to receive
C Runs to space A has left

Phase 2

A Has the ball, throws ball to empty corner
B Runs to empty corner to receive
A Runs to space B has left

Phase 3

B Has the ball, throws ball to empty corner
C Runs to empty corner to receive
B Runs to space C has left

Phase 4

C Has the ball, throws ball to empty corner
A Runs to empty corner to receive
C Runs to space A has left

Shooting drill

Pressure Training for the Shooter

Different teachers and coaches use different types of stretches. Before designing your programme check which type your teacher would prefer you to use.

AVOID ANY POSITION OF DISCOMFORT!

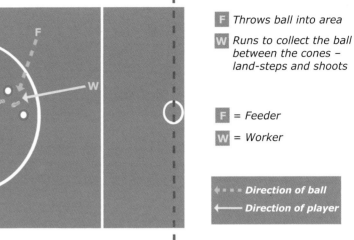

F — Throws ball into area

W — Runs to collect the ball between the cones – land-steps and shoots

F = Feeder

W = Worker

◄ - - - - Direction of ball

◄——— Direction of player

Increased intensity phases (2 minutes) – increased intensity phases similar to the game. These involve sprints and modified games, such as a 4 v 4 mini game using one third of the court and the circle.

What to do:

1. Using the ideas above – choose a different sport and devise and write out a warm up you would do for that sport.

Task 3

3 Appropriate Cool Down Routines

The aim of a cool down is to reduce the stresses on the body in a gradual way and to prevent discomfort after the exercise session. The phases of a cool down include reduced aerobic work phase and stretches phase. The aerobic work gradually become less intensive and the stretches are held for over 10 seconds.

Reason for cooling down

Aerobic exercise phase

- Gradually decrease the body's temperature.
- Remove waste from the body.
- Gradually reduce the stress on the muscles and body systems.

Stretch phase

- Decrease body temperature.
- Allows the muscles to relax.
- Prevent muscle soreness (delayed onset muscle soreness DOMS).
- Reduces the chance of dizziness and fainting as it stops blood pooling and gradually reduces the levels of adrenalin in blood.
- Stretch and lengthen the muscles to improve shape.

General cool down

Remember an appropriate cool down to prevent following discomfort

Cool down

5–10 minutes jogging or walking:

- helps to gradually decrease body temperature
- removes waste from the body.

5–10 minutes **static stretching**:

- concentrate on the muscle used in the event which could include – deltoids, pectorals, abdominals, latissimus dorsi, quadriceps, hamstrings and gastrocnemiusm biceps, triceps.
- decreases body temperature
- allows the muscles to relax
- helps prevent **DOMS** (delayed onset muscle soreness)
- reduces the chance of dizziness and fainting as it stops blood pooling and reduces the level of adrenalin in the blood.

Static stretches help the performer's body recover after the training session or competition.

What to do:

1. Select an activity.
2. State the muscles most necessary to stretch in a cool down.

Summary

Warming up gradually prepares the body for increased intensity and strain, reducing the likelihood of injury. A good routine will exercise the body parts needed in the game/competition. Not only should the heart, lungs, temperature, muscles and joints get a gradual start from a warm up, but it can also focus the mind to prepare for immediate competition too.

A cool down routine gradually reduces the exercise intensity to stave off aching and dizziness.

Warming up and cooling down are important parts of an exercise session.

Safe Practice: Assessing and Appreciating the Risks Involved in Chosen Practical Activities

What you will learn about in this section

1. Relevant Rules, Laws, Safety Precautions
2. Appropriate Levels of Ability/Participation

1 Relevant Rules, Laws, Safety Precautions

Rules give an activity its own individual character.

Each game has its own set of rules or laws. These rules are connected to the type of equipment and competition involved. They are designed to make the event safer and fairer. Its set of rules helps to give the game its own individual style.

The governing bodies of the sports make the rules. The players play to the rules. The referee, umpire or judge makes sure the rules are kept. Within the rules are a series of stages of discipline; often the player is given one warning to stop any bad play. If the foul play continues, a player will be asked to leave the game.

It is important to understand the rules/laws of your chosen activities in detail and how they help the game. There may be technical language to learn, correct procedures to follow and hand signals to perform when implementing these rules/laws.

Although there is often more than one official at a game, there will be normally only one official who has overall responsibility. A good example of this is in the game of rounders. Let's look at this in more detail.

There are two umpires, who have joint responsibility for clearly announcing the decisions and scores, checking the pitch, equipment, players' clothing and keeping records of the score and batters out. Each umpire can dismiss players from the pitch for unsporting conduct. As well as these dual responsibilities, each umpire has a specific role to play and a position to adopt during the game.

A second yellow (or violent act) earns a red card. Dennis Wise is ordered off.

The batter's umpire

- stands at the end of the batting line, so they can see the first post easily
- calls 'no-ball' if the bowler's action is not continuous, if the bowler bowls with a foot over the front line of the bowling square, if the ball passes above the head or below the knee of the batter or for any bowl that hits the ground before reaching the batter.

- calls 'rounder' or 'half rounder' when they are scored
- gives any decisions concerning the front line or back line of the batting square
- gives decisions on 'backward hits' and calls them when necessary
- gives decisions on the first and fourth posts
- gives decisions on all catches
- calls the next player (by name or number) to the batting square.

The bowler's umpire

- stands behind, away and to the right of the third post so they can see the pitch
- calls 'play' at the beginning of each innings
- calls 'play' to restart the game after a dead-ball situation
- calls 'no-ball' for wide bowls, balls that hit or would have hit the player if they had not moved or bowls passing on the non-hitting side of the batter
- gives decisions on the second and third posts
- calls 'no-ball' if the bowler's foot goes over the back line or side line of the bowling square
- ensures the waiting batters and those batters that are out stay behind their relevant lines.

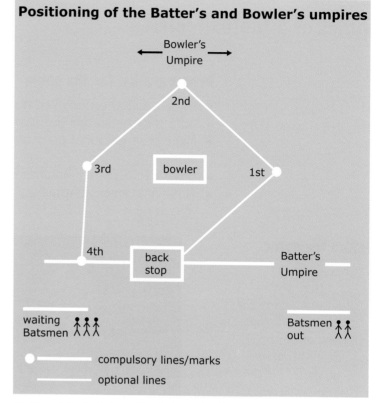

Position of the batter's and bowler's umpires in rounders.

We can see then from this short look at the two umpires in rounders, that it is important to know what your responsibilities are in the game, so you know when, and what, to call. Your chosen sport will have direct guidelines as to each official's responsibilities in its rule book.

To be a good official or referee takes time, practice and experience. The referees and umpires we see on television have worked hard to reach that standard. They have passed examinations, attended courses and kept up to date with developments in umpiring and refereeing in their sport to be the best they can.

Referees need a thorough knowledge and understanding of the rules and how they are applied in a game before beginning to referee. This allows them to use the correct terminology and hand signals when controlling the game. With practice and experience they gradually become more confident and efficient in applying rules appropriately.

What to do:

1. Using the rounders example, state which rules/procedures fit in the following categories:
   - safety
   - keeping order
   - making play fair

Duties of a referee/umpire

The duties of a referee/umpire are the jobs they are expected to perform. An umpire should check that they have the correct equipment before each match so that their job can be completed effectively and efficiently. Such equipment may include:

- watch to time the play (a back-up watch is recommended)
- pencil to record the score or official decisions (spare pencils are recommended)
- score pad set out for the particular game
- disciplinary cards to be shown for foul play.

Duties of a football referee

In preparation for the game

- Have a full knowledge of the rules of the game.
- Gain experience for the standard of the match.
- Make sure personal presentation is of a high standard.
- Have all necessary equipment.
- Achieve a level of fitness to meet the demands of the game.

Before the game

- Check the condition of the playing surface for safety.
- Check equipment:
  – match ball
  – goals.
- Check players:
  – dress
  – jewellery
  – equipment.

During the game

- Concentrate throughout the play.
- Watch play all of the time.
- Keep up with play.
- Keep play within the laws of the game.
- Work as a team with the other officials.
- Make decisions efficiently.
- Communicate clearly with players and officials.
- Keep an accurate record of the score fouls.

After the game

- Record the score.
- Make sure both teams know the final score.
- Write a match report (if necessary).
- Send scores (and report) to the relevant body.

Correct Skills/Techniques

Some rules of an activity are clearly there to make competition or performance safe. These rules often have a direct bearing on the technique permissible. The nature of some activities results in them having danger elements.

The form of danger can be due to the equipment. A hockey ball or stick can be hazardous to others if not controlled. Therefore within the rules of hockey there are clear restrictions on lifting the ball and stick. Certain footwear can allow the performer to maintain steady footing and change direction efficiently. Studs on football boots can also be dangerous to others. The laws of football are clear on dangerous play to do with raised boots and two footed tackles, infringements of this kind attract severe penalties.

The physicality of rugby makes it a joy to watch and play. Tackling can be spectacular to watch but incorrectly performed can be dangerous too. The rules on 'high tackles' protect the runner from being unfairly and dangerously brought to ground.

Each activity has its own rules affecting technique and skills. It is important to know and understand the rules of your chosen activities. It is the responsibility of the pupils to learn the rules of the game they are playing, for safety purposes.

2 Appropriate Levels of Ability/Participation

In contact sports there are rules that keep similar age groups together and that separate the sexes at certain ages. This is an attempt to make the competition even and safe by keeping the experience and strength of the players at a similar level. Different factors are taken into account to ensure a **balanced competition**. These include:

- grading
- skill level
- weight
- age
- sex.

Summary

Rules not only give the activity its character but they also intend to make competition fair and safe. Rules can have a direct bearing on the skills and techniques of an activity often for the overall safety of the performers. Other ways of making a competition fair and safe are to have the competitors matched by age, weight, height and experience. This will even out the competition, making injury less likely and also more of a competitive match.

Safe Practice: Assessing and Appreciating the Risks Involved in Chosen Practical Activities

What you will learn about in this section

1. How to Use Correct Equipment Safely – Lifting, Carrying, Placing
2. Specific Equipment and Safety Equipment to Use/Wear

1 How to Use Correct Equipment Safely – Lifting, Carrying, Placing

Coaching is essential to all levels of sport. The coach is responsible for giving the performer an understanding of the game. The skills learned will be within the laws of the game and prepare the player for competition. The correct techniques are learned, not only for success but for risk prevention: this is especially important for tackles and lifts.

Training improves the body so it is strong enough to deal with the stresses of the event. This reduces the possibility of fatigue, which often leads to injury. Coaching trains the performer to complete skills in a technically correct way. Body alignment is important in take-offs and landings, especially in activities like gymnastics, trampolining and volleyball, to reduce the risk to the bones and tissues of the body. Knowledge and experience of how to control the equipment for the activity comes about through training. A hockey stick used without training can become a danger to all on the pitch, not just the opposition.

Gymnastics

There are many specialised pieces of equipment used in gymnastics. Lessons on the instruction of setting and putting away are integral parts of gymnastic sessions. Each piece needs clear tuition on its movement.

Trampolining

Movement and setting out of a trampoline needs well-trained teamwork. Each person should know their role and be able to carry it out at the correct time, at the correct pace and in the correct way. An awareness and understanding of the energy and resistance the springs contain should help to reinforce how important everyone's role is.

It can take a team of six people to set out a trampoline safely. In general the procedure is as follows:

- Move to the site and align squarely to the space and on a level surface
- Remove the wheels and store them safely
- Lever over the ends
- Engage the braces
- Check the braces and safety cushions are in place
- Arrange the mats around the trampoline.

Good lifting technique

Poor lifting technique

Using the correct techniques can reduce the risk of injury.

Example
Carrying a bench:
two to a bench
one at each end
Face the way you are to travel
Bend knees to grasp sides of the bench
Lift together
Walk to the placement area
Bend knees to place the bench down carefully

●●●●● ⚠ **A note of caution**

Remember to keep elbows out of the way whilst the trampoline levers over.

2 Specific Equipment and Safety Equipment to Use/Wear

The clothing for team events not only gives a feeling of unity to the group but can also play its part in safety. Each sport has a unique type of clothing, which has developed due to the nature of the game. It may allow protective guards underneath or be close fitting so it does not catch on equipment. Importantly, it provides free movement so the full range of skills can be performed in each sport.
Clothing should:

- be in good order
- not catch on equipment
- ensure the performer can keep a clear view ahead
- not flap in the opposition's face and hinder their performance
- allow free movement to perform the skills of the game.

Sports equipment and clothing should be checked regularly. Repairs should be made so that there is nothing to act as a hindrance or danger to anyone. The correct design of equipment should be used for the job. Specialised equipment should always be worn properly. Loose straps and poorly fitting helmets can be a danger.

Footwear to fit the event

Footwear is a specialised part of sports gear; each sport has its own design. Some sports have several different technical designs to suit a variety of conditions. The correct footwear helps in many ways: it gives support, protection, grip, greatest or least amount of movement and is an aid to performance and streamlining.

The condition of studded footwear should be smooth so that studs do not cut into another player. Checking studs is the job of a referee at the beginning of the game and referee's assistants can be seen checking the studs of football substitutes. There are specific rules set out in certain sports in which some footwear may be seen as dangerous. It is therefore essential to keep footwear in good order.

What to do:

1. Study the pictures above. Notice that each sport has a different kind of footwear.
2. Say which sport is shown in each picture.
3. Give a reason why the footwear has been developed in that way for each sport.

> Look at the differences in the sole, strapping, material and weather conditions.

Protect and be safe

Each activity needs its own protective equipment. Each item of protection guards against a different kind of injury. These injuries could take the form of: impact of another player, the playing surface, the ball, external conditions, forces put on the body by lifting, friction caused by repeating the skills of the event.

What to do:

1. Choose a type of sportsperson and list the items they would need to dress for safety.

Use the pictures above to help with this task.

••••▶ Active Challenge

With a partner, discuss and decide on as many items of protection in as many sports as possible. Now link each item of protection with an incident that could happen in a game.

Work down from head to toe, thinking of the protection a player may need.

Jewellery

Before a team game begins, players are checked for any jewellery they may be wearing. This may seem petty, but each type of jewellery has its own hazards. Sometimes players put a plaster over earrings so they are not as dangerous. In games where physical contact regularly occurs, it is essential that there is no jewellery to mark the wearer or the opposition.

Rings   If fingers are jarred or a ball knocks the end of the finger (called 'stumped finger') the finger swells; a ring could be stuck on the finger and cut into the flesh. Also rings could get caught and cut the performer or an opponent.

Necklaces   If caught and pulled could cause a scar around the neck.

Earrings   If caught could injure the wearer or an opponent.

Personal presentation

Fingernails need to be clipped to prevent catching and scarring, especially in games like netball and basketball in which reaching for the ball around head height is common.

Hair should be tidy and not in the performer's eyes so players can see where they are going and it does not flick into another player's eyes.

If glasses are worn they should be made of plastic so if they break they do not shatter and injure someone.

Clothing worn for sport should be kept in good order. Ripped or frayed clothing can catch and be a danger.

What to do:

1. Read the two columns of parts of sentences.
2. Link the beginnings of the sentences with the endings.
3. When the sentences are complete, write them in your book.

Beginning of sentence
1. Players are checked for
2. If a ball jars a finger
3. Long fingernails can catch and scar
4. Wearing correct clothing in gymnastics is important
5. Studded footwear is important in rugby
6. Helmet, facemask, pads and gloves

Ending of sentence
a. but they must be kept in good order
b. protect the hockey goalkeeper
c. a player wearing a ring could cut their flesh
d. jewellery before a game
e. so the rules of netball state they should be short
f. so it does not catch on equipment

Summary

For many activities large apparatus needs to be positioned and set up prior to any action taking place. All involved should be well trained and have a full understanding of their role in the team.

All people taking part in an activity should be familiar with the relevant protective equipment. It is important that everyone understands that it should be worn in practice and competition and kept in good order.

Safe Practice: Assessing and Appreciating the Risks Involved in Chosen Practical Activities

What you will learn about in this section

1. How to Gather, Use and Respond to Information about the Environment
2. Organisation of Athletics Events
3. Surface Conditions and Weather on a Rugby/Soccer Field
4. Spotting in Trampolining
5. Mat Placement in Gymnastics
6. Appropriate Clothing in Dance
7. Swimming

1 How to Gather, Use and Respond to Information about the Environment

Where to get information about the weather

Information about the weather can be found:

- on the internet
- on the radio
- on the tv
- in the newspaper.

Assessing weather conditions before embarking on a journey

Before setting out on any expedition a detailed weather report should be studied. The Met Office can supply this for the British Isles. The weather at sea or in the mountains can change rapidly, so preparations should be made accordingly. By obtaining the weather report, predictions can be made as to whether it is viable to go out in the first place or what possible weather changes may occur during the day. If the elements are too much to handle, then it is sensible to turn back or take a safety route home. In mountainous areas the weather can bring wind, mist, rain, snow, heat, sun and storms all in the same day. The key is to prepare for the worst.

All conditions can and do occur on the same day – preparation is everything.

Effects of winds and temperatures

Whatever the ambient temperature the effect of the wind can reduce it by several degrees. This is called the chill factor and only affects living things. The wind leads to a cooling sensation of the body. This can have a great effect on any performer or team playing outdoors. It can especially have a bearing on outdoor and adventurous activities. The wind cools the body in two ways; It takes away the warm layer of air around the body and it evaporates the moisture on the skin's surface.

Altitude also affects the temperature. At the top of mountain it is colder than at the bottom. So whatever the temperature at the start of a hill walk it is going to get colder the more you climb. Any outdoor activity needs careful planning. The better the planning the less likely something will go wrong. Key factors to take into consideration are: experience, fitness, terrain, equipment and environment.

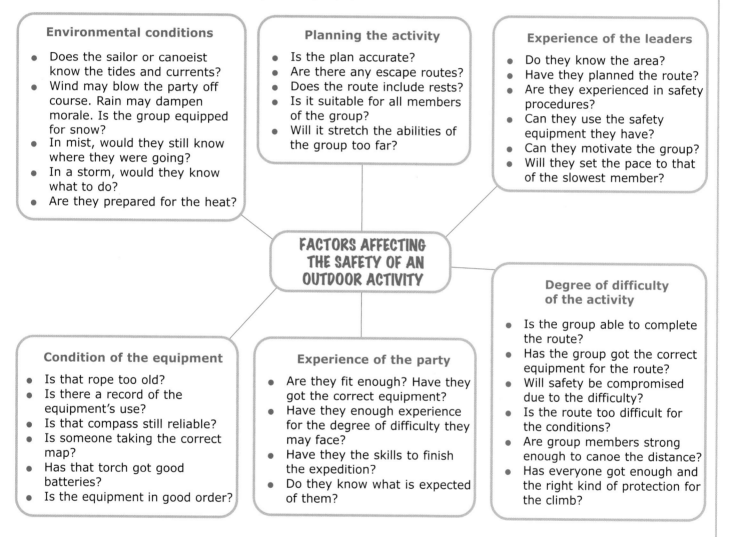

Environmental conditions

- Does the sailor or canoeist know the tides and currents?
- Wind may blow the party off course. Rain may dampen morale. Is the group equipped for snow?
- In mist, would they still know where they were going?
- In a storm, would they know what to do?
- Are they prepared for the heat?

Planning the activity

- Is the plan accurate?
- Are there any escape routes?
- Does the route include rests?
- Is it suitable for all members of the group?
- Will it stretch the abilities of the group too far?

Experience of the leaders

- Do they know the area?
- Have they planned the route?
- Are they experienced in safety procedures?
- Can they use the safety equipment they have?
- Can they motivate the group?
- Will they set the pace to that of the slowest member?

FACTORS AFFECTING THE SAFETY OF AN OUTDOOR ACTIVITY

Condition of the equipment

- Is that rope too old?
- Is there a record of the equipment's use?
- Is that compass still reliable?
- Is someone taking the correct map?
- Has that torch got good batteries?
- Is the equipment in good order?

Experience of the party

- Are they fit enough? Have they got the correct equipment?
- Have they enough experience for the degree of difficulty they may face?
- Have they the skills to finish the expedition?
- Do they know what is expected of them?

Degree of difficulty of the activity

- Is the group able to complete the route?
- Has the group got the correct equipment for the route?
- Will safety be compromised due to the difficulty?
- Is the route too difficult for the conditions?
- Are group members strong enough to canoe the distance?
- Has everyone got enough and the right kind of protection for the climb?

2 Organisation of Athletics Events

All surfaces to run on, throw from and jump off should be flat and free from obstacles and protruding objects.

Throwing events, such as the discus and hammer, require netting or a cage around the throwing area. These should be maintained regularly to prevent equipment escaping through gaps in the fencing. The throwing area should be clearly marked and marshalled. As the competition begins, warnings should be sounded to alert other judges, marshals and competitors that the throw is about to commence.

In jumping events, guidelines for the size, depth and composition of the landing areas are regulated by the governing body. Mats should have a continuous covering over them to keep them together. Throughout the high jump and pole vault competition a check should be kept on the correct placement of the landing area in relation to the bar.

Some equipment is dangerous, the javelin being an obvious example. There are special carry cages and trolleys for transporting awkward equipment. In schools, the training and drilling of moving such equipment, especially javelins and shot, should be reinforced in every lesson.

The throwing cage protects people at the event from a miss-throw. Dean Macey prepares to throw.

3   Surface Conditions and Weather on a Rugby/Soccer Field

It is the referee's job to check the surfaces suitability for play prior to the match starting. He checks not only the condition for play but also looks for any hazardous objects that could injure the players too.

Any grass surface will be affected by the environment. Too little moisture and it becomes hard and cracked, too much and it becomes waterlogged, the surface cuts up too easily and slipping becomes a danger.

With rugby it is important that the length of grass is longer than that of football pitches due to the nature of the game.

4   Spotting in Trampolining

Trampolining is potentially a dangerous activity. It is important that not only the equipment is in good order but the spotters are fully trained and their skills are routinely refreshed each session.

Their training could involve:

Positioning around the trampoline – at least one at the ends and two at the sides

Hand position whilst watching – on top of the protective cushion

Where to look whilst watching – at the upper part of the performer

An understanding of the weight distribution of the performer – top is the heaviest part

Hand position if performer travels in their direction – contact wrist and upper arm

Easing performer back to the trampoline centre – hold wrist and upper arm and gently push back onto trampoline

5 Mat Placement in Gymnastics

Whether training or competing, the landing areas should be safe and stable. Competition landing areas are 120–200mm thick and have safety mats around them to a depth of 22mm–60mm. The landing, after a vault, for instance, needs to be technically correct for a good overall mark and also for the safety of the performer. A two-footed landing on the toes, cushioning the force of landing, reduces the risk of a jarring injury to the back. The safety requirements for landing areas are set out by the governing body.

6 Appropriate Clothing in Dance

The surface the dance is performed on should always be safe and non-slippery. It should be smooth with no splinters. Costumes reflecting the dance and adding drama to the performance should be fitted to each performer securely and allow free movement during the event.

7 Swimming

All safety information and equipment should be clearly on display at the pool side. Any change of depth in the pool should be clearly marked on the pool edge and should be visible on the wall too.

The surface around the pool should be non-slip and clean to prevent injury and infection.

Although it may be seen as unglamorous, the swimming cap is a safety aid in a variety of ways. It keeps hair out of the eyes, giving a clear view of the direction for the swimmer and it keeps hair out of the swimmer's mouth, allowing clear, unhindered breathing. Keeping the hair in a cap also helps prevent loose hair entering and blocking the filters.

NO running.
NO fighting.
NO bomb-diving.
NO young children unsupervised.

Although a verruca can be painful, a person can still swim: they must take care when changing so they do not infect the floor and should wear a verruca sock when swimming to prevent it spreading.

Wearing goggles allows the swimmer to see underwater when their face is submerged. This allows turns to be made safely. Goggles also protect the eyes from the chemicals in the water.

Summary

Safety in many activities can often be down to good organisation, knowledge and experience of all concerned. Even with the best preparation a plan may have to alter due to environmental changes, especially in the case of outdoor activities.

All involved in an activity should be aware of the safety factors. Areas should be clearly marked out for competition, waiting competitors and spectators.

Trampolining may only take place if trained spotters are present. Their duty is to be alert and prepared for a mistake by the performer.

Even the simplest of rules and procedures are often simply common sense – but they can ensure safety.

Skill and Psychological Factors Influencing Performance – Skill Acquisition

What you will learn about in this section

1. Skill and its Definition
2. Ability and its Definition
3. Ways of Learning Skills
4. Performance and its Definition

Acquiring skill can be difficult for some depending on the person and the complexity of the skill. An element of natural ability will help a person to accomplish skills. All physical activities come with their specific mix of skills and to be good at that activity mastery of these is important. In invasion games for instance there may be a different set of skills required for players in specific positions – those for a defender may very well not be the same as those for an attacker. All performers will need to learn skills and be able to apply them to the game in order to play well.

1 Skill and its Definition

Skill is learnt through coaching and practice. The standard definition of skill is – 'a skill is a learned ability to bring about the result you want, with maximum certainty and efficiency'.

When a performer is seen to be skilful they can perform a task successfully. This success normally comes from hours of practice. Throughout his career David Beckham spent hours after full training on his free kick technique. He would attempt to kick a dead ball through a tyre hanging from the crossbar in the corner of the goal. He would use this target to fine-tune his skills to apply to the game.

Some skills are more complex. They may require more than one action in order to complete them correctly. Complex actions, such as breaststroke in swimming, need all the parts of the stroke to work in harmony so the skills are successful – arm pull, breathing and leg kick all need to be coordinated.

A complex skill like breaststroke needs all parts of the stroke to work in synchronisation.

Characteristics of a skillful performance

- Shots make the target – this shows that the skill is being performed with accuracy.
- A kick, serve, stroke, pitch of the ball all go where the player intended.
- A good cricketer, specialising in bowling, can place the ball on a chosen target by pitching the ball consistently around a chosen spot.
- The action often has a successful outcome – showing consistency. Hitting a target or completing a pass regularly requires skill. Making a pass in netball regularly from the centre to the goal attack gives the team a goal shooting opportunity.
- All parts of the body work in unison to affect the skill – this relies on coordination.
- When executing skills a performer maintains a smoothness to the technique even when responding to different and difficult situations.

- The correct weight/strength is put on a pass or hit, needing control. A tennis player can still play a winning shot despite having been defending, running across the base line for the ball and being late in the game.
- The action performed looks good and is aesthetically pleasing.
- The skill is performed with smoothness.
- It can apply the specific physical components appropriately to the skill – power, strength, agility, reaction, balance and speed.
- The technique used to perform the skill follows the correct technical model.
- The skill is performed with the maximum output but with minimum outlay of energy and time – this shows timing and coordination. A golfer may strike the ball with ease but it travels further than usual possibly making the next shot much easier.
- A skilled performer can easily adapt to changing circumstances and be successful. An attacking footballer may need to run back to make a tackle and then dribble out of trouble in a deeper position on the pitch than normal.
- A player is confident that his play will be successful and plays as such.

What to do:

1. Give six examples where you have witnessed skilled performance.

2. Develop four of these examples into sentences.

Characteristics of an unskilled performer

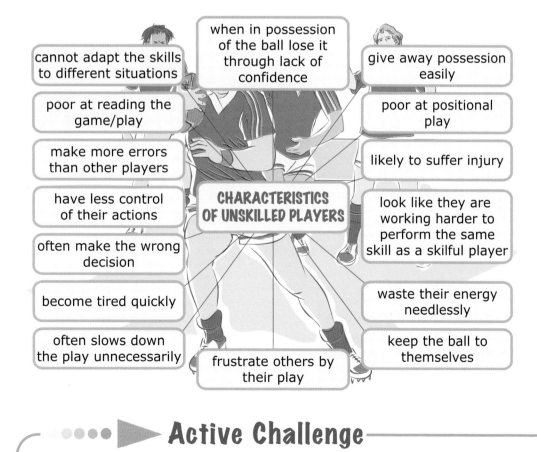

cannot adapt the skills to different situations

when in possession of the ball lose it through lack of confidence

give away possession easily

poor at reading the game/play

poor at positional play

make more errors than other players

likely to suffer injury

have less control of their actions

CHARACTERISTICS OF UNSKILLED PLAYERS

look like they are working harder to perform the same skill as a skilful player

often make the wrong decision

become tired quickly

waste their energy needlessly

often slows down the play unnecessarily

frustrate others by their play

keep the ball to themselves

●●●● ▶ **Active Challenge**

With a partner link the above information with a single chosen activity.

2 Ability and its Definition

Two definitions of ability are:

'A skill is a learned ability to bring about the result you want, with maximum certainty and efficiency' and

'Ability is an innate physical characteristic which facilitates movements.'

Ability, therefore, is an inborn, natural characteristic of the person. Despite being innate it can be trained and the natural state improved upon. It includes all the health-related and skill-related physical components. So, for instance, a person's natural flexibility can be trained and improved in order to develop that ability.

To be a good sprinter a person will have a basic natural capacity for speed and a good reaction time relying on fast twitch muscle fibres. A sprinter may be born with a higher percentage of these fibres in the body in comparison with a middle distance runner; the number will never change. An appropriate training programme will improve the condition of these fibres so allowing for greater speeds and quicker reactions.

Performing any skill relies on ability in certain skill-related physical components, for example:

| Driving in golf = coordination | Shot putting = power | Saving a goal = reaction time |

3 Ways of Learning Skills

What is learning?

Learning can be defined as:

'The act of gaining knowledge or acquiring skill'.

When learning a new skill guidance is required. This guidance is given by the coach or the teacher. Mixtures of different methods are often used to teach skills successfully.

Watching a coach explaining strategy gives learners a complete picture of the skill.

Visual

This is often the first method used, especially when learning a new skill. It shows the whole, overall skill enabling the learner to see a complete image of the skill and where it fits in with other actions.

This method is also appropriate when evaluating performance and giving feedback. The action can be repeated and its variation commented on as to what is regarded as the correct technique.

Visual guidance can take several forms, it can be:

- a demonstration from a teacher or skilled performer
- a playback of a video clip of top-class performers in action
- a playback from a special training video
- looking and observing the body position from a poster or a chart.

Verbal

Giving verbal guidance to performers learning skills can also be helpful. The words, phrases and sentences used must be clear, simple and straightforward. The language used should be appropriate to the skill and the level of understanding of the performer.

The language for instructing a skill can change and there may be several ways to express the same guidance; this gives the best chance for the performer to understand.

The same or similar instructions can be repeated over if necessary. Often this form is best used with other types of guidance. It is an especially good support to the visual guidance method linking verbal and visual images together.

The difficulty with this form of instruction is that the performer must be able to:

- understand the words used
- remember the instructions that have been given
- translate the words given into actions.

Manual

This method is used when the skills or movements being learned are potentially dangerous and complex. The teacher, coach or equipment applies a 'hands on' approach acting as a support or safety measure to the performer. This method gives freedom to the performer to attempt the actions without fear of injury, overbalancing or landing awkwardly.

Artificial aids help the performer, these include armbands for swimming or an overhead rig for trampoline, gymnastics or diving.

The presence of the safety measure gives confidence to the performer and it often affords the performer a one-to-one situation with the coach.

●●●● ▶ Active Challenge

With a partner discuss the three methods. Give each other examples of when you have learnt from those methods.

4 Performance and its Definition

What is performance?

Performance is how a skill is carried out. If an action is performed well then it will be technically correct and close to the 'perfect model'. Often if a skill is technically correct it has a greater chance of being successful.

Key Terms:

Skill	▶ 'a skill is a learned ability to bring about the result you want, with maximum certainty and efficiency'
Ability	▶ 'ability is an innate physical characteristic which facilitates movements.'
Learning	▶ the act of gaining knowledge or acquiring skill
Performance	▶ how a skill is carried out

Summary

Skills can be taught through coaching; developing and refining them takes up a large part of training sessions. Ability is inborn in the performer, but this can also be improved and enhanced with training.

When a performer is learning new skills or developing those already acquired, guidance is required. Using a variety of methods will give the best chance of improving a performance fully.

Skill Acquisition: Types of Skill

What you will learn about in this section

1. A Description of Basic and Complex Skills
2. The Open/Closed Continuum

1 A Description of Basic and Complex Skills

Basic/Closed Skills

These skills are performed in a situation that remains the same with no variations. The skills are unaffected by environment and are habitual in nature. They need few decisions to be made to perform them so are relatively straightforward to complete. The performer can control the pace of how the skill is executed. Swimming can be classed as a closed skill. It is not affected by the environment, other performers or pool conditions. The action to perform the stroke follows a prescribed pattern of movement, which are repeated habitually with little variation.

Complex/Open Skills

These skills are performed in an environment that is constantly changing. They are affected by the sports environment such as:

- other players' movements
- the angle the ball is approaching
- the pace of the ball
- the distance the ball must reach
- the height of the approaching ball.

Open skills require adaptability from the performer. So, although the skill is mastered it must be quickly modified to change with the needs of the environment. In order to complete the skill successfully decisions prior to its execution need to be made. The speed of play is often decided by others or the situation.

A plain forward roll is an example of a closed skill.

2 The Open/Closed Continuum

The continuum represents the degree to which a skill is open or closed. A skill placed to the left of the continuum shows that it is open and therefore complex, if placed to the right then it is closed and basic. Each skill will find its own place according to its habitual nature or variability.

open skill ⊢————————————⊣ closed skill

The tennis service example

Although the distance of the baseline, height of the net and the service box make this skill seemingly a closed one, there are factors that take this skill more towards the open end of the continuum.

Where the opponent is standing will influence where the ball is to be placed as the angle of the ball's flight will have to be changed.

The opponent may have strengths to avoid and weaknesses to exploit needing variations of the service action.

If playing outdoors the weather may have a bearing on the service – the wind may cause the ball to be blown in a certain direction so to compensate, the performer will have to adapt the ball toss to hit the ball in a different way or direction.

There may be a need to vary the type of service as the opponent may be getting used to the usual one. Putting spin on a serve, to take the opponent by surprise, gives them a new set of problems but also creates a variable with the skill too.

The pressure of the stage of the game may influence the serve. It may be important and necessary to make sure the service goes 'in' and apply caution rather than play a usual shot.

The crowd may also be a variable as they may become noisier and more partisan. A crowd cheering for one side or another evokes an emotional response that may affect the execution of the skill. The pressure of the occasion may cause the performer to tighten up or rise to the challenge.

It is likely that each of the pictured sports will sit on the open/closed continuum in a different place.

What to do:

1. Choose a sport.
2. List skills used in that sport.
3. Draw an open/closed continuum line.
4. Place the named skills on that line.
5. For each skill say why you have made that decision.

Key Terms:

Closed Skill
► basic skills unaffected by the sporting environment

Open Skill
► complex skills performed in constantly changing conditions

Summary

For games players to do their best the correct skills training should be followed, starting with basic individual skills, moving on to team play and then practice with the opposition. The top performers need to be able to adapt their skills to the situation at hand. Most team game sports involve open skills where this adaptability is vital although there are times in a game where a closed skill, like a penalty shot for instance, is necessary. Some sports, such as gymnastics, totally rely on the ability to repeat closed skills consistently and to a high level of technical accuracy in order to succeed.

Skill Acquisition: Information Processing

What you will learn about in this section

1. Information Processing (basic)
2. Feedback
3. Memory
4. Motivation
5. Goal Setting

1 Information Processing (basic)

Input

Input is all the information received by the body from the senses including influences from both inside and outside the body. All of these inputs add to the experience of the performer coming in the shape of:

- Skills
- Practice
- Game play
- Emotional responses
- Pleasure in performance
- Fear and apprehension
- Good experiences
- Bad experiences
- Decision making

Decision making

The brain processes all of the information received and makes a decision. It interprets the information of how it sees the situation (perception) and decides on the response to make. For this to happen it has to search both the short and long-term memory. After filtering out the necessary information the brain tells the muscles what to do.

Selective attention

In a game situation a player will be aware of many stimuli which will influence his actions. These will range from the actual game play to effects from those watching the match. It is important that a player focuses only on the important issues relevant to the game. This is called selective attention. By keeping their attention only on matters concerning play, their brain has a better chance of making clear, quick and correct decisions. Being able to 'Selectively attend' is achieved as a result of **memory** and **perception**.

Task 1

What to do:

1. Choose a major sport.
2. Make a list of the important information that a player must keep focused on during a game.

> For example
> The sound of the ball being kicked giving a clue to the pace of the pass.

Output

Output is the action that comes about from the brain's decision. If the brain has memory of varied skills practice; quality training, good advice and constructive feedback for instance, then the output has the possibility of greater success.

Often a retired player can give advice to a young, up and coming one. Such suggestions can help the novice, adding to his experience and improving his play as a result.

Feedback

Feedback responds to the output. It can comment on success, strengths and weakness. It should influence the next decision to be made and possibly improve the performance as a result of the experience.

Active Challenge

With a partner choose a sport and discuss what relevant feedback a player receives from a performance.

2 Feedback

Every player or athlete needs feedback on their performance in order to improve. Any information can go towards helping develop future attempts, training or play. Comments made should refer to both the strengths and weaknesses of a performance and should serve to motivate the player. Highlighted points will indicate the need for changes and aspects to work hard on during training.

Knowledge of performance (KP), of both its good and bad points, helps the learning process and will shape the future actions and refine skills of the performer. Feedback reinforces the correct actions and tells the player what they should do next time in order to improve that skill.

During the game statistics may be kept of different aspects of the activity; these may be recorded and analysed at a later date and training adapted according to the needs of the performer. Having a knowledge of results (KR) provides evidence of the successful and unsuccessful aspects of the performance.

Intrinsic feedback

This happens internally to the performer. They know that the skill they effected was not quite right or that it was the best it could be. Intrinsic feedback is assessed by the senses – 'did the shot feel good?' When cricketers middle the ball, they hit the ball forcibly, with what seems little effort. When the ball is hit on the 'sweet spot' in this way, the sound of the contact is different too. If, in addition to the feeling of the shot, it is placed in a gap in a scoring position as well, the batter forms in his brain the intrinsic feedback. The resulting positive feelings are those of satisfaction, pleasure and confidence about their play.

What to do:

1. Refer back to a competition or match you have been involved in.

2. List the examples of intrinsic feedback you experienced during the event.

Extrinsic feedback

This type of feedback comes externally to the performer. It can present itself in many forms:

- Watching a video of their own performance.
- Listening to a coach remarking on the skill.
- Having a professional instruct you on skill technique – this happens often in golf when the professional tells the player about the grip, stance and address of the ball.

- The final score of a game.
- Studying the match analysis.

Therefore there are two lines of External Feedback:

- Knowledge of results (KR) – the outcome of the performance.
- Knowledge of performance (KP) – law will be performed rather then the results.

Giving feedback to the performer

For feedback to be useful it needs to work positively for the performer and give them the motivation they need to make the changes for success.

should be frequent enough to help but not too often that there is too much information given and therefore cannot be taken on board

accurate

concise

immediate

should relay information

easy to understand

constructive – saying how perceived weaknesses can be improved

positive – highlight strengths and suggest how they can develop them

suit the needs of the performer

Active Challenge

With a partner discuss the examples of extrinsic feedback given to you about your performances in sport over the past two weeks. How are you going to help it improve your play?

3 Memory

Short-term memory

Information does go into the brain but only stays for a short time. It is important that the recipient pays attention or the memory fades away quickly. Applying greater concentration helps move the information from the short-term memory to the long-term memory banks.

Long-term memory

Long-term memory is like a library holding a store of information until it is required. This type of memory holds images, actions and feelings with which a person is familiar. It can store a limited amount of information permanently in the brain.

Long-term memory stores knowledge of the sports skills a person has learned, so when performing an action, it is this type that allows the recall of how that action is performed.

Incoming information is processed, interpreted and a response is made from a search of the memory by the brain and an action results. In sporting terms the following hockey example can happen:

A player sees the actions of the opponent, the brain interprets what is seen and an action ensues resulting from information stored in the long-term memory.

Incoming information – A player sees an opponent change body position to make a pass.

Interpretation – the playing is going to pass to the right.

Action – the player reverses their stick, outstretching it to make an interception.

4 Motivation

Motivation can be defined as:

'Amount of enthusiasm and determination a person has for a given sporting performance or activity'.

People can be motivated in many different ways. Some motivations work the internal drive of a person – intrinsic. Others are to do with incentives provided by the external of the person – extrinsic. Both ways can motivate a person to produce a better performance.

Intrinsic motivation

Intrinsic motivation is all about 'self' and how a person can inspire oneself into doing well. The internal drive of a person is enough to enthuse them to participate, train and compete. All the encouragement to do well comes from internal sources.

Often, people who are self-motivated, take part for the sheer enjoyment of the activity, with no other gain in mind. Enjoying the sport for no other rewards than how it makes them feel is enough to generate commitment to the activity.

Self-motivated people often have an internal desire to be the best and personally need to be the best in order to be satisfied.

Extrinsic motivation

Extrinsic motivation is all about a person needing and receiving praise, external gratification and rewards as an incentive to do well. A person motivated in this way needs more than enjoyment in order to participate.

The inducement of rewards is required in order to do well. These rewards can come in different forms:

- certificates
- following the goals set and so improving in stages and at an appropriate pace
- trophies
- receiving good teaching/coaching
- money
- receiving praise
- team success
- acclaim
- personal successful performance
- reaching for attainable and realistic goals
- badges
- team spirit-all working for one goal making each other work hard
- awards
- being in a competition suitable to their ability

Disadvantages of extrinsic motivation

Although rewards and acclaim can be seen as a motivator, not all people regard them as important to the activity. For some, the struggle to achieve the reward can be too difficult and may discourage participation, so reducing the amount of people having the chance to benefit from the activity. For others the reward for success in a competition may be so great that it puts too much pressure on the performer to do well and rather suffer this pressure they choose not to compete at all.

Where victory is all important and winning stops then the performer may be discouraged and may even choose to stop competing all together. In some cases rewards for the activity are too easy to gain; undervaluing the activity in this way may also prevent people taking part.

Where winning is everything to a team or individual they will do anything to achieve success. Winning at all costs could lead to cheating, use of artificial substances and hostility. When rewards are the motivator often the initial fun and enjoyment of the activity can be lost.

Task 3

What to do:

1. From your own experience recall six examples of ways you have been motivated.
2. Detail these examples.
3. Say whether they are intrinsic or extrinsic.

5 Goal Setting

Goal setting is important to the performer. By setting out staged and achievable goals a coach/teacher can keep the performer motivated. Having knowledge of the phases, shows the way forward and keeps the athlete focused on the task reducing the possibility of boredom.

These goals can keep the performer working hard and focused on the task giving a better chance to improve fitness and skills. Reaching a stage and moving on signposts the athlete's physical progress.

Goals can mentally prepare the performer for an activity or competition. Each stage may train the individual in a way that grooms them for a more challenging situation so when it arrives they can handle the conditions, taking it in their stride, without it affecting their level of performance.

Reaching goals indicates the progress of training. It shows how the performance is developing in relation to the structured time settings and point out the need for changes to the training.

Knowing the stages gives an element of control to the performer. As each stage is reached and passed the athlete can see the progress and rather than worry about his ability can be confident that development is on track. Athletes, for instance, gain much confidence when in training they reach a personal best time or distance.

Goals need to be SMARTER.
When planning goals they should focus on seven points:

S – specific – to the sport – could be a time or distance for an athlete

M – measurable – results can be measured and so set against recognised norms

A – agreed – both the performer and coach agree on the way forward – so both working together and on the same wave length – they agree on the specific goal as they are in accord with the targets helping with motivation

R – realistic – the goal aiming for should be realistic to the level of skill and fitness of the performer

T – time-phased – timetable of training set out can give a target for a certain level of performance to be attained – the plan would follow the goals set – it would allow time for improvement to be made – the time would also relate to the amount of weekly training sessions to be undertaken

E – exciting – the type of training/practice needs to keep the attention of the performer and motivate them to continue with tasks set

R – recorded – results and progress should be recorded to compare with past and future results to show how the performer has moved on and where they should be aiming for in the next stage

For some the hard work pays off.

Task 4

What to do:

1. Choose a sport.
2. Apply SMARTER to your choice.
3. Describe, in sentences, how each point would apply to that sport.
4. List two main targets you have for a particular sport.

Short and long-term goals

The difference between the two types is time. Short-term goals are achievable sooner than long-term goals. In order to achieve a long-term goal, short-term goals must be met first. So smaller achievable targets are reached which will eventually bring the long-term goal nearer. Often in sport the goals are time specific, due to the fact that the long-term goal may have a particular date set to it, like an athletics event or a major tournament.

A committed athlete trains in all weathers focusing on the long-term goal.

Short-term

These are often set in training programmes and can act as incentives to train hard.

They can work as a signpost indicating whether the performer is on target for success.

There may be several different levels to a short-term goal, for instance an athlete may have the following stages:

- Train hard to achieve a good distance which qualifies them for an event.
- They may win that event.
- They then may be selected for the county team.
- Then they may be selected to represent the county in a competition.

Long-term

These targets are often the culmination of several training programmes and can possibly lead to a competition or final event. There are two types of sporting goals; Outcome Goals, which are linked to results of performance competition and Performance Goals which are concerned with previous ones.

- To run for the country.
- To be selected for the Olympics.

What to do:

1. For a sport of your choice list the short and long-term goals needed for success.

Key Terms:

Extrinsic feedback	▶ external information gathered by the performer, based on what they see or hear, at the time of the action
Selective attention	▶ blocking out other thoughts and concentrating on the performance only
Intrinsic feedback	▶ internal information gathered by the performer at the time of the action about how they feel the performance is going
Motivation	▶ level of enthusiasm and determination a person has for a given subject
Goal setting	▶ series of phases, setting out achievable goals for progress

Summary

For a performer to do their best both body and mind need to be trained to compete. In an important competition, spectators and the opposition may play their part in making the challenge more difficult. By controlling thoughts and using selective attention, the player can ignore distractions and concentrate on the performance only. A person training can be kept motivated by knowing the plan and seeing where on the plan they are. Using feedback after training or a competition can show where adjustments are needed for the future.

Guidance and Practice

What you will learn about in this section

1. Guidance
2. Visual Guidance
3. Verbal Guidance
4. Manual/Mechanical Guidance
5. Links with Feedback
6. Types of Practice

1 Guidance

Guidance is required whenever new skills are being learnt. Coaches or teachers will offer ongoing guidance to those learning from their own personal experience. The knowledge to give support and direction comes from training, observations, personal participation, discussions with others in the same field and experience gained from recognised courses.

A coach will inform the performer of how well they are doing and give them instructions in training, showing them the way forward and how to progress. Therefore guidance and feedback are linked together so progress can be made.

2 Visual Guidance

When learning a new skill often visual guides are given to the performer. These can take the form of demonstrations, photographs or videos of the skill in question. A recording of a performance may be made and replayed back in a training session indicating areas on which to work.

3 Verbal Guidance

Here the coach tells the performer what is needed to be done for improvement. Informing the performer of the aim of the action and describing the skill in question, breaking down what each part of the body does can help in the future execution of the skill. Such instructions can be repeated and made in several different ways suiting a variety of circumstance.

4 Manual/Mechanical Guidance

This method is used with complex skills that are difficult to perform. The coach supports manually or with specialised equipment, giving confidence to the performer to try the action. Artificial aids can include armbands in swimming and overhead rigs for gymnastics, trampolining and diving.

Armbands are an example of mechanical aids.

5 Links with Feedback

There is an ongoing link with feedback and guidance provided by the coach. There are several times when this link occurs and the timing has a different effect on the performer:

Before training Prepares the performer and focuses their mind on the job in hand.

During a training session A problem can be identified and worked on straight away.

Immediately after training Highlights successes and failures whilst they are clear in everyone's mind.

The day after training Here everyone is calmer and fresher and so feedback is often more prepared and thorough.

Before a competition or match Prepares and focuses the performer for the task in hand. The coach also has a chance to 'psyche up' the team.

During the competition or match This is dependant on the game or event. Time-outs in basketball are especially designed so the coach can give feedback to the team.

Immediately after the match All exhausted so only a general response is appropriate.

The day after the match A measured reflective response can be given with the possibility of match statistics taken into consideration.

The basketball coach gives feedback during the game.

6 Types of Practice

The type of practice chosen depends on the skills to be improved. Some are simple, others more complex. There are a series of different methods that better suit particular complexities of skills. The aim of practice is to help the performer learn how to complete the skills successfully, so not only is it important to choose the correct method for the action but also a way to deliver the instructions to suit the personality of the athlete too.

Whole practice

This method suits practicing simple skills and involves repeating the whole of the action at once. These skills are unlikely to confuse the performer due to their simplicity and so can be practiced in this way in order to get the feel of the action.

Gymnastic skills like simple jumps from a box, such as a pin, star or tuck jump, can be practiced in this way.

Games skills that are difficult to split into parts also suit this method. Dribbling in football and basketball or catching in netball or rugby are skills that lend themselves to be taught in this way.

As the action is simple and quick to carry out, the performer can repeat it over and over again, each time, having listened to the feedback of the coach, modifying it according to the instructions.

Whole practice is used to learn simple skills.

Part practice

This method is best suited to skills of a more complex nature, which have several different parts making the whole. The triple jump is a good example of a skill that would complement this type of practice.

In many cases it helps if the performer attempts the whole skill first. By doing this they see and understand the need to break down the skill into its component parts, learn them separately and gradually build up to the whole action.

For this method to work the key parts to the skill need to be identified. As the different parts are rehearsed the performer receives feedback accordingly. When a stage is performed well a new stage is practiced.

A tennis serve is such a skill that can be broken down into several parts. These include: ● ball toss ● transfer of weight ● racket preparation ● throw action ● contact ● follow through.

Parts and sometimes all of this skill can be practiced without the ball in shadow fashion.

What to do:

1. Study the following complex skills:
   - Breaststroke in swimming
   - Triple jump
   - Lay up shot in basketball
   - Gym routine
2. Choose one of these complex skills. Break it down into the component parts a performer would practice.

Whole-part-whole practice

This method is also usually used for complex skills. It involves a combination of the whole and part practice approaches.

The whole action is attempted; this allows the performer to experience the action and get a feel of the skill. The action is then broken down into parts, practiced section by section and then reassembled into the whole action again.

This method is complicated in itself as it can be technically difficult to reassemble the whole action. As a result of its complexity this type of practice is often suited to already skilled or experienced performers. This method suits long and triple jumps in athletics.

Fixed practice

Fixed practices are suitable for closed skills – those that can be performed in the same way on each repetition. These conditions for practice always remain the same, rarely varying. The skill is continually repeated, feedback is given to the performer and necessary adaptations are made. Examples of skills that benefit this type of practice include gymnastic skills like forward and backward rolls, penalty kick taking in football and tumble turning in swimming.

Variable practice

Open skills adapt to variable practice as the sporting conditions change during the execution of the skill. When training for invasion games, like netball, hockey and basketball for instance, variable practices are often used. These exercises aim to simulate the changing situations that might occur in a game. By presenting the player with these problems they may be better prepared for competition conditions. During practice time feedback is given on the performance, indicating further changes necessary for improvement.

Netball can be used as an example to show some ways of how variable practice can work.

A free throw is always taken from the same distance from the basket with no defence.

Task 1

Once a potential goal attack has reached a suitable level of success and is able to dodge an opponent and can regularly score goals from different places in the circle unopposed, variable practices will demand that these skills are adapted to cope with competitive conditions.

The goal attack will be faced with increasingly more difficult conditions, simulating those likely in a game, these may include finding a way to score against the following opposition:

1 marker stopping the shot
2 markers – one blocking her pathway to the circle, one marking the shot
3 markers – two blocking and one marking in the circle.

Each time the shooter will have to adapt the skills learnt to overcome the new problems.

What to do:

Using your understanding of practice

1. Study the list of different types of practice below:
   - Fixed
   - Varied
   - Whole
   - Part
   - Whole-part-whole

2. Using one or more sports match a skill with the most suitable type of practice on the list.

Football coaches are able to give instructions to their team from the technical area.

Key Terms:

Guidance	► help and instruction given to complete a task
Whole practice	► repeating the complete action in training
Part practice	► completing part of a complex action in training
Fixed practice	► repeating closed skills in the same conditions in training
Variable practice	► performing whole skills in changing conditions in training

Summary

Coaches and teachers help develop skills by being able to offer constant guidance and instructions to the performer. There are several methods used to help learning and different skills are suited to one or more of them. In training it is important that the practices or drills are performed at speed and are similar to situations of the competition; this will allow the athlete/player to transfer skills readily to the competitive environment.

Application of Skill and Psychological Factors: Observation, Analysis and Evaluation

What you will learn about in this section

1. Choosing the Right Activity to Analyse
2. Gaining Observational Experience and Understanding
3. Plan Your Observations
4. Expectations of the Observer
5. Knowledge of Skill-Related Fitness
6. The Perfect Model
7. Evaluate a Performance by Comparing it to the Perfect Model
8. Knowledge of the Activity
9. Analysing Performance
10. Ways to Analyse
11. What Can be Analysed?

Applying your knowledge and experience of sport and physical activities will help when working with others to improve performance. Setting out clearly what to analyse, how to carry that evaluation out and how to feedback the information for future improvement will show how well you understand the subject.

This chapter can be used to improve the ability to analyse performance and help with the learning and development of this skill. The various ideas and techniques will provide a bank of information of how to successfully analyse a performance.

The information can directly help with the implementation of assessing a practical performance. It could bring about an awareness of the many factors needing to be addressed, which will lead to sound, accurate analysis. The recording of the student's analysis of performance may, as a result, have more depth and accuracy when recorded in their Exercise Log.

Areas of the assessment criteria the section will help:

- selecting and applying skills to assessment
- strategies for assessment
- analysing performance
- linking theoretical components with performance and assessment
- improving performance.

1 Choosing the Right Activity to Analyse

Many people can watch an activity but only the trained eye can understand the skills and actions of the performance. The observation and analysis part of the course requires you to train these observation skills and make judgements on quality, success, and ways of improving a performance.

You can choose any activity to analyse. You are likely to find that the activity that you are most familiar with, in terms of experience and knowledge of the rules, is likely to be the easiest one to tackle. The more you know about your activity, the better the foundation from which to observe and analyse.

Your personal experiences of playing, being coached and observing top quality performances should give you a clear understanding of what the activity should look like when performed correctly.

2 Gaining Observational Experience and Understanding

There are different ways you can build up your observational skills and understanding of an activity. Using as many methods as you can will give you the broadest information base from which to work.

- Know as much about the activity as possible. This will allow you to anticipate the action, prepare a mental picture of the best performance and compare it with what you see. The expectation of the action aids an understanding of how effective the performance observed has been.
- Watch top class play of the activity, live or recorded.
- Discuss a performance with others to develop knowledge, language and understanding of what you see.
- Listen to the coaching points given by your teacher in class or coaches at your club and compare them with how a person performs the activity. This will develop your experience of linking the description of the correct action with a beginner's attempt.
- Read appropriate coaching manuals and books. This will give you knowledge of what the perfect model should look like. When comparing this knowledge with the novice performer, the differences will become apparent and will therefore develop your observational skills.
- Understand the components of skill required in order to perform well.
- Video class performance and study what you see. You can then build up your observation and appreciation of the whole action after several replays.
- Study photographs of sports performers who are expert in their sport.
- Study the progression of time-lapsed photography.
- Watch specialised coaching productions on video or CD-ROM.

3 Plan your Observations

Choose the best place from which to view. Different positions will give a different view of the action; more than one viewpoint may be necessary for a full picture of an activity. In many cases, a raised position allows you to see more.

Have the correct equipment at hand – record sheets, pencils (pencils are better for outside as they keep working in the rain!) and something to lean on are all basic and obvious requirements to do the job.

Work out which key points you need to watch; this will help you focus your observation. You may prefer to photograph or video the performance. In which case, greater planning is necessary in order to book the equipment before the date.

4 Expectations of the Observer

Many factors can influence a performance. These are sometimes in the control of the performer and sometimes not. When observing an activity a distinction should be made between the two, and comments and feedback given should be adapted accordingly. For instance, a player may well have shown success or great skill in an activity in the past, but changes in the weather could cause the skill to break down, for example, the ball toss for the serve in tennis might be a problem on a very windy day but at no other time.

ALWAYS HAVE IN MIND THE PERFECT MODEL	FACTORS AFFECTING THE PERFORMER	REACTION AND COMMENTS MADE APPROPRIATELY

Rules

May be complex and competition strong so mistakes made.

Skills may be good but rules broken in performance.

Fitness

The performer may drop in standard due to lack of fitness.

Experience

Player may be relatively new to the game.

Weather

May make surface slippery.

Standard of game

A player's own skills may be fair but those of the other players may be poor.

Degree of difficulty of skill

The skill being performed may be complex and difficult to complete.

Open skills

May be affected by the actions of others or the environment.

Closed skills

Should not be influenced by the people and conditions around the performer.

Comment on good aspects of performance.

Comment on poor aspects of performance.

Have a knowledge of how the bad points can be improved.

Suggest ways to improve.

Make allowances for difficult circumstances.

Factors influencing the expectations and reactions of the observer.

5 Knowledge of Skill-Related Fitness

What you have learnt about skill-related fitness and its application to different sports will help with your observations. You will know which components to look out for in your chosen activity. This knowledge will enable you to break down the action into smaller parts, helping you to analyse.

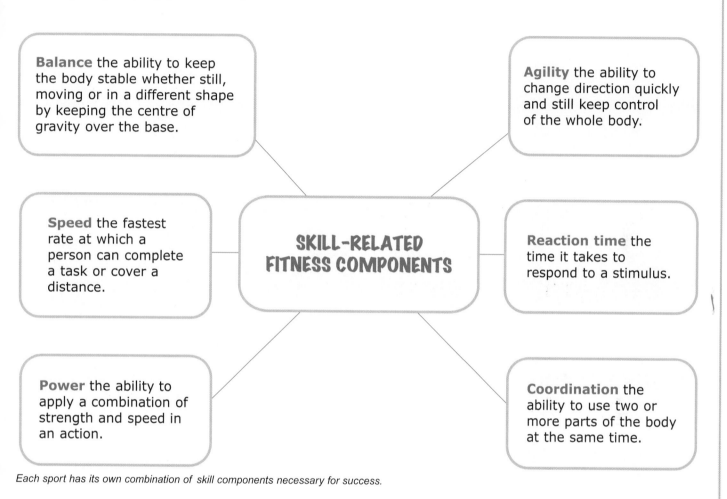

Balance the ability to keep the body stable whether still, moving or in a different shape by keeping the centre of gravity over the base.

Agility the ability to change direction quickly and still keep control of the whole body.

Speed the fastest rate at which a person can complete a task or cover a distance.

SKILL-RELATED FITNESS COMPONENTS

Reaction time the time it takes to respond to a stimulus.

Power the ability to apply a combination of strength and speed in an action.

Coordination the ability to use two or more parts of the body at the same time.

Each sport has its own combination of skill components necessary for success.

6 The Perfect Model

The perfect model is how top-class performers perform the activity at their best. The image of such skills and abilities should be clear in your mind when completing your analysis of performance.

Your knowledge of the activity will also provide you with an image of what the action should look like. A good knowledge and practical experience of the activity will lead to a more comprehensive understanding of how the activity should be performed.

You should understand the various types of skill and conditioning the activity relies on for success. Is it necessary for a player to change direction quickly, work at a moderate-to-hard rate for long periods or is their hand-eye coordination essential?

Usually an activity will require a mixture of skills, types of fitness and body conditioning.

Watching video recordings of matches and performances of top performers can help develop an understanding of the perfect model. By replaying, slowing and pausing the action, you can fully appreciate the performance in question.

When looking at a performance, the shape of the body in action will indicate how close it is to the 'perfect model'. Some areas to look for are the head position, where the centre of gravity is, a balanced body position and how the weight is distributed.

Take every opportunity to compare, at length, evidence of the performance to the perfect model.

BOYS HURDLES. Photo: Tony Henshaw/Action Plus.

Colin Jackson

- Head placed low in a forward position
- Lead leg outstretched forward
- Arm still in running action
- Body leaning forwards and low
- Shoulders square
- Trail leg close to hurdle
- Whole body close to hurdle going forwards

Schoolboy

- Head high
- Lead leg bent
- Arm too far to the side
- Body upright
- Shoulders turned
- Trail leg – knee position at an angle
- Whole body too high and going upwards

7 Evaluate a Performance by Comparing it to the Perfect Model

This is the process after analysis when the coach or observer works out the success or failure of an activity. Evaluation tells us where strengths and weaknesses are and how training should be adapted to the findings in order to make progress.

Knowledge of the perfect model may come from a photograph, video or coaching manual. Understanding the perfect model will make it easier to evaluate what is seen and suggest improvements to be made.

The evaluation process may look like this:

1 Perfect model – know what you are looking for
2 Make observations of the performance.
3 Compare the performance with the perfect model.
4 Decide on and state the main positive point to express.
5 Decide on and state the main fault and express it.
6 Communicate how the performance can be improved at the next attempt (short-term).
7 Communicate how training will need to be adapted and a new plan made (mid-term).
8 See changes in the performance in a targeted event or competition (long-term).

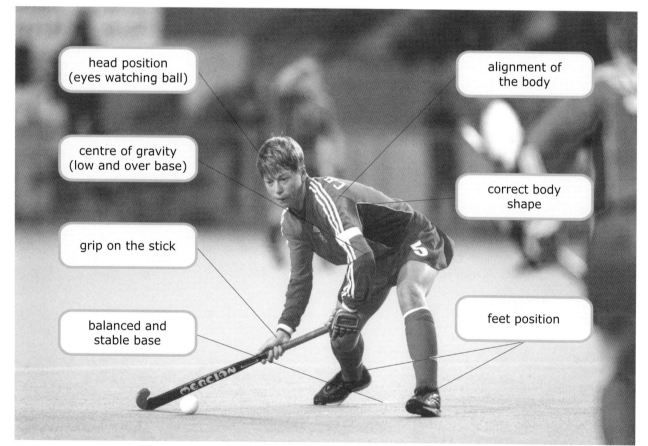

Factors building up to the perfect model.

8 Knowledge of the Activity

Each activity has its own special combination of skills, skill-related components and body conditioning. Identifying these areas will give an idea of the parts of the body and the body systems required to train and develop for success. It is essential to know what is needed in the sport in order to include the correct methods, exercises and practices in training. This knowledge can then be adapted to an individual performer to form a workable and relevant personal exercise programme (**PEP**) for them.

The analysis section will give you an example of how to apply the following to a variety of activities:

- knowledge
- training principles
- training methods
- training practices.

Suggestions of how to monitor and evaluate progress will also be given. In order to use the information for your own chosen activity and give the best response for your final exam mark, you will be required to adapt the text by applying your own understanding, knowledge and personal experience to the chosen area.

You may feel the need to develop your knowledge and understanding of your chosen activity. Do this by:

- reading coaching manuals to increase your knowledge
- using Internet sites for up-to-date information on training
- watching coaching videos or CD-ROMs
- discussing coaching points with your teacher or coach
- developing your own skills to the highest standard
- watching top-class performers.

9 Analysing Performance

To successfully analyse performance you need to be able to recognise the strengths and weaknesses of a performance, and understand and demonstrate ways to improve them. Analysis is part of the whole process a coach would use in order to improve a person's performance.

The Coaching Model on page 221 has all the components for what you need to study for this section. The following coaching model is useful when breaking down the parts that are important for analysis.

An interpretation of the Coaching Model.

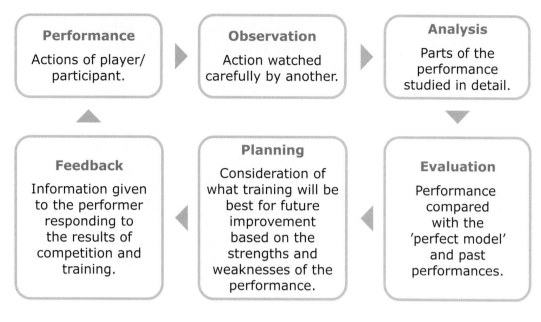

Performance	Observation	Analysis
Actions of player/participant.	Action watched carefully by another.	Parts of the performance studied in detail.

Feedback	Planning	Evaluation
Information given to the performer responding to the results of competition and training.	Consideration of what training will be best for future improvement based on the strengths and weaknesses of the performance.	Performance compared with the 'perfect model' and past performances.

10 Ways to Analyse

Comments made on a performance can be based on a person's opinion or factual evidence: each can comment about the same action but in a different way.

Subjective

Subjective analysis is related to how the observer thinks the player is performing in comparison with the other players. This type of analysis is based on opinion. As two people may have a different opinion about a performance, a bank of reasons why you have that opinion is necessary. Examples of subjective statements are:

'That's the best goal I've seen him score.'
'She looks to be serving better.'
'He is moving quicker to the ball.'
'I thought that shot had more pace.'
'There seem to be fewer double faults than in previous sets.'
'She is crossing the ball better.'
'He has more energy than the others.'

Objective

Objective analysis is based on fact, not personal opinions. The aim of this type of analysis is to have results and statistics to back up the observations. This is very helpful to the coach and performer, as it identifies explicitly the strengths and weaknesses of the performer. Objective analysis provides:

- a statistical record of aspects of the performance
- records of heights jumped, distances thrown, speeds run or number of successful attempts at a particular skill
- comparisons made between the performer and the decided criteria (perfect model).

11 What can be Analysed?

There is a variety of areas that can be analysed when looking at performance. Some are more complex than others. The most straightforward are individual, closed and basic skills; the most complicated are open, complex and advanced skills.

There are different skills required by different players on the pitch so the observer must be mindful of this in the analysis. An attacker may not need information on the number of tackles they make, but for a defender, this would be an important part of the analysis. A strong team may be often on the attack, so the defence is only rarely involved. As a result, a defender may only make a few passes in the game, so for them, the percentage rather than the actual number of successful passes made may reveal more about their personal play.

The skills required for good play are different for a defender and attacker.

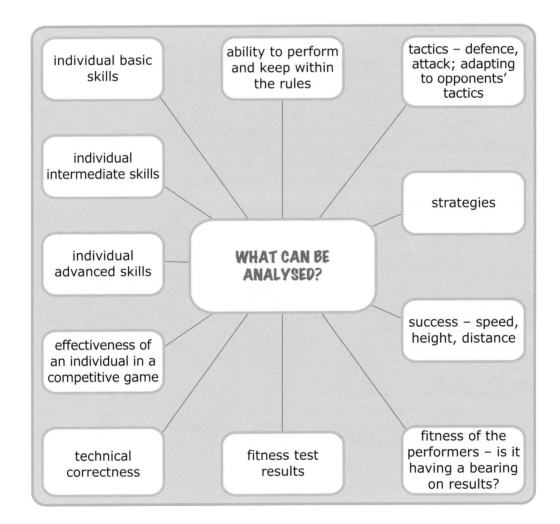

- individual basic skills
- ability to perform and keep within the rules
- tactics – defence, attack; adapting to opponents' tactics
- individual intermediate skills
- strategies
- individual advanced skills
- **WHAT CAN BE ANALYSED?**
- effectiveness of an individual in a competitive game
- success – speed, height, distance
- technical correctness
- fitness test results
- fitness of the performers – is it having a bearing on results?

Conclusion

When preparing to analyse be mindful of the following:

- have an idea of the types of comments you are going to make
  - subjective
  - objective
- begin by assessing straightforward 'closed' skills
- attempt 'open skill' assessment once you are more experienced
- analyse the player on the skills most relevant for their position
- compare what you see with what is considered to be an ideal or expert performance of the same skill or activity (the perfect model)
- remember, the whole team may be losing, but the player you are assessing could be having a good game
- record your findings and keep them safe for future reference.

Communication

After studying a performance, information can be related to the individual or group concerned. Sharing you findings with others will come in different forms:

- Discussing with others about performance.
- Giving a short talk on practical work.
- Summaries of articles read.
- Relaying information in different ways – charts, letters and so on.

Ways of recording reactions and views

There are many ways of recording information, so it is best to choose the method most suitable for you, the activity and the performer. The record of the feedback sessions will form part of your coursework, so keep it safe and in order. If there is anything left outstanding, complete it in good time.

Using questions and answers

Question and answer sessions are similar to questionnaires, but verbal questions and responses are given and recorded. It can add a personal touch to the process, but it can be difficult to hand-write the responses quickly, and taking time to keep your handwriting legible may make the procedure boring. Using this method, however, gives the opportunity for the interviewer to further explain a point if the question is found to be difficult. One way of overcoming this is to tape the session, though you will need to ask the performer's permission. Answers can be written out later at your convenience.

Examples of possible questions that can be used:

About the personal exercise programme:

- Were you tested before the programme started?
- Did the programme make you work hard?
- Was the programme easy to complete?
- Was the programme varied enough to keep your interest?
- Did you get feedback after each session?
- Before you were tested did you think that you were stronger than you actually were?
- Which part of the programme was your favourite?
- How were you motivated throughout the programme? (self/coach/teacher/friends)
- Did you need motivating in the programme?
- What surprised you about the re-testing after the programme was finished?

Analysis of performance is an integral part of the course. Of the 60% of marks awarded for practical activities, 10% is awarded for the ability to analyse performance. Therefore, understanding what is necessary to analyse, practicing this skill frequently and accurately recording your assessments in the Exercise Log will add to the overall final mark.

Glossary

A

Abduction   moving a limb or bone away from the body

Ability   an innate physical characteristic, which facilitates movements

Adduction   moving a limb or bone towards the body

Aerobic   'with oxygen'; when exercise is moderate and steady, the heart can supply all the oxygen the working muscles need

Aesthetic quality   how good an action looks

Agility   the ability to change the position of the body quickly and to control the movement of the whole body easily

Altitude training   training at a place situated high above sea level

Alveoli   tiny air sacs of the lungs where gaseous exchange takes place

Anaerobic   'without oxygen'; when exercising in short, fast bursts, the heart cannot supply blood and oxygen to the muscles as fast as the cells can use them, so energy is released without oxygen present

Antagonist   a muscle whose action counteracts that of another muscle and so allowing movement

Aorta   the main artery of the body, blood vessel transporting oxygenated blood to the body tissues

Arterioles   blood vessels that are sub-divisions of arteries, leading into capillaries

Asymmetric bars   a piece of Olympic gymnastic equipment used by females with bars at different heights

Atrophy   decline in effectiveness; when muscles atrophy they weaken and lose their strength and size

B

Balance   the ability to retain the centre of mass (gravity) of the body above the base of support with reference to static (stationary) or dynamic (changing) conditions of movement, shape and orientation

Balanced competition   grouping based on size, age or experience for an even match

Balanced diet   daily intake of food containing right amounts and types of nutrients

Bar chart   information set out in blocks to show an amount over a period of time

Basal metabolic rate   the level at which energy is used without exercise

Blood doping   method of increasing the oxygen carrying capacity of the blood, by increasing haemoglobin levels and red blood cell count

BMI   Body Mass Index

Body composition   the proportion of body weight that is fat, muscle and bone, normally measured as a percentage

C

Calcify   harden by conversion into calcium carbonate

Calcium   an essential element for strong healthy bones; dairy products provide a good source of calcium

Capillaries   blood vessels of hair-like thinness that connect the arteries with the veins

Carbohydrate loading   eating large amounts of carbohydrate-rich foods to build up glycogen levels in the body to use in endurance events

Cardiac muscle   only found in the heart, never tires

Cardiac output   the amount of blood pumped by the heart in one minute

Cardiovascular   relating to the heart and blood vessels

Cardiovascular fitness   the ability to exercise the entire body for long periods of time; this is dependent on the fitness of the heart, blood and blood vessels

Cartilage   whitish, tough, flexible tissue found at the end of bones; more widespread in infants, as during growth it is replaced by bone

Cervical vertebrae   bones of the vertebrae forming the neck

Chill factor   the combination of wind speed and air temperature and its effect on the living organisms

Circuit training   a series of exercises completed in order and for a certain time limit

Circulatory system   transports blood, using the heart, through all parts of the body

Classification   a way of sorting or organising groups

'Climbing Higher'   document compiled by the Welsh Assembly, setting out a strategy for sport and physical activity

Closed skill   basic skills unaffected by the sporting environment

Coccyx   small fused triangular bone at the base of the vertebral column

Compact bone   strong, hard bone

Compound/open fracture   break of the bone that pierces the skin, causing a risk of infection

Concussion   injury to the brain, caused by blow to the head, may cause a person temporarily to lose consciousness

Continuous training   aerobic exercising, at a moderate to high level, with no rests lasting for a sustained period of time

Cool down   exercises after the main activity gradually bringing the body systems back to near resting state

Co-ordination   the ability to perform complex moves using two or more body parts together

D

Dehydration   extreme lack of water in the body, usually as a result of exercising in hot conditions or heavy sweating

Diaphragm   a dome-shaped muscle that divides the chest cavity from the abdominal cavity

Dilate   open up or become wider

Dragon sports   sports programme for the young, resulting from the Welsh Assembly's initiatives

Drugs   substances (other than food) that, when taken into the body, cause a change; socially unacceptable drugs are drugs that are illegal to possess

Dynamic   relating to energy and forces producing movement

E

Ectomorph   body type with little fat or muscle and a narrow shape

Element   a part that contributes to the whole

Endomorph   body type that is apple or pear shaped, with a large amount of fat

Endothelium internal space of the blood vessels

Endurance the ability to keep working over a period of time without tiring or losing skill

Energy drinks fluids containing carbohydrates

Epiphysis end of a long bone

ESTYN Her Majesty's Inspectorate for Education and Training

Etiquette a code of polite behaviour

Evaluation to set out the value of a certain task or sport

Exercise a form of physical activity done primarily to improve one's health and physical fitness

Expiration breathing out, exhalation

Extension increasing the angle at a joint

Extrinsic feedback external information gathered by the performer, based on what is seen or heard, at the time of the action

F

Fartlek training 'speed play': changing speed, distances and times of exercise, with rests in the same session

Fast twitch muscle fibres used in events requiring quick reactions and power; muscles contract rapidly providing strength and so tire quickly

Fatigue extreme tiredness and physical exhaustion

Fitness ability to meet the demands of the environment

FITT frequency, intensity, time and type

Fixator muscles which steady parts of the body to give prime movers a firm base on which to work

Fixed practice repeating closed skills in the same conditions in training

Flexibility joints' ability to move to their full range

Flexibility training training which increases the total range of motion of a joint or collection of joints

Flexion decreasing the angle at a joint

Forced breathing breathing during exercise

Friction action of two surfaces rubbing together creating heat

G

Gender male or female

Glycogen the form in which carbohydrates are stored in the muscle and liver

Goal setting series of phases, setting out achievable goals for progress

Governing body a group responsible for rules, procedures and fixtures of a particular game or event

Guidance help and instruction given to complete a task

H

Haemoglobin found in red blood cells; transports oxygen to body tissue

Health a state of complete social, mental and physical well-being

Heart rate the number of times the heart beats per minute

Heat exhaustion fatigue brought on by the body temperature rising

Hypertrophy when muscle increases in size due to regular exercise

Hypothermia condition of the body when its core temperature falls below 35°C

I

Individual needs personal requirements for training

Infringement action in a game that breaks the rules

Insertion the point where a tendon attaches a muscle to bone where there is movement

Inspiration the drawing in of breath, inhalation

Interval training mixing periods of hard exercise with rest periods

Intrinsic feedback internal information gathered by the performer at the time of the action about how they feel the performance is going

Involuntary muscles muscles that work automatically, controlled by the involuntary nervous system

Isokinetic the muscles shorten and contract at a constant speed

Isometric muscular contraction muscle contraction with no movement; there is increased tension but the length of the muscles does not alter, e.g. when pressing against a stationary object

Isotonic muscular contraction muscle contraction that results in limb movement

J

Joint the point where two or more bones meet

L

Lactic acid produced in the muscle tissues during strenuous exercise, as a result of insufficient oxygen availability

Leverage the use of force or effort (muscle power) to overcome resistance

Ligament tough, rounded, elastic fibre attaching bone to bone

Line graph a graph using various coloured lines to show the rise and fall of a particular subject matter

M

Main activity period of training, competition or performance when all-out effort is applied

Maximum heart rate calculated as 220 minus age

Media the means of communication that reach a large number of people, ie television, newspapers etc

Mesomorph body that is characterised by being muscular

Metabolic rate the speed at which energy is used up

Minimum level of fitness (for health) the resulting fitness level when over a period of weeks three to five exercise sessions of 20 minutes, raising the heart rate to 60–80% of its maximum, are completed

Minority sports ones which have fewer competitors and less media coverage than more popular sports

Mobility training exercises include dynamic stretching, related to the activity, which could form part of a warm-up

Moderation   balancing training and not over-training

Modified game   a game with adapted rules, equipment and playing area based on a full game

Motivation   level of enthusiasm and determination a person has for a given subject

Movement   in motion, could be an action like running or swinging a racket at a ball

Muscle definition   muscle shape

Muscle tone   muscles in a state of very slight tension, ready and waiting to be used

Muscular endurance   the ability to use voluntary muscles, over long periods of time without getting tired

Muscular strength   the amount of force a muscle can exert against a resistance in one attempt

N

National Curriculum   government instructions on what is to be taught in schools

Newton   a unit of force

O

Obese   a term used to describe people who are very overfat

Open skill   complex skills performed in constantly changing conditions

Optimum weight   ideal weight for a person, giving them the best chance of success in an activity

Origin   the point where the tendon attaches the muscle to a fixed bone

Osteoclasts   bone-eroding cells

Overfat   a person having more body fat than is recommended for their gender and height

Overload   following the principle that the body can only be improved through training more and harder than normal

Overuse injury   this can be caused by using a part of the body too much or by too much repetitive training

Overweight   having weight in excess of normal; not harmful unless accompanied by overfatness

Oxygen debt   the amount of oxygen consumed during recovery above that which would have been consumed in the same time at rest (this results in a shortfall in the oxygen available)

P

Part practice   completing part of a complex action in training

Percentile ranking   data recorded from target groups showing percentage of success

Performance   how well a task is completed

Performance-enhancing drugs substances that artificially improve personal characteristics and performance

Periosteal collar   also known as periosteum, membrane surrounding the shaft of a bone

Personal exercise programme (PEP) training designed specifically for one individual

PESS   Physical Education and School Sport

Plyometrics   a method of training combining speed and strength and so developing power and explosiveness

PNF stretches   Proprioceptive Neuromuscular Facilitation – muscles contract before the stretch to achieve relaxation, allowing a greater range of movement

Posture   the way the muscles hold the body when still or in motion

Power   the ability to complete strength performances quickly; power = strength x speed

Prime mover   contracting muscles that cause movement

Principles of training   ideas behind effects of training

Progression   starting slowly and gradually increasing the amount of exercise completed

Protect   guard against threat

Protocol   a code of behaviour

Pulmonary circuit   system of blood vessels that transports deoxygenated blood from the heart to the lungs and re-oxygenated blood back again

R

Reaction time   the time between the presentation of a stimulus and the onset of a movement

Recovery rate   the time it takes for the heart and metabolism to return to resting after exercise

Regularity   repeating exercise sessions in a week to bring about improved fitness

Rehabilitate   recovery from injury

Reliability   how the test can be marked and set against other norms

Residual volume   the amount of air left in the lungs after a maximal breath out

Resting heart rate   number of heart beats per minute when the body is at rest

Reversibility   any adaptation that takes place as a consequence of training will be reversed when a person stops training

Rotation   movement in a circular or part-circular fashion

S

SAQ training   exercising concentrating on speed, agility and quickness

Shaft   long, thin part of a long bone

Shape   form or outline

Skeleton   the arrangement of the 206 bones of the human body

Skill   'a skill is a learned ability to bring about the result you want, with maximum Certainty and efficiency'

Skill-related fitness   physical motor abilities of the body adapted to specific sports

Skin-fold calliper   equipment used to measure a fold of skin with its underlying layer of fat

Slow twitch muscle fibres   muscle fibres required in endurance events

Somatotype   particular body type and shape of an individual. There are three types: ectomorph, endomorph and mesomorph

Specificity   concentrating on specific kinds of activity or exercise to build specific body parts

Speed   the differential rate at which an individual is able to perform a movement or cover a distance in a period of time

Sports Council for Wales   Governing body for sport in Wales

Static strength   contracting muscles beyond the normal range and holding position for short periods of time

Statistics   applying knowledge of numbers to a given subject

Stress   a state of mental or emotional strain leading to anxiety and nervous tension

Stress-related illnesses   illnesses such as heart attack, ulcer, high blood pressure

Stroke volume   the amount of blood pumped out of the heart by each ventricle during one contraction

Subscription   fee paid weekly, monthly, annually or at each session

Synergists   two muscles are called synergists when their contraction leads to movement in the same direction about the axis of a joint

Synovial capsule   tough fibre surrounding the synovial joint

Synovial fluid   fluid helping to lubricate a synovial joint

Synovial joints   freely movable joints with ends covered in cartilage

Synovial membrane   lining inside joint capsule where synovial fluid is produced

Systematic training   planning a programme for an individual as a result of the effect of previous training

Systemic circuit   part of the circulatory system concerned with transporting oxygenated blood from the heart to the body and deoxygenated blood back to the heart again

T

Target zone   level of effort applied, often keeping within aerobic levels but depending on specified training intensity

Tedium   ensuring that the training keeps the interest of the performer

Tendon   strong, non-elastic tissue attaching bone to muscle

Testing   ascertain the worth or endurance of a person using various examinations

Thoracic vertebrae   bones of the vertebrae in the chest area

Threshold of training   level of intensity above which exercise begins to have an effect on the body

Throwing cage   a secured enclosure around a throwing area

Tidal volume   amount of air breathed in or out at rest

Training   a planned programme which uses scientific principles to improve performance, skill, game ability and motor and physical fitness

Trend   a general direction or mode

U

Unconsciousness   state of unawareness, an unwakening sleep

V

Validity   a recognised and appropriate test carried out in a prescribed way

Valves   openings allowing blood flow in one direction, found in the heart and veins

Variable practice   performing whole skills in changing conditions in training

Vascular shunt   the redistribution of the cardiac output

Vasolidation   widening of the vessels under the skin

Vena cava   blood vessel transporting deoxygenated blood back to the heart

Vertebral column   irregular bones (vertebrae) that run the length of the body from head to rear; the column protects the spinal cord

Vital capacity   the maximum amount of air that can be forcibly exhaled after breathing in as much as possible

VO$_2$ max   maximum amount of oxygen the body can take in

Voluntary muscles   skeletal muscles, attached to the skeleton, work consciously by the brain

W

Warm-up   exercises gradually putting stresses on the body systems in preparation for the main activity

Weight training   progressively lifting heavier weights to improve strength or lifting weights more often to improve stamina

Welsh Assembly   Governing body in Wales

Whole practice   repeating the complete action in training

Index

lottery funding 45, 64, 82, 84, 86–7

lungs 22, 129–30

M

machine weights 25

manual guidance 210

manual learning 201

maximum weight 27

measuring and testing fitness 11, 99, 107–25

mechanics (in training) 35

media

coverage of sport 44, 49, 51, 73–9

types of 72, 76–7

membership fees 63, 88

memory 204, 206–7

mental health 61

mental preparation 208

merchandising 64

minerals 159

minimum level of fitness 14

minority sports 44, 66, 78, 79

mobility training 33–4

motivation 10, 16, 23, 207–8

muscle tone 169

muscles

contraction of 152–3, 156

energy in 30

fibres in 156

in relation to bones 142, 144, 146–51, 170

insertion point 146, 149

locations of 150

origin point 146, 149

producing heat 126

types of 146

working 127, 131, 133, 135, 136–7, 146, 159

in pairs 146

muscular endurance 6, 7, 11, 13, 24, 99, 104–5

difference from muscular strength 118

tests 11, 115–16

muscular strength 6, 7, 14, 98, 99, 103–5, 148, 153

difference from muscular endurance 118

tests 117–18

musculoskeletal injury 62

N

netball 86–7, 105, 183–4, 198, 211, 212–13

O

obesity 166

objective analysis of performance in sports 221

observation of performance in sports 214–19

open skills 202–3, 212

opioid analgesics 92, 97

opportunity for success, providing 174

opportunity to play sport, providing 80

optimum weight 165

output 204–5

over-extension 8

overload 14–15, 16, 27

oxygen 32, 100, 113, 126, 127, 129–31, 133, 156, 177

debt 137, 139

oxyhaemoglobin 129, 131

P

participation levels in sport 44–7, 49, 51–2, 53–5, 66, 79, 90–1

partner activities 22

'pay per view' television 74

percentile rankings 110

U

umpires 186–8

unskilled performer, characteristics
    of 199

V

validity of tests 107

vascular shunt 133

verbal guidance 210

verbal learning 200–1

visual guidance 210

visual learning 200

vital capacity 130–1, 135

vitamins 158

VO_2 maximum 113, 131, 135, 177

voluntary muscles 146, 149–50

volunteers 84

W

warm-up 10, 15, 30, 32, 35, 38–9,
    98, 148, 179–84

water, drinking 157, 162

weather conditions 12, 192

weight lifting, training 15, 24-6, 37, 43,
    48–9, 144, 154

weight problems 96, 165–6

well-being 168

winds 195

women's participation in sport
    48–50, 83

Y

young people's participation in sport 51–2,
    70, 82, 90–1; *see also* school